THE ITALIAN
SALT-FREE DIET
COOKBOOK

Merle Schell

THE ITALIAN SALT-FREE DIET COOKBOOK

NAL BOOKS

NEW AMERICAN LIBRARY

NEW YORK AND SCARBOROUGH, ONTARIO

Published simultaneously in Canada by The New American Library
of Canada Limited.

 NAL BOOKS TRADEMARK REG. U.S. PAT. OFF. AND FOREIGN COUNTRIES
REGISTERED TRADEMARK—MARCA REGISTRADA
HECHO EN HARRISONBURG, VA., U.S.A.

SIGNET, SIGNET CLASSIC, MENTOR, ONYX, PLUME, MERIDIAN
and NAL BOOKS are published *in the United States* by NAL PENGUIN
INC., 1633 Broadway, New York, New York 10019, *in Canada*
by The New American Library of Canada Limited, 81 Mack Avenue,
Scarborough, Ontario M1L 1M8.

Designed by Julian Hamer

Library of Congress Cataloging-in-Publication Data

Schell, Merle.
  The Italian salt-free diet cookbook.

  Bibliography: p.
  Includes index.
  1. Salt-free diet—Recipes.   2. Cookery, Italian.
I. Title.
RM237.8.S285   1988   641.5′632   87-20919
ISBN 0-453-00568-3

First Printing, January, 1988

1 2 3 4 5 6 7 8 9

PRINTED IN THE UNITED STATES OF AMERICA

*To Harry and Jason...
for the goodness and joy
and pure love
you brought to my life.*

Acknowledgments

No one writes a book totally alone. Over the years, I have been fortunate to have many people give of themselves, their experience, and their knowledge in helping to bring my books to fruition: doctors, nutritionists, food authorities, restaurateurs, and friends.

For this book, I want to single out a few who were particularly generous with their time and support: my dear friend Amy Shouse who was always there through the long days and longer nights of assembling, organizing, computing, typing, proofing, and revising the manuscript; my editors, Irene Pink and Molly Allen, for their patience; and my son, Harrison, whose arrival and good nature brought me the joy and energy I needed to complete this work.

And to my readers. Your satisfaction and thanks are my best reward.

Contents

Foreword by Len Horovitz, M.D.   xi
Foreword by Elizabeth Siber   xiii
Author's Note   xv

The Regional Cuisines and Their Differences   1

Northern Cuisine   1
Southern Cuisine   5
Central Cuisine   9

The Ingredients and Where to Find Them   12

An Italian Pantry   12
A Low-Sodium Pantry   21

For Ease of Preparation   27

Utensils   27
Preparation and Assembly   27

How to Adapt Your Favorite Italian Recipes   30

Other Diet Tips   32

Food Watching   32
Travel and Other Pleasures   37

RECIPES 39

Antipasti 43
Soups 63
Breads 79
Salads 95
Fish and Shellfish 117
Poultry 137
Meat 159
Pasta, Rice, Polenta, and Beans 183
Vegetables 213
Sauces and Dressings 239
Desserts 261

An Italian Menu for Entertaining 277

An Italian Diet 295

Tables of Nutritional Values 339

BIBLIOGRAPHY 349
INDEX 351

Foreword

I am happy to write this introduction to Merle Schell's newest book because I endorse both its health premise and the thoughtful, gratifying way in which Ms. Schell has incorporated sound nutrition with eating satisfaction.

In the last two decades, the medical establishment has become increasingly aware of the dangers of the average American's excess sodium (salt) intake. Numerous disorders, from hypertension and arteriosclerotic heart disease to the edema of pregnancy, have been linked to high levels of dietary sodium. In addition, nutritionists have noted that Americans tend to favor fats and refined sugars over complex carbohydrates, legumes, and fiber sources. This has resulted in an unacceptable proportion of people well above ideal body weight. Some investigators are now attempting to implicate obesity and dietary imbalances with some cancers and even immunological disorders.

By the clever use of herbs and spices (long believed to have medicinal and diuretic properties), Ms. Schell brings a vibrancy to her dishes that will please even the most salt-addicted palates. With helpful hints and common sense advice for good eating and healthier living, Ms. Schell continues to make available to all of us the artful combination of high nutritional principles and eating pleasure.

—LEN HOROVITZ, M.D.
Attending Physician,
Lenox Hill Hospital,
New York, N.Y.

Foreword

Merle Schell's newest book is an important addition to every cook's collection because it meets the needs and wants of today's consumer.

Taste has always been the primary definition of good food. But as people's eating habits and taste preferences have evolved, quality, convenience, health, natural ingredients, and ethnic variety are also key ingredients.

The Italian Salt-Free Diet Cookbook meets all of the criteria outlined above. First, it is a carefully researched, nutritionally balanced diet book, covering many dietary needs, including low fat, low carbohydrate, and low calorie, as well as low sodium. The more than 240 recipes, each with nutrient content per serving plus the party menus and the diet program all prove how easy it can be to adapt your personal requirements to your life-style.

Second, Italian food, currently the most popular ethnic cuisine, is the subject. Last, and singularly important, the recipes have been artfully developed to deliver authentic taste and eating pleasure.

As the former manager of several leading restaurants, and now as proprietor of a gourmet food store, anticipating my customers' wants and bringing them the latest and best new food experiences are continuing sources of personal delight and pride. I am happy to say Merle Schell's book fills both these requirements perfectly.

—ELIZABETH SIBER
Proprietor, Food & Co.,
Washington, D.C.
Formerly manager,
Windows on the World,
New York, N.Y.

Author's Note

Like many of us, I grew up thinking of Italian food in the same way I thought of hamburgers and french fries, ice cream and Oreo cookies. It was delicious and fun. But I never thought of whether it was healthy, and I certainly never thought of it as ethnic.

To me, Italian food meant lots of tomato sauce, melted cheese, garlic, and oregano. I was only vaguely aware that these flavors were but a small sampling of southern Italian cooking. Of the northern and central cuisines, I knew very little.

Today, things are different. Our collective awareness and appreciation of the many varieties of Italian food have broadened considerably. Indeed, of all the ethnic foods we Americans enjoy, none has become so much a part of our regular diet as Italian cuisine—whether eaten out, ordered in, or made at home. In a study published on December 23, 1985, the Futures Research Division of the Security Pacific National Bank reported that among those who eat out or take out, Italian food ranks first, the choice of 36 percent, followed by Chinese at 23 percent and Mexican at 20 percent.

This same study confirms that at home, too, Italian food is the favorite. Think of the wonderful aroma of meatballs simmering in a rich, chunky tomato sauce, chicken parmigiana crusty with bread crumbs and cheese, fettuccine swimming in creamy broth, or shrimp fragrant with garlic. There is something familiar and comforting in all these dishes.

Italian food makes you feel good. So it is easy to understand its enormous popularity . . . which is precisely why I wanted to write *The Italian Salt-Free Diet Cookbook*. No one should be denied the pleasures of Italian cuisine—not the salt-restricted dieter, or the cholesterol-conscious, or the sugar-watcher, or the calorie-counter. Not anyone. Yet for all the Italian food we consume, for all the Italian cookbooks on the market, there is no book, no advice, no recipes specifically for the millions of people with hypertension, cardiovascular problems, diabetes, etc. For the millions more who want to eat better to insure a better quality of life, the availability of pertinent and practical information is equally paltry.

The Italian Salt-Free Diet Cookbook aims to redress this problem. For it is more than a cookbook. Like my two previous books in this series (on Chinese and Mexican cuisines), this book explains how to easily and comfortably adapt your personal needs to suit your lifestyle. It contains such practical advice as how to read labels, where to find special diet foods, how to order in restaurants, what to do when you travel, and more. In addition, the book shows you how to plan no-fuss parties sure to please the palates of the special dieter and non-dieter alike.

And, of course, there are the recipes . . . more than 240 from every region of Italy . . . all low in calories, fat, and carbohydrates, as well as salt. Every recipe has been tested and retested to assure its authentic taste and your satisfaction whether your preference is northern, southern, or central Italian cuisine. Finally these same recipes form the basis of a sample two-week diet plan, nutritionally sound yet sure to start you on your way to a slimmer, healthier body.

If I sound enthusiastic, it is because I am. Italian food is more than good-tasting. With its emphasis on pasta and rice, and its abundance of vegetables, Italian cooking can be good eating in every sense of the word. What it needs are the adjustments in fat, sugar, and salt which, I hope you will agree, are provided in *The Italian Salt-Free Diet Cookbook*.

As I stated earlier, I grew up loving Italian food and continue to do so today despite my own dietary restrictions. So this book was a special joy to do because it allowed me to share with all of you the marvelous delights of Italian cuisine.

Good health and *buon gusto*.

Note: If you are on a special diet, check with your doctor for eating do's and don't's before using the recipes in this—or any other—cookbook.

The Regional Cuisines and Their Differences

Italian food is a product of many cultures, and each province of the country is marked by its own unique culinary heritage. Most of us tend to overlook the fine distinctions and label Italian cuisine either northern or southern. But the central region is one no serious cooks ignore because, as a bridge between northern- and southern-style cooking, it offers some of the finest food in Italy.

Northern Cuisine

If the southern region is synonymous with Mediterranean passion and volatility, northern Italy is characteristically continental in style and outlook. Indeed, bordered by France, Switzerland, Austria, and Yugoslavia, northern Italy is also known as European Italy. Accordingly, its cuisine is not just one, but a mix of many influences, and its beginnings can be traced back to the Roman Empire.

During the second century B.C., Roman armies conquered the Celtic tribes then living in the northeast corner of Italy, bordering Austria. To this region, called by the double name Trentino/Alto Adige, the Romans introduced the first grape vines and started the cultivation of such well-known Italian wines as Bardolino, Valpolicella, Asti Spumante, and Pinot Grigio, to name but a few.

For the 600 years of the Dark Ages, the Austrian Empire and, to a lesser degree, France dominated the north. The long-term presence of these powers explains why such seemingly unlikely foods as sauerkraut and chopped liver are popular in northern Italian cuisine, and why wine is a more important cooking ingredient here than in the southern region.

Venetian sailors added three more staples to the northern Italian kitchen, first in the fourteenth century, when they brought back rice from the Orient, and again in the sixteenth century, when they transported corn and beans from America.

The convergence of these influences has resulted in a cuisine which is at once heavier and less spicy than that of southern Italy. What is more, although each region of the north has its own distinct cooking style, they all share a preference for rice, beans, or polenta to pasta; butter to olive oil; and beef and veal to pork and lamb.

Piedmont

Its name means foot of the mountain, and this region of north-west Italy, along with the tiny province, Valle d'Aosta, does indeed lie in the Alpine country that extends into both France and Switzerland. These towering, glacier-topped peaks, which include the Matterhorn and Mont Blanc, offer some of the best skiing in the world. They surround the Piedmont on the north, west, and south; and to the east, the plains of the Po Valley seem to stretch endlessly until they reach Milan.

The Piedmont typifies northern Italy, for it is a harmonious combination of industry, beautiful mountain playgrounds, and agriculture. Turin, the capital city, is also Italy's automobile capital, and once served as the power base for the Savoys—the French family which ruled the Piedmont on and off from the eleventh century until Italy was unified in 1861.

The French influence is still very much in evidence today in the cooking style of the region, which favors hearty stews and wine-enriched dishes reminiscent of French country fare.

Wine-making is an important part of Piedmont economy, and the region produces some of the finest wines in Italy. In addition to the popular Asti Spumante, other notable wines include Dolcetto, Barbera, Freisa, and Barbaresco, this last prized by wine connoisseurs.

Butter, garlic, milk, and cheese are common ingredients in Piedmont dishes, and no meal would be complete without rice. Grown in the fertile lands surrounding the Po River, rice is served in every conceivable way from soup to dessert. Pasta, on the other hand, is reserved for special occasions, and almost always takes the form of agnolotti, meat-filled dumplings topped with meat sauce.

Any mention of Piedmont cookery must include its famous white truffles, which become yet another featured tourist attraction of this beautiful region during the fall truffle fair.

Lombardy

Lombardy, in the center of northern Italy, is a region of superlatives. It is the most industrialized, the richest, and one of the most beautiful in Italy, lying at the edge of the Swiss Alps and extending to the River Po. It is also the heart of the lake region. Maggiore on the west, Garda on the east, and Como, just north of Milan, all glisten in a peaceful tranquility that charms natives and tourists alike.

Milan, the capital of Lombardy, is considered by many to be the capital of northern Italy as well. It is a sophisticated city, at once a cultural mecca, an industrial hub, and the culinary center of the region.

For almost 2,000 years, Milan's strategic location made it both battlefield and eyewitness to European history, starting with the Emperor Augustus in 42 B.C. through the 200 years of Spanish rule (from 1525 to the beginning of the seventeenth century) to the crowning of Napoleon as King of Italy in 1805; finally ending with the Lombard and Piedmontese defeat of Austria, which resulted in the formation of the Kingdom of Italy in 1861.

In spite of, or perhaps because of, this tumultuous past, Milan and Lombardy have continued to grow intellectually, technologically, and artistically. Its cuisine, though varied, has a decided Swiss emphasis. Foods are often butter-fried in an egg batter, a tradition which started in the fifteenth century because the resulting golden color was thought to aid digestion. Breaded veal cutlets, hearty minestrone, cheeses, and fish from the lake region head the menu here. Buttery cakes are featured for dessert, the most famous being panettone, which is really not cake at all but a bread containing candied fruits and raisins.

We left for last Lombardy's most significant contribution to Italian cuisine: risotto, a creamy dish made from rice that is first fried in butter, often with onions, and then simmered in a rich meat stock. It is a flavorful addition to any meal.

Trentino/Alto Adige

Directly east of Lombardy, and sharing its northern border with Austria, lies the region of Trentino/Alto Adige. It is unusual in several respects, the most obvious that its people are bilingual, not surprising since Prussian nobles occupied this region from the eleventh century until the end of World War I.

After so many years of Prussian rule, so great is the Austro-German influence that not only is German the dominant language, but the food of the region is distinctly German as well. Rich varieties of goulash, light, flaky strudels, chopped liver, cornmeal and egg dumplings, and sauerkraut with smoked pork are among the region's most popular dishes.

This blending of two cultures continues today even outside the home via the Brenner Pass which connects the Alps Orientali of Austria with the spectacular Alto Adige mountain chain of reddish rocks, known as the Dolomites. Skiers and other travelers frequently use the Brenner Pass as a thoroughfare between the two countries, further encouraging cultural exchange.

Venice

In all of the north, the cuisine of the City of Canals is most special, for if rice, beans, and corn-based polenta are staples of northern cuisine, it is the Venetians who made them so. And with all due respect to Padua, Verona, Trieste, and the other great cities of the area, Venice is the culinary center of the Veneto region.

Situated at the delta of the Po River, Venice dominated the Adriatic Sea and all the trade routes to the East by the fourteenth century. By the sixteenth century, it controlled the waterways to the West as well. Thus although rice had been known to Europe since the eighth century as a very expensive commodity, Venetian sailors made it available to the masses by bringing back large cargoes of this grain on every trip from the Orient.

As its use became widespread, efforts were made to grow rice in Italy. Eventually Verona became the first city in Europe to master the art of rice cultivation. Today *risi e bisi*, a traditional Venetian dish of rice and peas, is a favorite throughout Italy.

In the mid-sixteenth century, Venetians adopted the corn brought from America and forever changed the staple polenta, a popular mush formerly made from wheat. Earlier in that century, between 1528 and 1532, Venetians also popularized American beans, which Pope Clement VII had previously introduced to Tuscany.

As might be expected of this city (so often called Pearl of the Adriatic), fish is a featured main course, with codfish (baccalà) the preferred selection. Liver, sausage, gnocchi, and every kind of vegetable also rank high with the Venetians.

The cooking style of Venice is very different from that of other northern provinces, for it echoes neither the food of France nor those of its Germanic neighbors, Austria and Yugoslavia. This is true perhaps because Venice was so long an independent power with free access to the worlds beyond its borders that it assimilated and made its own the foods and seasonings of far-off lands.

Southern Cuisine

The regions of southern Italy are all touched by the sea. Abruzzi, Molise, and Puglia border the Adriatic, Lucania has the Gulf of Taranto, while Calabria, Campania, and the islands of Sicily and Sardinia claim the Mediterranean as their own.

Together they represent a cuisine as generic as northern is disparate. Fish, pork, lamb, sweet ripe tomatoes, and a vast variety of pastas and pizzas are all seasoned with one or more of the distinctive flavors intrinsic to southern cuisine: oregano, basil, garlic, hot peppers, and nutty, rich olive oil.

In truth, southern Italian cuisine is a composite of the cooking styles of Greece, Africa, Arabia, Spain, and the Orient. It is the spicy food we most often think of when we think Italian, and our inclination, right or wrong, is understandable, for Italy, both geographically and in its soul, is primarily a Mediterranean country.

Italy is also credited as being the foundation of Western civilization. Ancient Greeks founded settlements in Sicily and Calabria in the eighth century B.C. They called their new land Magna Graecia (Greater Greece), and they lived there peaceably until they were overthrown by Rome in 200 B.C.

Today, magnificent Doric temples, amphitheaters, and other prime examples of Greek architecture can be found throughout the region from the Valley of Temples in Agrigento, to Syracuse, where Plato lived and taught, to the National Archaeological Museum, set amid the rambling hills of Naples. But the Greeks left behind more than archaeological treasures, for they bequeathed to Italy oranges, figs, lemons, limes, eggplant, almonds, and many other fruits and vegetables now intrinsic to the cuisine.

Sicily

Sicily, the island off the tip of the Italian boot, is a study in contrasts. Cliffs, pockmarked by volcanoes like the treacherous Mount Etna, loom over tranquil inlets and bays. Fertile farmlands on the east coast plain of Catania turn into stark plateaus along the southern coast facing Africa. The classic lines of Greek temples and monuments stand side by side Byzantine mosques and Baroque churches.

But high plateau or lowland, rich community or poor, the cuisine of Sicily remains constant. Vegetables flourish in the hot, humid climate, and are used in more ways and in greater quantities than in any other part of Italy. Local favorites include eggplant, wild asparagus, and a variety of cauliflower that Sicilians call broccoli.

Seafood is a mainstay on this richly endowed island, with tuna a special favorite. Various pastas and tomato sauces are also frequent offerings on the typical menu, often combined with chopped vegetables; the Marsala wine produced here and the famous Sicilian ice cream traditionally complete the meal.

Indeed, Sicily is noted for all its sweets, from candied fruits to sticky, delicious cannoli. Ice cream was invented here and is truly a specialty, whether creamy and rich with eggs and honey, or as the light and refreshing granita, which is simply chopped ice soaked with coffee, chocolate, or fruit-flavored syrup very much like the Italian ices we in America so often enjoy on a hot summer day.

Calabria, Lucania, and Puglia

As you travel north from Sicily, you will find few changes in the style, taste, and texture of the dishes. Any distinctions come from the foods that are available locally, and from the degree to which these key ingredients and seasonings are used.

For example, in Calabria, garlic is used sparingly, its pungent flavor generally replaced with large quantities of the local sweet onions of Tropia and generous portions of hot red peppers. This province along with Lucania and Puglia make up the toe, instep, and heel, respectively, of this boot-shaped country.

They are beautiful lands, filling the eye with miles of wheat fields and olive groves and, along the coast, quaint fishing villages. What is more, because these regions have not yet become fashionable with tourists, they remain relatively unspoiled.

Life goes on here very much as it did hundreds of years ago, amid artifacts from Greece, Africa, and the Orient. While the food is plain, it is hearty and naturally rich in local produce. Puglia produces more wine and olive oil than any other region in Italy. Fish is a perennial favorite, as are pork, lamb, and kid; other staples include artichokes, mushrooms, cheese, tomatoes, eggplant, and, of course, pasta. Pastas in the far south are well worth trying, not only because they are good but because names as exotic as *scilatelli*, *troccoli*, and *strascenate* deserve a taste.

Abruzzi and Molise

Molise boasts the highest site in this mountainous region; namely, the town of Capracotta, and shares with Abruzzi an agricultural economy.

Potatoes, beans, and fruit are primary crops, and sheep graze throughout the rugged hills. In fact, the shepherd is the symbol of Abruzzi, although wheat could also be a logical choice because Abruzzi is famous for its pasta. One particular favorite is *maccheroni alla chitarra*, so called because a utensil shaped like a guitar is used to cut the pasta into thin, stringlike strips.

Wholesome peasant food and scenic grandeur are the hallmarks of these too-seldom-visited regions.

Sardinia

In the middle of the Mediterranean Sea, west of Tuscany and Lazio, is the island of Sardinia. Despite its glittery jet-set resort, Costa Smeralda, Sardinia is poor in some areas, desperately so. Although the coastal and mountain regions are compelling in their beauty and attract thousands of visitors each year, more than fifty percent of the vast inland is made barren by heat, dust, the lack of natural springs, and a rocky terrain that cannot absorb rain.

Consequently, much of the land is unfit for agriculture, and not even the abundant surrounding waters of the Mediterranean can adequately feed Sardinia's one and a half million people. So the culinary staples include spaghetti, sausage, cheese, and the many wonderful varieties of flat bread which Arab invaders brought to Sardinia after the fall of the Roman Empire.

Arabs were not alone in coveting this island. Sardinia was once thought to be the center of the earth, and thus was besieged by one nation after another, starting with the Phoenicians around 500 B.C., and followed by the Carthaginians, Romans, Normans, Genovese, Arabs, Greeks, and Spaniards. In fact, Sardinia was the object of political turmoil until 1770, when the Treaty of London ceded the island to the Dukes of Savoy.

No wonder, then, that among the southern regions, Sardinia stands apart—philosophically as well as geographically. Its melting-pot heritage provides some of the most fascinating sights the island has to offer, such as Arab-style villages, prehistoric Nuraghic art, and ruins that reflect occupations by Rome, Pisa, Phoenicia, and Aragon, among others.

This heritage contributed to the cuisine as we know it today, for although the food is unmistakably southern, the use of such eastern spices as cloves, cinnamon, and nutmeg makes it uniquely Sardinian.

Campania

The culmination of all that is wonderful about southern cooking can be found in the food of Campania, which includes such legendary towns as Pompeii, Capri, Sorrento, Amalfi, and, of course, Naples. Like most of southern Italy, the region combines beautiful seashores set against a backdrop of craggy cliffs with flat plains and moutains that stretch from one end of this coastal region to the other. The beauty and desirability of the area did not go unnoticed, and Phoenicians, Cretans, and Greeks settled there around 1,000 B.C., followed by the Romans 300 years later.

The cuisine which evolved from these early cultures was completed centuries later when, in the 1440s, Spain occupied the region and introduced tomatoes from Peru. This fruit, now so intrinsic to Italian cookery, found a welcoming home in the moist, sun-drenched hills of Naples, and has given rise to some of the best tomato sauces you will find anywhere, as well as to the internationally popular pizza.

In Campania, vegetation thrives, and the wide fields and gentle hills provide excellent conditions for raising cattle, pigs, chickens, and sheep. With so much fresh bounty from land and sea, food needs no embellishment and the cooking style is justifiably simple. Fish, meat, and poultry are often grilled and basted with a light herbal marinade; vegetables are steamed or simmered in a casserole; and pasta is served with one of the many exquisite tomato sauces for which the region is renowned. Otherwise, one-dish meals are the standard.

The desserts of Campania are creamy and sumptuous. But the main dishes, as memorable as they are simple, are the real treats and remind us why southern Italian cuisine is enjoyed the world over.

Central Cuisine

While many of its accents are southern, the cuisine of central Italy is as interesting and diverse as that of the north. The resulting dishes are among the most unique and delicious in Italy.

Tuscany

One outstanding example is the cuisine of Tuscany, which lies to the north of Lazio (and Rome). This wedge-shaped region on the Ligurian Sea is steeped in history dating back to the Etruscans. Tuscany produces the finest olive oil in the world and puts it to good use in virtually every dish, including soup. But here the resemblance to southern cooking ends. For one thing, except for macaroni, pasta is not a particular favorite among the inhabitants of the region from Florence and Pisa to Siena. For another, although fish are in plentiful supply from the region's rivers and neighboring sea, poultry and meat are preferred. In fact, Tuscany is thought to serve the best steak in Italy.

Thanks to the rich valley soil of the Arno and Serchio Rivers, vegetables are in prodigious supply. They are mainstays of the Tuscan diet, along with bread, cheese, and the local wine, Chianti. Herbs and spices, used more lavishly in Tuscany than in any other region, further enhance this wonderful and varied food. Indeed, dishes seasoned to aromatic perfection, the liberal use of olive oil, and a relative indifference to pasta are the mark of this unpretentious cuisine, which some say is the best in Italy.

Emilia-Romagna

Separated from Tuscany by the Apennines, Emilia-Romagna is the other side of the mountain in more ways than one. Of the two regions, Emilia-Romagna is the wealthier, and the food is richer as well. Butter and cream are used freely; pasta is not the simple flour and water combination used in the south, but has the added flavor of eggs. Like its neighbors to the north, the area reflects the gastronomic influences of Austria and France.

Yet Emilia-Romagna also exhibits decidedly southern tendencies. The home of Parma ham (a world-famous prosciutto) and

Parmesan cheese, this region has an understandable affinity for pork and cheese dishes, and the use of tomato sauce as a staple is also very much in the southern tradition.

What the lush land of the Po River so amply provides, the cooks of Emilia-Romagna artfully use to blend the culinary styles of north and south into a whole that is truly greater than the sum of its parts. Indeed, this cuisine shares with Tuscany the reputation of being Italy's finest.

The Marches

Southwest of Emilia-Romagna is the Marches, a former papal dominion, of rocky coasts, mountains, and rivers which regularly overflow to form small pockets of fertile land. The agricultural output is consequently small but includes huge, succulent olives and the grapes from which Verdicchio wine is made. Fortunately, the Marches borders the Adriatic Sea, and its cuisine has developed around the large selection of seafood so close at hand.

Many of the foods here are breaded and fried in the northern tradition, then bathed in tomato, meat, or cheese sauces in the southern style. It is delicious, unassuming fare, the most elaborate dishes being the numerous baked pastas, loaded with vegetables and smothered in sauce, which very much resemble pot pies. In short, the cooking of the Marches proves it is not how much you have, but what you do with it that counts.

Umbria

Umbria, immediately to the west of the Marches, is one of the few regions that does not border a major body of water. Like most of Italy, it is a pretty land of rolling plains and hills. The terrain is not exceptional, yet there is a mystical quality about Umbria, due to the bluish haze which is constantly overhead. It casts an ethereal softness over the countryside, and the effect is one of timelessness, a still-life landscape. The look and feel of Umbria have caused it to be called the Green Heart of Italy.

The region is fertile as well as beautiful. Hills are terraced to maximize food production, and Umbria harvests excellent vegetables. Of particular note are the olives (and olive oil), tiny, sweet lentils, and, especially, truffles. This delicacy is so abundant in Umbria that it is freely used in every conceivable dish from breakfast to dinner.

Umbria is also famous for its crisp, dry white wine, Orvieto, named for the hill town in which the grapes are grown. It is a perfect companion to the traditional food of this region, which includes thick pasta, guinea hen, and pork. The latter is a staple of the local diet and is processed for prosciutto, sausage, and salami. Other meats here are generally grilled and seasoned with a variety of herbs and spices, a cooking style the Umbrians have mastered to perfection.

A meal might end with a bit of Perugina chocolate—another local product that has won international acclaim.

This region, which was home to St. Francis of Assisi, has much to offer. Dotted with relics of Italy's past, it is a lovely land of extraordinary charm whose pleasures are enhanced by the wonderful food.

Lazio/Rome

We have left Rome and the Lazio region for last, not because its cuisine is the most distinguished of the central region, but because it is Rome—the capital, the heart and soul of Italy.

Outside Rome, the countryside is bucolic, studded with medieval ruins, ancient monuments, and countless other testaments to the past. It is a rich heritage in a region now relatively poor in all things except food. And what food it is! Thick, spicy tomato sauces, fettuccine and gnocchi swimming in cream, milk-fed lamb, zuppa di pesce and other soups brimming with pasta and beans, batter-fried fish, grilled chicken, all kinds of vegetables, including tender globe artichokes sautéed whole with garlic and mint.

Of course, all this bounty and more can be found in Rome as well. The City of Seven Hills is wondrous to see. From the Trevi Fountain to the Sistine Chapel to the fashionable shops on the Piazza di Spagna, Rome is at once historic, cosmopolitan, elegant, and rich. The cuisine is a reflection of its style. Cozy trattorias serve peasant-style dishes from the country, while sophisticated restaurants offer selections representative of all Italy, prepared with an international flair that is singularly Roman. For Rome is the crossroads of the Mediterranean—a fact happily demonstrated in its cuisine.

As you can see, Italian food is not so easily categorized. To be sure, there are northern and southern and central distinctions, but even within these boundaries, there are myriad differences. This variety keeps it interesting and contributes to the universal and enduring popularity of Italian cuisine.

The Ingredients and Where to Find Them

Italian food is so much a part of our lives and its ingredients so generic that all the staples associated with it are generally available in supermarkets and food stores everywhere. Even the less common fennel and leek can be found at local vegetable stands. Consequently, preparing to cook from this book should be no more complicated than adding a few items to your grocery list.

Following are two alphabetized summaries of the ingredients you should stock. The first specifies Italian products (most of which you probably have). The second outlines the low-sodium items you will need; they will serve you well whatever cuisine you are cooking. For obvious reasons, we have not included such salted Italian products as anchovies and pimientos, but because substitutes and low-sodium options are detailed where appropriate, we think you will find your needs for authentic Italian cuisine more than satisfactorily met.

An Italian Pantry

ALCOHOL (See also individual listings)
Wine and sherry are often used to enrich the flavor of Italian dishes. Otherwise, alcohol, with the occasional exception of brandy, is seldom used in the cuisine. Although alcohol is low in sodium, its high sugar content may be unacceptable for diabetics who may either substitute orange juice or eliminate it altogether.

ALLSPICE
Although so named because its rich scent and flavor hint of a clove, cinnamon, and nutmeg combination, allspice is actually the

dried unripe berry of the evergreen family. The chocolate-brown allspice berry of Jamaica is considered the world's best because its higher essential oil content results in a richer aroma and flavor. But allspice trees are also native to Mexico, Guatemala, and Honduras. Allspice is available whole or ground in supermarkets everywhere and is most often used in baked goods or with sweet vegetables. Stored in jars in a cool, dry place, it will keep indefinitely.

ANISEED (FENNEL SEED)
Originally from the eastern Mediterranean and used as a medicine in ancient Syria, the small, grayish aniseed is a member of the parsley family. Its licorice flavor is occasionally found in Italian dishes, where it is used to accent meats and vegetables as well as baked goods. Aniseed and its taste-alike, fennel seed, are available in most supermarkets. Stored in jars or plastic bags and kept on a cool, dry shelf, both aniseed and fennel seed will keep indefinitely.

ARUGOLA
Although its slim, tapering leaves look like flat spinach, arugola is actually an herb which used to grow wild in Italian fields. Arugola's wonderfully pungent, nutty flavor makes it a delicious addition to any salad or a delicacy unto itself. Because it is fragile, arugola should be stored in a plastic bag in the refrigerator where it will keep its fresh snap up to one week.

BASIL
A member of the mint family, basil's warm, sweet flavor is matched only by its beautiful aroma; this heady combination gave rise to many, often contradictory myths about its powers. Ancient Greeks rejected it as not even fit for a she-goat, yet the Romans revered it as a symbol of love and fertility.

Basil is one of the easiest herbs to grow. Outdoors it flourishes in warm weather, but indoors, placed in a sunny window, it will thrive all year round. Accordingly, fresh basil is widely available in most supermarkets and vegetable stores and will keep up to one week in the refrigerator. Dried basil is always at hand in the spice section of all food stores and, if stored in tightly closed containers and kept in a cool, dry, dark place, it will keep indefinitely. It is particularly wonderful with tomatoes, which is why basil is so associated with Italian cuisine.

BAY LEAF
The dried leaf of the laurel tree, native to the Mediterranean, bay leaf probably came to Italy via Turkey, Portugal, or, most likely, Greece. Its slightly sharp taste is an optional flavoring for many of the soups, sauces, and stews that are featured at the Italian table. Stored in a tightly closed plastic bag or jar and kept in a cool, dry place, bay leaf will keep its delightful pungency indefinitely.

BRANDY
Although brandy is not used to flame Italian main dishes, it does make its presence known in many desserts. When brandy is called for, you may experiment by substituting any of the fruited varieties, like pear and peach. Brandy will, of course, keep indefinitely.

CAPERS
A true delicacy, the tiny green capers add a zesty, tangy taste to any and every conceivable dish, including antipasto, salads, seafood, and sauces. These heart-shaped fruits grow wild on the walls and cliffs along the Mediterranean coastline. Because they are very delicate and must be picked by hand, they tend to be expensive, but a little of their distinctive flavor goes a long way. Available in jars in the pickle section of most supermarkets, some capers come packed in brine, which is salt-filled and unacceptable. Others are packed in vinegar only and are recommended. Once opened, capers should be refrigerated where they will keep indefinitely.

CHEESE
Ranging from mild and creamy ricotta to sharp, hard Parmesan, cheese is a very important part of Italian cuisine. Indeed, cheese is often served along with fruit as the refreshing and palate-cleansing end to a meal.
Because Italian cheeses normally contain salt, we have substituted low-sodium options. For example, in place of the savory fontina, our choices are low-sodium Cheddar or Gouda. Low-sodium Swiss in combination with wine, herbs, and spices, is used in place of the more pungent Romano, Parmesan, Gorgonzola, and provolone. Fortunately, ricotta and mozzarella both have low-sodium equivalents which are quite good.
Available in supermarkets, health food stores, and cheese shops throughout the country, most low-sodium cheeses will keep up to one month in the refrigerator if tightly sealed in plastic or aluminum foil. If a white or green mold does form, simply cut it off (the

cheese is still good). There are a few exceptions: cartoned cheeses, such as cottage cheese and ricotta, will stay fresh only one week after opening. Mozzarella will start to soften and form a brownish mold two to three weeks after opening, but wonderfully, in this state, mozzarella tastes very much like Brie or Camembert.

Note: For the nutritional content of cheeses, consult the Tables of Nutritional Values (page 339).

CINNAMON

More than 2,000 years ago, cinnamon was prized in Egypt for its magical effect on the body and the emotions. The Romans thought its fragrance was of the gods and holy. Today, cinnamon is universally prized for its sweet, intoxicating flavor. Although used primarily in baked goods, it is finding its way into main dishes throughout the world, including Italy. Whether you use the milder Ceylon-type or the more aromatic and pungent Indian variety, cinnamon, in stick or ground form, is readily available everywhere. It will keep indefinitely if stored in a tightly sealed container on a dark, cool shelf.

CLOVES

Cloves are the dried seeds from tropical evergreens and were first discovered in the Moluccas of Indonesia. In ancient times, cloves were rare and so precious that those parents who could secure the seeds planted them to bless and honor the birth of a child. Today, cloves are readily available, ground or whole, in supermarkets everywhere. They lend a wonderful aroma and flavor to a number of Italian dishes. Stored in a tightly closed container and kept in a cool, dry place, they will keep indefinitely.

DILL

A member of the parsley family, fresh dill has a sweet flavor which gives a wonderful accent to salads and fish dishes. The dried form of the dill leaves is known as dillweed. The pickling ingredient dillseed is the dried fruit from the same plant. Either form is available in supermarkets everywhere and will keep indefinitely if kept in tightly closed containers on a cool, dark, dry shelf.

FENNEL

Although there is a bitter variety of fennel whose seeds are used in liqueurs, garden fennel, with its sweet, mildly licorice flavor, is the one prized in Italian homes. Rarely eaten raw, fennel is usually braised or simmered to allow its fibrous stalks to soften and its delicate flavor to come through. Although it resembles celery, fennel is actually a member of the carrot family and is most readily available in Italian markets and vegetable stores. It will keep up to two weeks in the refrigerator.

FENNEL SEED—See Aniseed.

GARLIC
This bulb plant probably originated in Siberia 5,000 to 6,000 years ago. Its succulent, nutty flavor and enticing aroma are synonymous with Italian cuisine, and it is used in a wide variety of dishes. Although garlic is available in many forms, including powder, flakes, and juice, the fresh is so easily found in supermarkets that we prefer to use it. Fresh garlic will keep several weeks if refrigerated. The various dried forms will keep indefinitely if stored in tightly closed containers, as will the juice, if refrigerated.

HOT PEPPER FLAKES
These fiery red morsels, which add a bit of fire to pizza toppings and other Italian dishes, are the dried form of red chilies. Available in the spice section of most supermarkets, hot pepper flakes will keep indefinitely on the shelf if kept in a tightly closed container.

LEEKS
A bulb plant, related to the onion, leeks have a delicate, slightly sweet flavor which adds a subtle charm to all kinds of dishes, including soups, salads, meat, fish, and poultry. Leeks are also delicious on their own, braised or simmered with a little wine or a dot of butter or margarine. Leeks are available in supermarkets and food stores everywhere and, if refrigerated, will keep up to three weeks.

MARJORAM
The gray-leafed marjoram plant, a member of the mint family, has myriad uses. Long known as a symbol of love, mythology records that Venus used it as the balm for a wound from one of Cupid's darts. In its more earthly form, marjoram is used to flavor lamb, vegetables, soups, and stews throughout central and northern Italy. Commonly available in dried and powdered form in the spice section of food stores, marjoram will keep indefinitely if stored in a tightly closed container in a dry, cool place.

MINT

Once known as a symbol of hospitality, mint adds a welcome and refreshing flavor to food. In Italian cooking, spearmint, native to the Mediterranean region, is the most widely used variety of this sweet-tasting herb, which is a staple in Tuscan cooking. Although it is easy to grow, spearmint is not easy to find in the more convenient dried form. However, since the somewhat stronger-tasting plain mint is readily available both fresh and dried in supermarkets, we use it throughout this book. Fresh mint will only keep about one week in the crisper section of your refrigerator. However, dried mint will keep indefinitely if stored in jars or plastic bags in a cool, dark place.

NUTMEG

Nutmeg, yet another product of the evergreen family, originated in the Moluccas. It was probably first discovered on an Arabian foray into the West Indies. The nutmeg spice, sold whole or ground, is actually the pit of the nutmeg fruit. It is available in all food stores and will keep indefinitely if stored in a cool, dark place.

OLIVE OIL

The fertile groves of Tuscany supply most of this distinct and richly flavored oil, which is a key ingredient in the cooking of central and southern Italy. From the purest, known as virgin oil, to more commercial and less heady blends, olive oil is available in food stores everywhere. Because its flavor and density are so concentrated, proportionately little is needed to cover surfaces and to release its full-bodied taste.

OREGANO

Some call it wild marjoram. The Greeks named it "joy of the mountain." But by any name at all, this sweet herb of the mint family, which thrives in the rich, warm soil of the Mediterranean region, has been a favorite of Italian cooks for centuries. Along with tomatoes and garlic, oregano is one of the constants of Italian cuisine. Although fresh oregano can be found in Italian and Spanish food stores, it is commonly available in dried or ground form, and will keep indefinitely if stored in a tightly closed container in a cool, dark place.

PAPRIKA

A key ingredient in many sausage recipes, and often used in pasta dishes, paprika plays an important role in Italian cuisine. Although the slightly sharp tang of Hungarian paprika provides the most distinctive flavor, the sweeter Spanish variety or the American blend, which is available everywhere, are fine for our purposes. Paprika will keep its flavor and rich russet color indefinitely if stored in a tightly closed container in a cool, dark place.

PARSLEY

Parsley's origins can be traced to the Mediterranean where it first came into use in cooking thousands of years ago. It is now grown worldwide, but Italian parsley is distinct because its leaves are larger and less curly than its cousins, and its taste milder and less sharp. Fresh parsley is available in supermarkets and food stores everywhere and will keep up to one week if refrigerated in a plastic container. Dried parsley is just as readily available and will keep indefinitely if stored in a tightly closed container on a cool, dry shelf.

PASTA

Despite the fact that northern Italians prefer rice, pasta is synonymous with Italian cuisine. Pasta comes in assorted shapes and sizes, and is delicious in every one. However, some forms lend themselves better than others to the various sauces which no respectable pasta would be without. For example, the most popular form, spaghetti, is best for plain butter, wine, and tomato sauces. Thin spaghetti and vermicelli are better in soups or for heartier sauces, such as those containing seafood or blended with olive oil. Meat-based, vegetable, and cream sauces need open-ended pastas like shells, macaroni, rigatoni, or the flat, broad lasagna noodle to catch their food morsels.

For best results, pasta should be cooked in water already at a rolling boil for 7 to 10 minutes, or until firm to the bite, otherwise known as al dente. Immediately thereafter, it should be drained, the sauce added, and then served. Although homemade pasta is a treat, before buying, do ask if salt has been added to the recipe. Interestingly enough, popular commercial brands are all low in sodium, approximately 4 milligrams to the ounce, and they will keep indefinitely if stored in tightly closed containers and kept in a dry place.

PEPPER

Long before salt was used as currency, there was pepper. Pepper was one of the sources of the city of Alexandria's wealth. Revenues from its sale were used to help establish the American merchant marine, and it was the foundation of the wealth of Elihu Yale, founder of Yale University. This little dried berry, known as a peppercorn, grows on vines and is native to the tropical area around the Equator. It was so prized (and still is today) because it enhances almost every food we eat—with the exception of desserts. Pepper is universally available whole, cracked, coarse ground, or fine. If stored in a dry place, it will keep its zesty bite indefinitely.

ROSEMARY

An evergreen shrub and another member of the mint family, rosemary has a delightful fragrance. Its intoxicating aroma did not escape the notice of the ancients who often used it in religious ceremonies and believed it to be a bond of faithfulness between lovers. Native to the Mediterranean region, rosemary is a classic spice in Italian cuisine and lends its appealing flavor to every kind of food. Although rosemary makes a lovely fragrant houseplant and will grow well indoors, commercially it is most commonly available in dried form in the spice section of supermarkets. If kept in a tightly closed container on a dark, cool shelf, it will keep indefinitely.

SAGE

Its Latin name means "to cure." The word itself is another name for wise man. For centuries past, this sturdy member of the mint family was valued as much as a medicine as it was as a seasoning. Sage thrives in the rocky hills of northern Italy, especially along the Adriatic Coast. It is a key ingredient in sausage making, but because its sweet flavor and aroma blend so well with other herbs and spices, it is often that "magic something" in all manner of dishes, ranging from soups to vegetables. Although sage is a hardy perennial and is easy to grow at home, commercially, fresh sage is not readily available. However, the dried and ground forms retain much of the delicately delicious flavor of the herb and are readily available in food stores everywhere. If stored in tightly closed containers in a dry, dark, cool place, sage will keep its taste and aroma indefinitely.

SHERRY
Dry sherry and red and white wines play a major role in Italian cooking. They are often used in marinades (to flavor or tenderize) as well as to impart a rich, heady flavor to foods as they cook. One important note: Never use the cooking sherry or cooking wines you find on your supermarket shelves. They all contain salt. Instead, choose any inexpensive regular sherry or wine for your pantry. They will provide the flavor you need, without salt, and will keep indefinitely on the shelf.

TARRAGON
This twisting, spiral herb, which owes its name to the Greek word for dragon, probably reached Italian shores when the Greeks began settling in Sicily centuries ago. Its strong, slightly anise flavor, tends to overwhelm other herbs, but is delicious in salad dressings and in fish and poultry dishes. Tarragon is most readily available in dried form in supermarkets. If stored in tightly closed containers in a cool, dry place, it will keep its flavor indefinitely.

THYME
Indigenous to the Mediterranean, this relative of mint probably came to Italy from the Provence region of France. It has a long and illustrious history, for thyme has won praise as a medicine, has been hailed as a source of courage and happiness, and was given as an offering to the baby Jesus. Its wonderful taste and scent flavor every type of regional Italian dish from salad dressings to sausages and stuffings. Fresh thyme may sometimes be found in Spanish markets, but the dried form is available in food stores everywhere. Thyme should be kept in a tightly closed container in a cool, dry, dark place to preserve its flavor and aroma indefinitely.

TOMATOES
Although it originated in Peru, this luscious fruit, which ripens to sweet perfection in the rich Italian soil, has been the symbol of Italian cuisine for thousands of years. Not only are tomatoes an important ingredient in many dishes, they are also the basis for many of the sauces that characterize Italian cooking.

VERMOUTH
Like sherry, dry vermouth is often used to add its rich, mellow flavor to foods, especially poultry and fish, as they cook. Any in-

expensive brand will serve the purpose admirably and will keep indefinitely on the shelf.

VINEGAR
The red, white, and cider vinegars used throughout this book are widely available. You need only remember to be wary of herbed, spiced, or seasoned blends, which sometimes contain salt. Vinegar will keep indefinitely on the shelf.

WINE, RED or WHITE
See Sherry.

A Low-Sodium Pantry

BAKING POWDER
When you consider that low-sodium baking powder contains only 2 milligrams of sodium per teaspoon compared to almost 500 milligrams for an equal amount of the salted version, and when you consider that they produce exactly the same results, there is no reason not to use the low-sodium form which is available today in supermarkets everywhere. It will keep indefinitely on the shelf.

BEETS, CANNED
Beets and, for that matter, a veritable cornucopia of other vegetables are widely available today canned in water for low-sodium consumption. You can find these items in the diet section of most supermarkets, as well as in health food stores. So popular have they become that, like their salty counterparts, they are usually available in two sizes (8 and 16 ounces), often produced by leading brand-name manufacturers. Because they are vacuum-packed, they have an indefinite shelf-life. In addition, there is a bonus: Because salt drains off the flavorful moisture of any food, the low-sodium products taste fresher and richer than the salty ones.
   Note: Although frozen vegetables are also acceptable, they often have added salt, so before using them, read the labels carefully.

BOUILLON, BEEF AND CHICKEN
Bouillon mixed with boiling water is a commonly used shortcut when a recipe calls for soup or stock. But there's a big difference between salted and unsalted bouillon. One teaspoon of salted beef

or chicken bouillon contains 1,143 milligrams of sodium—more than some of us are allowed all day. Compare that to unsalted beef bouillon, which has only 10 milligrams of sodium per tea-spoon, or unsalted chicken bouillon, which has only 5 milligrams of sodium per teaspoon—an amazingly healthy difference.

These low-sodium seasonings are widely available today in health food stores and supermarkets throughout the country. Some come in powdered form; others are granulated and packed in small jars. Although we prefer the powder, either form can be used for the recipes in this book. Low-sodium chicken bouillon is an instant "salty" pick-me-up for poultry, fish and shellfish, and vege-tables. Low-sodium beef bouillon has the same effect on all meats. Low-sodium bouillon has the added benefits of being low in fat, carbohydrates, and calories, and high in potassium. It will keep in-definitely on the shelf.

BREAD CRUMBS

Bread crumbs add a wonderfully crunchy texture and mellow flavor to sautéed and even baked foods. In addition, they are ex-cellent as food "stretchers" and in stuffings. But the commercial, salted brands contain approximately 410 milligrams of sodium per ¼ cup. Fortunately, low-sodium bread crumbs are also available plain and seasoned in supermarkets everywhere. The difference in the sodium is enormous: low-sodium bread crumbs contain less than 11 milligrams of sodium per ¼ cup. If kept in a tightly closed container in a cool, dry place, they will keep their fresh flavor indefinitely.

CELERY SEED

These tiny brown seeds from the root of wild celery are similar in taste but actually no relation to the celery commonly found in supermarket produce sections. Celery seed is found on the spice racks of these same markets and will keep indefinitely on your shelf if stored in a cool, dry place. They should always be used by the low-sodium dieter rather than celery flakes, which do con-tain salt.

CHEESE
(See also page 14.)
Low-sodium cheeses are so popular that you can find them in health food stores and supermarkets throughout the country. The variety is amazing and their flavor is excellent. Although not as long-lasting as their salty cousins, low-sodium cheese will stay

fresh in your refrigerator up to one month. For nutritional content, consult the Tables of Nutritional Values (page 339).

HOT CHERRY PEPPERS
Available in the pickle section of most supermarkets, low-sodium hot cherry peppers generally come in 16-ounce jars. Pickled in distilled vinegar, these spicy hot peppers contain only 7 milligrams of sodium per ounce compared to almost 400 milligrams of sodium per ounce for their brine-packed counterparts. Once opened, low-sodium hot cherry peppers should be refrigerated and will keep indefinitely.

KETCHUP
Ketchup, the delicious combination of pureed tomatoes and spices, was very likely an Italian invention. This condiment and its low-sodium counterpart are widely available in food stores throughout the country. One variation is low-sodium chili ketchup, which contains chopped onions and sometimes chopped pickle. Low-sodium ketchup and chili ketchup have only 5 to 10 milligrams of sodium per tablespoon compared to 298 milligrams for the salted products. Once opened, these low-sodium items should be refrigerated where they will keep indefinitely.

LEMON PEEL POWDER
Ground from dried lemon peel, this spice concentrate adds zip to any dish. It is available in the spice sections of food stores throughout the country. If bottled or tightly sealed in a plastic bag and stored in a cool, dry place, it will keep its full, pungent flavor indefinitely.

MAYONNAISE
Available in a wide variety of sizes, low-sodium mayonnaise is marketed by several leading health food manufacturers. Some brands are flavored with honey, others with egg yolks, and still others with lemon juice. All are delicious and, at only 4 milligrams sodium per tablespoon, a lot healthier than the salted commercial brands containing 85.5 milligrams sodium for the same 1 tablespoon. Once opened, low-sodium mayonnaise should be refrigerated immediately and will keep indefinitely.

MUSTARD
Hot, mild, Dijon, deli, or salad style, low-sodium mustard can be found everywhere. Although it contains only 3 to 7 milligrams

per ounce versus the 358 to 373 milligrams for the salty blends, low-sodium mustard has a pungent, zesty flavor that is every bit as tasty, if not tastier, than the salted varieties. Once opened, it should be refrigerated and will keep indefinitely.

ORANGE PEEL POWDER
Ground from dried orange peel. *See* Lemon Peel Powder.

PICKLES, BREAD AND BUTTER
Low-sodium pickles of every blend and type are widely available in food stores throughout the country. The sweet, crunchy bread-and-butter pickle is just one variety. Preserved in a sugar-based marinade, they—like all low-sodium pickles—are much lower in sodium than their salty counterparts, containing approximately 5 milligrams per ounce versus 192 milligrams. Once opened, low-sodium pickles should be refrigerated and will keep indefinitely.

SARDINES, CANNED
In this book, we rely on low-sodium sardines as replacements both for the salty variety and for anchovies when either are required. Low-sodium sardines are highly seasoned delectables, available in a wide variety of flavors and sauces: smoked, in chili sauce, in mustard sauce, and, of course, plain, to name but a few. Compared to their salty cousins and anchovies which contain a minimum of 510 and 400 milligrams sodium, respectively, per 3½ ounces, low-sodium sardines, at 120 milligrams sodium for 3½ ounces, are a find. Supermarkets everywhere keep a well-stocked selection on hand.

SALMON, CANNED
Low-sodium salmon has two distinct benefits over its salted counterpart. First, it is always packed in water so there is never any confusion with the high-calorie, oil-packed variety. Second, the difference in sodium for 3½ ounces is great: 70 milligrams compared to 473 for regular salmon. Low-sodium salmon is available in health food stores and supermarkets everywhere.

SUGAR SUBSTITUTES
Natural sugar—whether raw or processed—is a simple carbohydrate. Diabetics, of course, should avoid it altogether, and too much of it is unhealthy for all of us. The sugar substitutes on the market come in packets containing one- or two-teaspoon equivalents, and are sold in boxes. They will keep indefinitely on the

shelf. We recommend using only those made with calcium saccharine since these are low-sodium as well as sugar-free. Although aspartame is also low in sodium, we cannot recommend it at this time due to the controversy about its potential health detriments.

SWEET PEPPER HALVES
Available in the pickle section of most supermarkets, low-sodium sweet pepper halves generally come in 24-ounce jars. Made from sweet red peppers, these pickled delicacies, at only 7 milligrams of sodium per ounce, are the perfect salt-free alternative to pimientos, which are packed in salt. Once opened, low-sodium sweet pepper halves should be refrigerated and will keep indefinitely.

TOMATO PASTE
Low-sodium tomato paste, with only 3 milligrams of sodium per ounce, is widely available in supermarkets and health food stores across the country. It is rich and better tasting than its salty counterpart, which contains 57 milligrams of sodium per ounce. Although tomato paste is sold in cans to preserve its freshness, once opened, it should be transferred to glass or plastic containers, leaving ½ inch of headspace. It can be stored up to two months in the refrigerator, or indefinitely, in the freezer.

TOMATO PUREE
This thick, tomato-rich, subtly special blend is a great aid for perking up leftovers or freshening the flavor of a defrosted tomato-based dish. The low-sodium variety, containing only 3 milligrams sodium per ounce, is as readily available in supermarkets as the salty kind at 114 milligrams per ounce. Once opened, the puree should be stored in glass or plastic containers, leaving ½ inch headspace. Refrigerated, it will keep up to three weeks; frozen, indefinitely.

TOMATO SAUCE
Although in Italian cooking, tomato sauce is made from scratch with plump fresh tomatoes, low-sodium tomato sauce is a handy alternative to have in your pantry, and contains only 3 milligrams of sodium per ounce as compared to 86 for its salty counterpart. Many major manufacturers produce this basic sauce in 8- and 16-ounce cans and distribute it in supermarkets throughout the country. Once opened, low-sodium tomato sauce should be stored in glass or plastic containers, leaving ½ inch of headspace. Refrigerated, it will keep up to three weeks; frozen, indefinitely.

TUNA, CANNED
Like low-sodium salmon, low-sodium tuna is available in food stores everywhere. It also has the same health advantages versus its salty alternate, namely, that it comes packed in water rather than oil and that it contains only 51 milligrams of sodium compared to 800 milligrams for the salted varieties.

WORCESTERSHIRE SAUCE
This spicy blend with a soy sauce-and-vinegar base was created in Great Britain more than 400 years ago. It adds a marvelous, tangy bite, which is especially good in tomato-based dishes. A low-sodium version is available in health food stores and most supermarkets throughout the country. It will keep indefinitely on the shelf.

For Ease of Preparation

Utensils

Good Italian food requires no special utensils other than those you have in your kitchen. The exquisite creations of *la buona cucina* (the good kitchen) rely instead on the choicest and freshest foods, and—never to be underestimated—a talent for imaginative improvisation. It is, indeed, the ability to trust and take pleasure in your own taste which will prove your most valuable, if intangible, "utensil."

Preparation and Assembly

Preparing and cooking Italian food is a joy because most dishes can be made in 10 to 15 minutes. Those that require 45 minutes or more allow you time to do something else. As with any cuisine, assembling your ingredients is key to reducing your time in the kitchen. Many of these, like onion, garlic, or vegetables for a minestrone, can be diced, chopped, or sliced the day before, wrapped, and refrigerated until you are ready to use them. Others, such as a pork roast or veal scallops, usually require seasoning and perhaps the addition of vinegar or wine when you are ready to cook.

Italian cooking is so easy because there are only four basic methods of preparation.

Sautéeing

A great many Italian dishes are sautéed. Tuna Sautéed in Wine (page 130) and Veal with Artichokes and Mushrooms (page 180) are just two examples in this book. A majority of the recipes call for onion and/or garlic to be sautéed before adding the main ingredients, and this technique should be mastered to insure the finest flavor.

If you want the onion and garlic cooked to the same degree, add the onion first because garlic browns more quickly, acquiring a nutty flavor as it does so. For best results, barely melt the oil or butter (margarine, in this book), then add the onion. When the onion is just wilted and pale gold, add the garlic.

Italian cooks might use ½ cup of oil or more to sauté two or three onions and a few cloves of garlic over medium or high heat. But, in this book, to minimize fat, we sauté over a very low heat, and thus generally require no more than two to three tablespoons of fat for those same three onions. In this way, the food's own moisture is as much responsible for the cooking process as is the fat.

Deep Frying

The key to successful deep frying is this: Never crowd the pan. Hot oil will cool if overloaded with food, producing soggy results. The best method is (1) to have enough oil in the pan to cover the food; (2) to heat that oil until it crackles, and a bit of batter quickly sizzles and rises to the surface; and (3) to fry a few pieces of food at a time.

If you follow this procedure, food will fry quickly and evenly, using very little oil. Proper draining on brown paper bags or heavy toweling will absorb much of the remaining excess fat.

However, because of the dietary considerations of this book, whenever possible we use alternate methods to frying. The fat your body needs is amply supplied in the balanced meals you eat, or should eat, every day.

Roasting

In Italy roasting is somewhat unique in that it is most often done on top of the stove. First, the meat is browned over high heat in a little oil or butter. This process seals in all the natural juices. Then, the heat is reduced to low, and a small amount of wine or broth is added (just enough to generously cover the bottom of the pot—preferably a Dutch oven). Finally, the pot is covered with the lid slightly askew to allow steam to escape.

During the cooking process, additional liquid may be added, if necessary, to keep the meat from burning, but once the meat is done, any excess liquid should be boiled away.

This method offers the best combination of oven- or dry-roasting and braising, which is moist cooking done in a tightly closed pot. The final product has the texture and rich flavor of dry-roasted meat with the added moistness and tenderness of braising.

The oven-roasted or stove-topped braised recipes in this book may all be adapted to this technique; two candidates are Braised Chicken with Applesauce (page 138), and Italian Beef Stew (page 160).

Boiling

Whether boiling vegetables or pasta, the rule in Italy is the same: cook al dente, which means "to the tooth," or, in our vernacular, tender crisp.

With all vegetables (except leafy greens) and pasta, the method is simple. A pot of water, large enough for the food to float freely, should be brought to a rolling boil. The vegetables or pasta are added, and boiled about 5 to 7 minutes, or until fork tender. Drain instantly and rinse in cold water to prevent further cooking.

Leafy greens are cooked in a closed pot just large enough to contain them and with only the water left on the leaves from washing them. They will cook in their own moisture in 2 to 3 minutes.

No matter what cuisine you prefer, the Italian method of cooking vegetables is really ideal because the food cooks quickly and evenly, the color stays bright, the texture is firm, and the taste is fresh and sweet. When you try some of the recipes in our chapter on Vegetables (pages 213–38), you will be sure to agree.

How to Adapt Your Favorite Italian Recipes

After writing three cookbooks prior to this one, I think I have been able to persuade my readers that any cuisine can be adapted to be salt-free and still retain the flavor and authenticity of the original. What it takes is imagination, common sense, some know-how, and a little encouragement.

At this point, so many people have discovered the health benefits of living salt-free and have mastered the art of tasty, salt-free cooking (due, in part, I hope, to my efforts) that it remains to me to continue to supply the know-how and encouragement. This I am most happy to do. So let me repeat here those tips that have proven true over time and through many experiments:

- Any pungent or hot spice will give food a zesty flavor. These include: cayenne pepper, black pepper, hot pepper flakes, cumin, lemon peel powder, chili powder (salt-free, of course), garlic powder, paprika, and fennel seed. You get the idea.
- Even sweet spices and herbs like basil, dill, cinnamon, cloves, nutmeg, and orange peel powder trick the mind and palate into thinking sweet rather than salty.
- Condiments that have an acid content really do give foods a salty flavor. Marinate or cook meat, fish, or poultry with vinegar, lemon juice, low-sodium ketchup, mustard, or wine, and you will be a believer.
- One final tip: Low-sodium bouillon, either beef- or chicken-flavored, will instantly give you the taste of salt. Whether you are using the granulated or powdered form, just stir it into any dish, and everyone will think you have added salt.

Of course, not all of the herbs, spices, and condiments noted above have application to Italian cooking. But many do. Perhaps more interesting is the fact that Italian food is not an overtly salty cuisine. Much of its spiciness comes from the acidity of the lemons, tomatoes, wine, and vinegar so frequently part of the recipes, as well as from the distinctive flavors of basil, oregano, and garlic. To these, add the ripe, also slightly acidic, taste of olive oil, and you will realize that, of all cuisines, Italian is seemingly easy to adapt for the salt-free dieter.

But to paraphrase an old cliché: Easy is as easy does. Most Italian recipes still call for a degree of salt, or use salty foods such as anchovies, Parmesan cheese, and use non-dietetic canned tomato products, which are processed with salt. Eliminating salt so subtly used, and replacing it with equally undetectable amounts of herbs, spices, and condiments to yield the same flavorful authenticity, required many hours of trial and error, and finally success in my kitchen. The resulting recipes are offered here for your pleasure. We believe they will satisfy the salty palates most of us have acquired through life-long eating habits.

The purity of Italian cooking is such that salt can actually detract from the fullest enjoyment of a recipe's flavor. As we hope this book will demonstrate, if you follow the tips outlined above, you, too, can adapt your favorite Italian recipes, and pass up the salt.

Other Diet Tips

Every magazine in this country today has regular articles or columns devoted to the latest information on maintaining health on special diets, and on physical fitness. Consumer interest has never been higher. The more we know, the more we want to know. And we are putting this knowledge into practice in our daily lives.

A few years ago, all the warnings, suggestions, and product labelings would have been intimidating and, for the most part, probably ignored. Special needs were thought to be reserved only for an unfortunate minority with problems that somehow carried the social stigma of sickness. Today we know better. First, we realize that preventive care can benefit all of us, often staving off or lessening serious illness. Second, knowledge breeds confidence and confidence wins converts, so we may find ourselves part of a comfortable majority, albeit a newly enlightened one.

Food Watching

Salt, sugar, cholesterol, calcium. How much do we need? How much is too much? What consumer aids and information exist to help us observe healthier dietary principles? There is now a medical and nutritional consensus in response to these questions.

Salt

Despite increased consumer cutback on salt, too many Americans still consume 12,000 to 20,000 milligrams of sodium per day—far more than the range of 1,000 to 3,000 milligrams considered more than adequate. Indeed, many medical experts believe that 250 milligrams daily is all that any of us—man, woman or child, of whatever height, weight, or build—require, and that more than 250 milligrams is excessive.

In a world seemingly saturated with salt, a limit of 250 milligrams seems impossible to achieve. Less than a decade ago, this was true, but not any longer. First, today's marketplace is flooded with low-sodium products of every kind. Second, full-disclosure labeling has long been voluntarily practiced by a majority of manufacturers. Third, effective July, 1986, per ruling of the Food and Drug Administration, any products offering ingredient and nutritional information must include the sodium content in milligrams per serving. And finally, those products already making a sodium claim must conform to FDA regulations, which are listed below for your information:

- *No salt added.* These products may have been processed with salt or sodium without extra salt added for flavor. No-salt-added products should be avoided by everyone on salt-free diets.
- *Low-sodium.* Containing at least 75 percent less salt than their salty counterparts, low-sodium products average 140 milligrams per serving. They are fine for those on moderately restricted diets, but should be avoided by those who must not exceed 1,000 milligrams sodium or less per day.
- *Very low-sodium.* At 35 milligrams of sodium per serving, or less, these products are acceptable for those with even the most severe salt restrictions.
- *Sodium-free.* No one need worry about these products which contain less than 5 milligrams of sodium per serving.

For those products whose ingredients may contain salt, hidden behind another name, here is a three-point guideline:

- Avoid everything from saccharin to soda that contains salt or a sodium compound, such as sodium benzoate, disodium sulfate, sodium saccharin, brine, sodium bicarbonate (baking soda, baking powder), etc.
- Avoid products that still list "natural ingredients," which is often the deceptive label for, among other things, salt.
- Avoid all packaged goods and canned goods that are not labeled "low-sodium."

With so much information and so many products now available to the salt-free dieter, it is really quite easy not only to stick to your diet, but to enjoy as much variety and taste as you did in saltier days. The Italian Diet on pages 295–338, which never exceeds 300 milligrams of sodium per day, should be sufficient proof.

Sugar

The issue for most Americans is not sugar, but sugar substitutes. Like many foods, sugar has a bad reputation because we overdose on the wrong kind of sugar—the kind that makes up the empty calories in soft drinks and sweets.

We all know that the fructose sugar found in fruits is healthy. Even granulated sugar, in moderation, is not harmful, and at only 16 calories per teaspoon, it can hardly be considered anathema to the dieter. Moreover, today many medical professionals believe that, in very small amounts, sugar is not harmful even to the diabetic.

The watchword is moderation, which should be applied to sugar substitutes, as well. Because these sugar alternatives contain minimal calories, we tend to believe we can consume any or all of them, regardless of the amounts. It is important to remember that most sugar substitutes are chemical compounds and that even those approved for commercial distribution may not be right for your body.

In regard to this last point, the FDA banned cyclamate in 1970 because it was linked with cancer. That relationship has been virtually disproved, but other concerns have arisen. Studies in medical laboratories throughout the country indicate that cyclamate can cause the chromosome defect resulting in Down's syndrome and that, in the body, cyclamate changes to cyclohexylamine which can cause male sterility. Because of its many potentially harmful effects, it is highly unlikely that cyclamate will be made available to consumers at any time in the near future.

Even sorbital, approved for most diabetic diets, is clearly not for everyone. Although widely used in many products, especially candy, this artificial sweetner produces severe reactions, including diarrhea, in up to 30 percent of whites and 52 percent of blacks with diabetes.

Aspartame, commercially sold under the name Nutra Sweet, is the newest sugar substitute on the market and is supposed to be the best because it produces the taste equivalent of sugar without the bitter aftertaste of saccharin. However, some concerns have been raised regarding aspartame's possible negative effects on the body.

On the market since 1981, this amino acid compound may be linked to headaches, depression, and dizziness which have been reported after its use. To date, studies at the Centers for Disease Control in Atlanta have been unable to corroborate any causal relationship between these disorders and aspartame. However, experts generally agree that some people exhibit a high sensitivity to the sweetener. In particular, those with the genetic disorder phenylketonuria could suffer mental retardation from aspartame because they must restrict their intake of one of its key components.

Saccharin is still the most widely used of all sugar substitutes. Although, in 1977, studies with laboratory rats indicated that saccharin is a low-level carcinogen, years of subsequent research continue to substantiate its safety. So if this is the sweetener of your choice, be aware that saccharin comes in two forms: sodium saccharin and calcium saccharin. The latter carries the label "sodium-free" and should be the choice of all salt watchers.

What all this means is that no artificial sweetener is 100 percent safe. Consult your doctor to determine which sugar substitutes you are allowed. Then read labels to be sure that the products flagged "dietetic" are truly all right for you. We offer this information not to dissuade you from using sugar substitutes, but in the belief that an aware consumer is a healthier one.

Cholesterol

Cholesterol presents another health controversy. Everyone agrees that too much can be harmful and can lead to heart disease and circulation problems. But because individual cholesterol tolerance varies, it is hard to establish a firm, prescribed minimum/maximum at this time. However, the majority of medical authorities recommend holding consumption to 250 to 300 milligrams of cholesterol per day. The ultimate purpose is to control the body's blood cholesterol level which should be maintained under 200 milligrams throughout life.

Contrary to popular belief, although cholesterol is found only in animal-derived foods, it is not synonymous with fat. For example, chicken contains the same amount of cholesterol with skin or without. What is more, at 48 milligrams of cholesterol for 2 ounces of white meat and 53 milligrams for dark, chicken is on a par with pork and beef.

Dairy products contain about 30 milligrams of cholesterol for an average portion. Eggs, at more than 100 milligrams, are the exception in this food group. A similar anomaly exists in the seafood category. Fish generally contain under 40 milligrams of cholesterol per 2-ounce serving, whereas shellfish exceed 100 milligrams for the same amount.

The amount of cholesterol in foods is always a factor to consider. It is also important to note that not all cholesterol is bad for you. There are two types of cholesterol: HDL and LDL. It is the latter which clogs the arteries and can lead to the health problems noted above. On the other hand, HDL-cholesterol actually protects against heart disease.

According to the May, 1986, issue of the Tufts University Diet and Nutrition Letter, recent studies at the University of Texas Health Science Center in Dallas, under the direction of Dr. Scott Grundy, suggest that monounsaturated fats, particularly olive oil, may be directly responsible for lowering the levels of LDL-cholesterol in the blood.

So you see, being aware of the latest scientific findings coupled with a common-sensical balanced diet are the surest means of keeping your cholesterol level within proper limits.

Calcium

As a child, how many times did your mother urge you to "drink your milk" to build healthy bones? Probably quite often. Your mother, like mothers everywhere, wanted to be sure you had the proper amount of calcium. But the need for calcium in the body goes beyond bone structure. Calcium plays a critical role in controling muscle contraction (including the heart), in blood clotting, and in the transmission of nerve impulses.

Despite the need, the typical American diet, particularly among adults, is far too low in calcium, averaging 500 milligrams a day, half of the current RDA. Indeed, many doctors and nutritionists believe that teens, pregnant women, and nursing mothers require 1,200 milligrams, and that post-menopausal women need 1,500 milligrams per day.

Unfortunately, most foods high in calcium, like dairy products, are also high in calories and sodium, which are the overriding concerns of the moment for most of us. Apart from dairy products, there are other high-calcium foods that are low-sodium and low-calorie in average servings. Some of them include: broccoli, 140 milligrams per cup; tofu, 154 milligrams per cup; and sardines, 400 milligrams per 3.8-ounce can. For more information on calcium and how to provide your body with its daily allowance, we suggest you read *The Calcium Bible* by Patricia Hausman.

However, because there is no medical proof that calcium is better absorbed from foods than taken in alternate ways, you might want to consider one of the many calcium supplements available. These are made from a variety of compounds: calcium carbonate, calcium phosphate, calcium lactate, to name a few. They also come in different forms, including tablets, powder, and chewable tablets.

Whichever you choose, consider two things: your own health and the elemental calcium content per dose. For your health, avoid bone meal or dolomite calcium, which may contain lead and be toxic. If your doctor finds your stomach has a low acid content, avoid calcium carbonate and calcium phosphate. If you have a lactose intolerance, avoid calcium lactate.

Elemental calcium is that part of a calcium compound your body will actually ingest. It is usually considerably less than the weight of the calcium product. For example, a calcium tablet containing 1,000 milligrams of calcium phosphate might supply your body with only half that amount. To determine the elemental calcium content of a given product, carefully read the label, front, side, and back.

In the final analysis, safeguarding your health comes down to being aware and taking an active part in selecting what is best for you. Today all the literature on the market and the regulations currently in effect make it much easier than it once was, but taking advantage of them is up to you.

Travel and Other Pleasures

Good thoughts bear repeating. That is why we want to restate here the tips detailed in our two previous salt-free diet cookbooks in order to help you maintain a salt-free diet outside the home.

The travel and hotel industries have always shown the greatest awareness of special diet problems. With 48 hours' notice, any airline will provide one of a number of special diet meals, including low-calorie, vegetarian, seafood, kosher, diabetic, and low-sodium. These meals are special in more ways than one, for often they are much tastier than regulation airline fare.

Hotels will also try their best to accommodate your dietary needs. On request, they will install a refrigerator in your room (usually for a modest daily rate) so you can keep any special foods or medication on hand. What is more, if you explain your problem and requirements to room service, the restaurant maître d', and the hotel manager, they will generally be understanding and helpful. But one word of caution: Wherever you are and whatever the circumstance, if the food you get is not the food you ordered, send it back. Never, but never, settle for less than perfection when your health is at stake.

By the way, it is always a good idea to carry a few low-sodium snacks and canned goods when you travel, in case an emergency arises or boredom sets in. A small container of your favorite spices will also come in handy for perking up a meal "out."

Closer to home, you will have many more occasions to eat out. Today restaurants are much more sensitive to the special dieter than they were a decade ago. I used to carefully explain to the waiter or captain what I needed and why, to emphasize how important my requests were. They would listen politely but with slightly bemused expressions, and would often reply, "Ah, yes, Madame is watching her figure." Funny to think about now, but maddening and often disastrous then. They did not take me seriously, and my food, when it arrived, was predictably unacceptable.

But times have changed. Today that same waiter in that same restaurant will nod with understanding and faithfully see that your order is prepared exactly as you like it. This applies not only to salt-free requests but to any dietary need.

In any restaurant, including Italian, certain foods should be avoided because they are prepared ahead of time and usually contain salt. These include soups, sauces, dressings, and condiments. However, because Italian food is so basic, a simple tomato sauce may be all right for you. Just ask how it is prepared before you place your order.

The rule of thumb for dining out is simple: Avoid all foods made in advance; stick to dishes broiled with nothing more than herbs and spices or a little wine; request steamed vegetables with no salt added to the water; in Italian restaurants, ask for the pasta to be boiled in unsalted water. And, most important, when in doubt, ask before you order or taste. You will be surprised how many dishes are available to you in Italian restaurants, or in any other.

As for visiting, do not be shy. Tell your friends the problem. Chances are they will want to prepare food you can enjoy. If that is not possible, brown-bag your own. It is as easy as that.

Always be aware, however, that even with the best intentions, people can make mistakes. Be glad they are receptive and want to be helpful, but, fortified with the tips outlined above, you should—and must—always be the questioner, the final judge of, and the last word on what is best for you.

Recipes

The most ardent Italian cooks will tell you that there is no great mystery to fine Italian food. The secret, if any, lies in preparing the freshest ingredients available in the simplest way. Even herbs like basil, rosemary, thyme, mint, and oregano are used as much for their aromatic scents which fill the air with contentment as for their singular flavors.

However, there is no doubt that, like other ethnic cuisines, Italian food is distinguished by its use of particular herbs and spices. Most are indigenous to the Mediterranean region, while others, garlic for one, came from as far away as Siberia. But their origin is beside the point because these herbs and spices are now irrevocably associated with Italian food, especially when they are blended with wine, vinegar, lemon juice, and tomatoes. These highly acidic ingredients and the Italian style of cooking them down to produce a rich, concentrated flavor, create a "salty" taste that virtually eliminates the need for salt itself.

It is not hard, therefore, to adapt Italian food for the salt-free dieter while still maintaining the style and taste of the original. Equally important, Italian cuisine can also be adjusted to suit the needs of those who must restrict their fat and calorie intake as well. For example, in this book, we have taken the liberty of reducing the amount of cooking fat and calories by using very low heat for browning and frying. What is more, even diabetics can enjoy most of the recipes—with the exception of pasta main dishes and pastries—because every attempt has been made to keep the carbohydrate content to a moderate level.

Italian cuisine really does hold the promise of good food for just about everyone. But only half the pleasure is in the eating. The other half comes from the actual dining experience. Meals in the Italian home tend to be basic and, for that very reason, comforting. Indeed, eating together is a beloved family tradition, marked by a warmth and lusty unself-consciousness characterized by the phrase *buon gusto*.

In Italy, the big meal is generally a multi-course affair served in the evening. A first course of antipasto is followed by soup, pasta or rice, and then by a hearty main dish, often accompanied by one or more cooked vegetables. During the meal, wine is the preferred beverage.

Because wine is produced in every province in Italy, Italians are delightfully casual about it. They do not care one bit about drinking red wine with meat, or white wine with poultry or fish. What they do care about is which wine will provide the most pleasure at a particular moment. At meal's end, they abandon wine altogether, preferring a liqueur or whiskey with dessert.

This habit of eating so heavily right before bedtime is not the healthiest for two reasons: First, there is no opportunity to work off the calories consumed, and, second, the digestive system has the disadvantage of having to work literally lying down. Luckily, this practice is, to some degree, counteracted by the very healthy penchant for energy-packed mini-meals throughout the rest of the day.

At breakfast, foaming cups of cappuccino are usually accompanied by cornettos (the Italian version of French brioche). Pizza, hot from the ovens of local bakeries, is the favorite coffee break and lunch snack. These carbohydrate foods burn calories and simultaneously generate energy. Lunch and dinner are still the biggest meals although some Italians now opt for their version of nouvelle cuisine at dinner. In general, smaller portions are served and less oil used at all meals, but dinner is lighter than lunch only when eaten at home.

All things considered, Italian food is nutritionally sound and is basically good for everyone. Furthermore, as we noted earlier, adjustments for the special dieter are easily accomplished. You may wonder then why we do not simplify things further by using salt and sugar substitutes.

With regard to the former, there are three reasons. First, too much of anything is unhealthy, and indiscriminate use of salt substitutes (potassium chloride) can, over time, be just as harmful as overdosing on salt. Second, salt, in any form, masks the true flavor of food. Our purpose is to enhance it, which we can do most deliciously and easily with the extensive selection of Italian seasonings abundantly available. Third, Italian food normally requires little salt, and since we can make up the difference with natural ingredients, there is no need to opt for chemical additives.

We have also avoided sugar substitutes for three reasons. First, as noted earlier in this book, some diabetics cannot tolerate sugar replacements. Second, sugar substitutes break down under the heat of cooking to produce a bitter, lingering aftertaste. Third, on a per-serving basis, the amount of sugar found in any of our recipes is fairly small and may be allowed on the diabetic's diet.

"May be" is the key phrase and must be qualified, for whether your problem is sugar, salt, fat, or calories, you should never play guessing games with your health. So always check with your doctor before using this or any diet book.

Just two reminders before you begin:

1. The calorie, sodium, carbohydrate, and fat contents given for each recipe include all ingredients called for, but do not include any of the suggested accompanying dishes.
2. For convenience, we have used dried rather than fresh herbs and spices in these recipes, unless otherwise noted. However, do use fresh whenever you can because nothing tastes quite as good. Just remember: Because the flavor in dried, ground, or powdered herbs and spices is concentrated, you will need three times the amount in fresh form.

There is nothing more to add, except when in Rome, do as the Romans do: *mangia*, and enjoy.

Antipasti

In the United States, the word "antipasti" promises wonderful morsels of Italian persuasion: broiled stuffed mushrooms, chunks of spicy sausage, miniature pizza. The greater the variety, the better we like it, because we enjoy antipasti as party delicacies, independent of any meal.

But in Italy, antipasti are planned as carefully as we plan our appetizers. That is, what is served and whether it is served hot or cold is carefully designed to complement the meal that follows. In Italy, antipasti are not finger foods, but rather the first course of the main meal—quite literally those foods served before the pasta, which is how they got their name.

So do not reserve the recipes in this chapter for cocktails only. As Italians know all too well, antipasti can set a memorable tone for any meal.

Mixed Vegetable Appetizer MAKES 12 CUPS

A true Sicilian medley—as colorful as it is tasty. Leftovers make a wonderful topping for hamburgers, cold fish, or cold chicken.

2 eggplant, peeled and diced
2 tablespoons low-sodium beef bouillon
7 tomatoes, chopped
4 tablespoons dried basil
4 tablespoons dried parsley
1 teaspoon celery seed*
¼ cup cider vinegar

¼ cup sugar
2 tablespoons olive oil, divided
3 onions, chopped
3 zucchini, diced
Black pepper to taste
2 teaspoons paprika
⅛ teaspoon hot pepper flakes

1. In Dutch oven, place eggplant. Sprinkle with bouillon. Weight down with a heavy plate. Let stand 2 hours.
2. In saucepan, combine tomatoes, basil, parsley, and celery seed. Turn heat to low and simmer 1 hour, stirring occasionally.
3. Add vinegar and sugar, stirring to blend thoroughly. Let simmer 1 hour more.
4. While tomatoes are cooking, in skillet, heat 1 tablespoon oil over medium-low heat. Add onions and cook 3 minutes, or until onions are golden brown, stirring frequently. Transfer to platter.
5. To skillet, add remaining oil and zucchini. Cook 5 minutes, or until zucchini are tender, stirring often. Transfer to platter.
6. Drain eggplant and place in same skillet. Cook 3 minutes, stirring often.
7. Stir onions, zucchini, and eggplant into tomato mixture, blending thoroughly.
8. Stir in remaining ingredients. Cover and simmer ½ hour.
9. Pour mixture into jars, leaving ½-inch headspace and close tightly.
10. If refrigerated, will keep up to 1 month. If frozen, will keep indefinitely.

Per recipe: 1,293.4 calories; 178.4 mg. sodium; 255.8 gm. carbohydrates; 41.1 gm. fat.
Per cup: 107.8 calories; 14.9 mg. sodium; 21.3 gm. carbohydrates; 3.4 gm. fat.
Per tablespoon: 6.7 calories; 0.9 mg. sodium; 1.3 gm. carbohydrates; 0.2 gm. fat.

* Do not use celery flakes, which contain salt.

Sweet Pickled Vegetables   MAKES 12 CUPS

Nobody can make pickled vegetables as zesty or as spicy, yet as sweet, as the Italians do. The recipe below is patterned on the style of Calabria, the region at the tip of the Italian boot.

4 carrots, parboiled,* sliced in
⅛-inch rounds
6 cups cauliflowerettes,
parboiled*
12 white onions, sliced thin
12 cloves garlic, minced
2 tablespoons dried mint

3 tablespoons dried parsley
16 radishes, sliced in ⅛-inch
rounds
6 cups water
2 cups white vinegar
½ cup sugar

1. In bowl, combine first 7 ingredients. Toss to blend. Set aside.
2. In saucepan, combine water and vinegar. Turn heat to medium and bring to a slow boil.
3. Stir in sugar and continue stirring 2 minutes, or until sugar is completely dissolved.
4. Pour vinegar mixture over vegetables.
5. Spoon vegetable mixture into jars, leaving ½-inch headspace. Cover tightly and let stand ½ hour.
6. Refrigerate and vegetables will keep indefinitely.

Per recipe: 1,864.8 calories; 485.0 mg. sodium; 480.3 gm. carbohydrates;
4.9 gm. fat.
Per cup: 155.4 calories; 40.4 mg. sodium; 40.0 gm. carbohydrates; 0.4 gm. fat.
Per tablespoon: 9.7 calories; 2.5 mg. sodium; 2.5 gm. carbohydrates;
0.03 gm. fat.

* Do not add salt to water.

Antipasto Mixed Fry

SERVES 24

You do not have to be Italian to enjoy this traditional dish from the Abruzzi region. Serve with Hot Sauce (page 250).

4 eggs
¾ cup water
¾ cup all-purpose flour
2 tablespoons low-sodium beef bouillon
2 teaspoons lemon peel powder
2 teaspoons dried oregano
¼ teaspoon black pepper
2 cups vegetable oil
2 cups broccoli flowerettes, steamed al dente*

2 cups cauliflowerettes, steamed al dente*
2 green peppers, sliced in ½-inch rings
1 pound shrimp, shelled and deveined
24 radishes, halved
3 lemons, cut into wedges

1. In bowl, beat together eggs and water. Set aside.
2. In second bowl, combine flour, bouillon, lemon peel powder, oregano, and black pepper, blending thoroughly. Set aside.
3. In skillet, heat oil over medium heat until oil starts to crackle.
4. While oil is heating, dip broccoli, cauliflower, green peppers, and shrimp into egg mixture. Then dip into flour mixture.
5. With slotted spoon, lower half the vegetables and shrimp into oil. Fry 5 minutes, or until batter turns golden brown.
6. With slotted spoon, transfer mixed fry to paper towels. Drain.
7. Repeat Steps 5 and 6 with remaining vegetables and shrimp.
8. Transfer mixed fry to platter. Skewer with toothpicks.
9. Garnish with radishes and lemons.

Per serving: 82.3 calories; 45.0 mg. sodium; 8.4 gm. carbohydrates; 2.6 gm. fat.

* Do not add salt to water.

Baked Stuffed Mushrooms

MAKES 48 CANAPÉS

Italian chefs are renowned for their baked stuffed antipasto dishes. Oysters, clams, eggplant, zucchini—every food imaginable takes on its own special magic when stuffed and baked Italian style. This recipe and the one that follows are two variations.

1 tablespoon olive oil	1 teaspoon paprika
48 large mushrooms, stems reserved and chopped	1 teaspoon dried oregano
1 can (6½ ounces) low-sodium tuna, including liquid	3 tablespoons heavy cream
1 tablespoon dried parsley	4 ounces low-sodium Swiss cheese, minced
	4 tablespoons unsalted margarine

1. In skillet, heat oil over medium-low heat. Add mushroom stems, tuna, including liquid, parsley, paprika, and oregano. Cook 5 minutes, stirring constantly.
2. Transfer tuna mixture to bowl. Add cream, blending thoroughly. Then mash.
3. Stir in cheese.
4. Preheat oven to 350°.
5. Dot bottoms of mushrooms with margarine and stuff with tuna mixture.
6. Place mushrooms in 9 x 13-inch ovenproof casserole and bake 20 minutes.

Per canapé: 35.1 calories; 7.6 mg. sodium; 1.4 gm. carbohydrates; 2.3 gm. fat.

Mushrooms in Mustard Marinade

MAKES 24 CANAPÉS

A delicious variation of marinated mushrooms which traditionally call for vinaigrette dressing.

24 large mushrooms, stems removed
3 cups Mustard-Garlic Sauce (page 256)

½ teaspoon hot pepper flakes
1 onion, chopped
2 tablespoons dry sherry

1. In bowl, combine all ingredients. Cover and refrigerate at least 4 hours to allow flavors to blend.
2. May be refrigerated up to 2 weeks in tightly closed containers.

Per canapé: 48.1 calories; 5.2 mg. sodium; 2.7 gm. carbohydrates; 3.8 gm. fat.

Zucchini Strips

SERVES 8

These crisp and sweet finger foods are as popular here as they are in the southern regions of Italy.

2 tablespoons olive oil, divided
4 zucchini, cut into ½-inch strips, 2 inches long, divided

2 tablespoons low-sodium beef bouillon
¼ teaspoon black pepper
3 tablespoons lemon juice

1. In skillet, heat 1 tablespoon oil over medium heat. Add half the zucchini and fry 2 minutes, stirring constantly. Transfer to warm platter.
2. Repeat Step 1 with remaining oil and zucchini.
3. Sprinkle bouillon and pepper over zucchini. Toss to blend.
4. Sprinkle lemon juice over zucchini.

Per serving: 63.2 calories; 8.5 mg. sodium; 5.5 gm. carbohydrates; 4.6 gm. fat.

Stuffed Eggs Genovese   MAKES 12 CANAPÉS

Very spicy and very good.

1 tablespoon unsalted margarine
6 scallions, chopped, including
  greens
1 can (3⅜ ounces) low-sodium
  sardines
1 teaspoon low-sodium mustard

½ green pepper, minced
⅛ teaspoon cayenne pepper
2 teaspoons dried parsley
6 hard-cooked eggs,* peeled and
  halved lengthwise

1. In skillet, melt margarine over low heat. Add scallions and cook 3 minutes, stirring often. Set aside.
2. In bowl, combine sardines, mustard, green pepper, cayenne pepper, and parsley, blending thoroughly.
3. Stir in scallions.
4. Scoop out egg yolks and add to sardine mixture. Mash thoroughly.
5. Stuff egg white hollows with egg yolk mixture.
6. Transfer stuffed eggs to 9-inch square casserole. Cover and refrigerate at least 2 hours to allow flavors to blend.

Per serving: 71.8 calories; 40.7 mg. sodium; 1.3 gm. carbohydrates; 4.1 gm. fat.

* Do not add salt to water.

Sweet Pepper-Stuffed Eggs

MAKES 12 CANAPÉS

Even people who do not like hard-cooked eggs will love this light and luscious specialty.

6 hard-cooked eggs,* peeled and halved lengthwise
⅛ teaspoon celery seed†
1 teaspoon dried tarragon
1 teaspoon paprika
⅛ teaspoon dried thyme
Black pepper to taste
2 halves low-sodium sweet peppers, chopped

3 tablespoons liquid from low-sodium sweet peppers
1 tablespoon low-sodium mayonnaise
3 scallions, minced, including greens

1. Scoop out egg yolks and place in bowl. Mash.
2. Add all remaining ingredients, except egg whites, blending thoroughly.
3. Spoon egg yolk mixture into egg white hollows.
4. Transfer stuffed eggs to 9-inch square casserole. Cover and refrigerate at least 2 hours to allow flavors to blend.

Per canapé: 54.2 calories; 32.4 mg. sodium; 1.9 gm. carbohydrates; 2.0 gm. fat.

* Do not add salt to water.
† Do not use celery flakes, which contain salt.

Baked Stuffed Oysters MAKES 24 CANAPÉS

Clams oreganato, the international favorite from Tuscany, is the
inspiration for this recipe. We have used oysters because they are
much lower in sodium than clams.

1 tablespoon olive oil
2 cloves garlic, minced
1 pint oysters, shucked and
  chopped, liquid and shells
  reserved
Black pepper to taste
2 teaspoons low-sodium chicken
  bouillon

¼ cup low-sodium seasoned
  bread crumbs
1 teaspoon dried parsley
1 teaspoon dried basil
2 ounces low-sodium Cheddar
  cheese, minced

1. Preheat oven to 375°.
2. In skillet, heat oil over low heat. Add garlic and cook 10
   minutes, or until garlic is lightly browned, stirring often.
3. Add oysters, pepper, bouillon, bread crumbs, parsley, and
   basil. Cook 3 minutes, blending thoroughly.
4. Transfer oyster mixture to bowl. Add oyster liquid and cheese,
   blending thoroughly.
5. Spoon oyster mixture into oyster shells.
6. Place aluminum foil on bottom rack in oven. Put shells on foil
   and bake 10 minutes.

Per canapé: 33.0 calories; 12.3 mg. sodium; 2.1 gm. carbohydrates; 1.8 gm. fat.

Garlic Shrimp

MAKES 24 CANAPÉS

Venice and other ports along the Adriatic Sea inspired this irresistible dish. It is so good you may want to feature it as a main course for 4.

1 tablespoon olive oil
6 cloves garlic, minced
2 dozen medium shrimp, shelled and deveined
Dash of hot pepper flakes
1 tablespoon unsalted margarine

2 tablespoons low-sodium seasoned bread crumbs
¼ teaspoon dried oregano
1 teaspoon dried parsley
2 halves low-sodium sweet peppers, chopped

1. In large skillet, heat oil over low heat. Add garlic and cook 5 minutes, stirring often.
2. Raise heat to medium. Add the shrimp and hot pepper flakes and cook 5 minutes more, or until shrimp turn pink all over, stirring constantly. Transfer mixture to bowl.
3. In same skillet, melt margarine over low heat. Add bread crumbs, oregano, and parsley. Cook 5 minutes, stirring often.
4. Spoon bread crumb mixture over shrimp. Toss to blend.
5. Add sweet peppers. Toss to blend.
6. Skewer shrimp with toothpicks.

Per canapé: 36.9 calories; 29.7 mg. sodium; 2.0 gm. carbohydrates; 1.3 gm. fat.
Per serving as an entrée: 211.2 calories; 178.2 mg. sodium; 12.3 gm. carbohydrates; 7.9 gm. fat.

Salmon Spread

MAKES 1¾ CUPS

A most spectacular dip from the northern regions, this spread is wonderful with raw vegetables and low-sodium crackers. For variety, you may replace the salmon with either 2 cans (6⅜ ounces) low-sodium sardines, or 1 can (6½ ounces) low-sodium tuna.

1 can (7¾ ounces) low-sodium salmon, including liquid
1 onion, chopped
2 cloves garlic, minced
⅛ teaspoon fennel seed
1 teaspoon dried parsley

¼ teaspoon dried sage
1⁄16 teaspoon hot pepper flakes
½ teaspoon mustard powder
1 tablespoon capers*
½ cup low-sodium ricotta cheese
2 tablespoons lemon juice

1. In bowl, combine all ingredients, blending thoroughly. Cover and refrigerate at least 2 hours to allow flavors to blend thoroughly.
2. May be refrigerated up to 3 days in tightly closed containers.

With salmon:
  Per recipe: 573.5 calories; 172.9 mg. sodium; 31.2 gm. carbohydrates; 28.5 gm. fat.
  Per cup: 327.7 calories; 98.8 mg. sodium; 17.8 gm. carbohydrates; 16.3 gm. fat.
  Per tablespoon: 20.5 calories; 6.2 mg. sodium; 1.1 gm. carbohydrates; 1.0 gm. fat.
With sardines:
  Per recipe: 722.7 calories; 294.7 mg. sodium; 31.2 gm. carbohydrates; 40.9 gm. fat.
  Per cup: 413.0 calories; 168.1 mg. sodium; 17.8 gm. carbohydrates; 23.4 gm. fat.
  Per tablespoon: 25.8 calories; 10.5 mg. sodium; 1.1 gm. carbohydrates; 1.5 gm. fat.
With tuna:
  Per recipe: 473.7 calories; 122.6 mg. sodium; 31.2 gm. carbohydrates; 17.8 gm. fat.
  Per cup: 270.7 calories; 70.1 mg. sodium; 17.8 gm. carbohydrates; 10.2 gm. fat.
  Per tablespoon: 16.9 calories; 4.4 mg. sodium; 1.1 gm. carbohydrates; 0.6 gm. fat.

* Preserved in vinegar only.

Broiled Chicken Wings in Tomato Sauce

MAKES 16 CANAPÉS

These Neapolitan chicken morsels are simply delicious.

2 cups Tomato Sauce I (page 242)   16 chicken wings
2 teaspoons dried tarragon

1. Preheat oven to broil.
2. In 9 x 13-inch ovenproof casserole, combine first 2 ingredients, stirring to blend.
3. Add chicken wings and broil 6 inches from heat 6 minutes, or until skin starts to brown.
4. Turn wings and broil 5 minutes more.
5. Transfer wings to platter. Serve hot or warm.

Per canapé: 77.5 calories; 23.5 mg. sodium; 3.2 gm. carbohydrates; 3.5 gm. fat.

Wine-Baked Chicken Wings

MAKES 16 CANAPÉS

The subtle marinade lends a northern elegance to this dish.

1 cup red wine   **¼ teaspoon garlic powder**
¼ cup lemon juice   **1½ teaspoons dried oregano**
½ teaspoon onion powder   **16 chicken wings**

1. In 9 x 13-inch ovenproof casserole, combine first 5 ingredients, blending thoroughly.
2. Add chicken wings. Cover and marinate at least 4 hours, turning wings occasionally.
3. Preheat oven to 350°.
4. Bake, covered, ½ hour.
5. Turn wings. Bake, uncovered, 10 minutes more.
6. Transfer wings to platter. Serve hot or warm.

Per canapé: 75.5 calories; 22.2 mg. sodium; 0.9 gm. carbohydrates; 3.2 gm. fat.

Chicken Liver Spread

MAKES 3 CUPS

An unusually tasty blend that is as elegant as the finest pâté.

1 tablespoon unsalted margarine
2 onions, chopped
2 cloves garlic, minced
1 pound chicken livers
2 tablespoons dry sherry
3 tablespoons low-sodium
   seasoned bread crumbs

2 teaspoons dried oregano
⅛ teaspoon hot pepper flakes
2 tablespoons cider vinegar
3 tablespoons low-sodium
   mayonnaise

1. In skillet, melt margarine over low heat. Add onions and garlic. Cover and cook 15 minutes, or until onions are lightly browned, stirring occasionally.
2. Add livers and sherry. Cook, uncovered, 10 minutes more.
3. Turn livers. Add bread crumbs, oregano, hot pepper flakes, and vinegar. Cook 10 minutes more.
4. Transfer mixture to blender. Grind to a coarse paste.
5. Transfer mixture to bowl. Stir in mayonnaise. Cover and refrigerate at least 1 hour to allow flavors to blend.
6. May be refrigerated in tightly closed containers up to 1 week.

Per recipe: 1,255 calories; 378.8 mg. sodium; 83.5 gm. carbohydrates;
   63.4 gm. fat.
Per cup: 418.3 calories; 126.3 mg. sodium; 27.8 gm. carbohydrates;
   21.1 gm. fat.
Per tablespoon: 26.1 calories; 7.9 mg. sodium; 1.7 gm. carbohydrates;
   1.3 gm. fat.

Marinated Chopped Beef

MAKES 3 CUPS

A modified version of steak tartare, with the added Italian flavors of garlic and capers, this dish is simmered to perfection. Serve warm or chilled as a spread for low-sodium crackers.

¾ pound chopped beef, divided
3 cloves garlic, sliced
Black pepper to taste
1 jar (3½ ounces) capers,*
  including liquid

2 tablespoons olive oil
¼ cup lemon juice
3 tomatoes, chopped

1. In blender, combine 2 tablespoons beef plus garlic. Grind to a paste. Transfer to bowl.
2. Add all remaining ingredients, blending thoroughly. Cover and refrigerate overnight.
3. In skillet, place beef mixture. Turn heat to low. Cover and simmer ½ hour, stirring occasionally.

Per recipe: 1,379.4 calories; 188.7 mg. sodium; 33.1 gm. carbohydrates; 100.3 gm. fat.
Per cup: 459.8 calories; 62.9 mg. sodium; 11.0 gm. carbohydrates; 33.4 gm. fat.
Per tablespoon: 28.7 calories; 3.9 mg. sodium; 0.7 gm. carbohydrates; 2.1 gm. fat.

* Preserved in vinegar only.

Meatballs in Creamy Mustard-Garlic Sauce

MAKES 48 CANAPÉS

The subtle delicacy of the sauce and the spiciness of the meatballs produce a savory delight. This dish also makes a perfect main course for 8.

1 pound chopped beef
2 tablespoons dried basil
1 teaspoon dried oregano
1 tablespoon paprika
½ teaspoon dried sage
⅛ teaspoon black pepper
2 tablespoons low-sodium ketchup

⅓ cup low-sodium mustard, divided
2 cups water
1 cup dry red wine
4 cloves garlic, minced
¼ cup heavy cream
⅛ teaspoon ground nutmeg

1. In bowl, combine first 7 ingredients, blending thoroughly.
2. Stir in 3 tablespoons mustard, blending thoroughly.
3. In Dutch oven, combine water, wine, and garlic. Stir in remaining mustard. Turn heat to low and cook 5 minutes.
4. While wine mixture is cooking, form beef mixture into 48 walnut-size meatballs.
5. Add meatballs to wine mixture. Cover and simmer 45 minutes.
6. Add cream and nutmeg. Cover and simmer 15 minutes more.
7. Transfer meatballs to platter. Pour sauce over all.
8. Skewer meatballs with toothpicks.

Per canapé: 38 calories; 5.4 mg. sodium; 0.5 gm. carbohydrates; 2.4 gm. fat.
Per serving as an entrée: 227.9 calories; 32.4 mg. sodium; 3.1 gm. carbohydrates; 14.3 gm. fat.

Melon and Pork
MAKES 36 CANAPÉS

The combination of melon with prosciutto is one of the most famous antipasto dishes. Our variation substitutes a spicy roast pork for the salty, smoked prosciutto. For variety, replace the melon with 6 large MacIntosh apples, peeled, cored, and sliced.

1 large cantaloupe, peeled, seeded, and sliced thin

Braised Pork (page 173), sliced very thin

1. On platter, alternate slices of melon and pork. Cover and chill at least ½ hour.
2. With toothpicks skewer together a slice of melon and a slice of pork.

Per canapé with cantaloupe: 99.7 calories; 28.5 mg. sodium; 3.4 gm. carbohydrates; 4.7 gm. fat.
Per canapé with apples: 111.9 calories; 25.9 mg. sodium; 8.1 gm. carbohydrates; 4.9 gm. fat.

Rosemary Lamb Kebobs
MAKES 8 CANAPÉS

The central regions of Umbria and Abruzzi are famous for their lamb specialties. This dish is one example.

½ pound lamb shoulder, trimmed and cut in 1-inch chunks
½ cup orange juice
1 tablespoon olive oil

1 teaspoon dried rosemary
1 tablespoon low-sodium chicken bouillon
Black pepper to taste

1. In shallow baking dish, combine all ingredients. Cover and refrigerate 2 hours, turning lamb occasionally.
2. Drain meat, reserving marinade.
3. Preheat oven to broil.
4. Thread lamb onto skewers and place on rack in baking dish. Broil 3 inches from heat 4 minutes.

5. Turn lamb. Baste with reserved marinade and broil 3 minutes more.
6. Transfer kebobs to platter, and skewer with toothpicks.

Per canapé: 35.7 calories; 23.5 mg. sodium; 2.4 gm. carbohydrates; 4.7 gm. fat.

Combination Cheese Dip   MAKES 6 CUPS

As refreshing as it is delicious. Serve with raw vegetables and low-sodium crackers.

1 cup low-sodium ricotta cheese	Black pepper to taste
1 cup low-sodium cottage cheese	1 tablespoon dried tarragon
2 tablespoons dried parsley	1 package (8 ounces) low-sodium
8 scallions, chopped, including greens	cream cheese
	2 tablespoons dry sherry
2 tablespoons lemon juice	2 cucumbers, diced

1. In bowl, combine first 4 ingredients, blending thoroughly.
2. Stir in lemon juice, pepper, and tarragon.
3. Fold in cream cheese.
4. Stir in sherry and cucumbers. Cover and refrigerate at least 2 hours to allow flavors to blend.

Per recipe: 1,801.9 calories; 202.8 mg. sodium; 50.2 gm. carbohydrates; 128.8 gm. fat.
Per cup: 300.3 calories; 33.8 mg. sodium; 8.4 gm. carbohydrates; 21.5 gm. fat.
Per tablespoon: 18.8 calories; 2.1 mg. sodium; 0.5 gm. carbohydrates; 1.3 gm. fat.

Fried Cheese Puffs　　　MAKES 32 CANAPÉS

These popular morsels can be found in every trattoria along the Mediterranean coast, from Genoa to Marsala. Now you can enjoy them in your own home.

1 cup all-purpose flour
1 tablespoon olive oil
1 tablespoon low-sodium chicken bouillon
⅓ cup water
½ cup low-sodium ricotta cheese
2 ounces low-sodium Swiss cheese, minced

2 ounces low-sodium Cheddar cheese, minced
⅛ teaspoon dried sage
½ teaspoon dried rosemary
Black pepper to taste
2 cups vegetable oil

1. In bowl, pour flour. Push flour to sides of bowl. To well created in center, add oil, bouillon, and water.
2. Fold flour into oil mixture, blending thoroughly.
3. Turn dough onto lightly floured board. Knead briefly. Turn dough into greased bowl and turn to grease all over. Cover with damp cloth and let stand in warm, dry place 2 hours.
4. In second bowl, combine cheeses, sage, rosemary, and pepper, blending thoroughly. Set aside.
5. Turn dough onto lightly floured board. Roll out to ⅛-inch thickness.
6. Cut dough into 2 x 4-inch rectangles.
7. Spoon 1 rounded teaspoon cheese mixture onto top half of each rectangle.
8. Fold bottom half of rectangle over cheese. Crimp edges together. Place on waxed paper, side by side.
9. In skillet, heat oil over medium heat until it is crackling hot.
10. With slotted spoon, or steel spatula, gently lower 8 puffs into oil.
11. Turn heat to high and fry 4 minutes, or until golden on each side, turning only once. Transfer to paper towels to drain.
12. Repeat Steps 10 and 11 until all puffs are fried.

Per canapé: 59.3 calories; 1.8 mg. sodium; 5.7 gm. carbohydrates; 3.1 gm. fat.

Spiced Apple Relish

MAKES 10 CUPS

This marvelous relish will be gone before you know it. Serve it with raw vegetables, low-sodium crackers, or as an accompaniment for any meat or poultry dish. For variety, replace the apples with 1 medium eggplant, peeled and diced.

6 apples, peeled, cored, and
  chopped
2 lemons, chopped
2 onions, chopped
1 cup golden raisins*
1 cup brown sugar

1½ cups cider vinegar
3 cups water
⅛ teaspoon hot pepper flakes
⅛ teaspoon ginger powder
¼ teaspoon ground cinnamon
2 green peppers, chopped

1. In Dutch oven, combine all ingredients, except green peppers. Turn heat to medium and bring to a slow boil, stirring occasionally.
2. Reduce heat to low. Cover and simmer 1½ hours, stirring occasionally.
3. Add peppers. Cover and simmer ½ hour more, stirring occasionally.
4. Remove from heat and let cool 20 minutes.
5. Pour mixture into jars, leaving ½-inch headspace. Cover tightly.
6. If refrigerated, will keep up to 3 months; if frozen, will keep indefinitely.

With apples:
  Per recipe: 2,463.8 calories; 236.0 mg. sodium; 656.6 gm. carbohydrates;
    9.5 gm. fat.
  Per cup: 246.4 calories; 23.6 mg. sodium; 65.7 gm. carbohydrates;
    1.0 gm. fat.
  Per tablespoon: 15.4 calories; 1.5 mg. sodium; 4.1 gm. carbohydrates;
    0.1 gm. fat.
With eggplant:
  Per recipe: 1,939.3 calories; 237.7 mg. sodium; 521.0 gm. carbohydrates;
    3.7 gm. fat.
  Per cup: 193.9 calories; 23.8 mg. sodium; 52.1 gm. carbohydrates;
    0.4 gm. fat.
  Per tablespoon: 12.1 calories; 1.5 mg. sodium; 3.3 gm. carbohydrates;
    0.03 gm. fat.

* Preserved in non-sodium ingredient.

Tomato-Plum Relish   MAKES 16 CUPS

A puckery delight, this sweet-and-sour relish is sure to please. Serve with raw vegetables, low-sodium crackers, or as an accompaniment for any meat or poultry dish.

3 pounds tomatoes, chopped
8 plums, pitted and chopped
4 onions, chopped
2 green peppers, chopped
1 cup golden raisins*
1 tablespoon orange peel powder
1 tablespoon garlic powder

2 teaspoons ground cinnamon
2 teaspoons dried basil
1 teaspoon hot pepper flakes
2 cups sugar
2 cups cider vinegar
2 cups water

1. In Dutch oven, combine first 10 ingredients, stirring to blend thoroughly.
2. Add remaining ingredients. Bring to a slow boil over medium heat.
3. Reduce heat to low and cook 1½ hours, or until mixture thickens, stirring often.
4. Remove from heat and let cool 20 minutes.
5. Pour mixture into jars, leaving ½-inch headspace. Cover tightly.
6. If refrigerated, will keep up to 3 months; if frozen, will keep indefinitely.

Per recipe: 3,572.6 calories; 254.1 mg. sodium; 959.9 gm. carbohydrates; 5.0 gm. fat.
Per cup: 223.3 calories; 15.9 mg. sodium; 60.0 gm. carbohydrates; 0.3 gm. fat.
Per tablespoon: 14 calories; 1.0 mg. sodium; 3.7 gm. carbohydrates; 0.02 gm. fat.

* Preserved in non-sodium ingredient.

Soups

Fifteen hundred years ago, Italy was not a country but a cluster of adjoining fiefdoms, kingdoms, principalities, and dukedoms, all continually at war with one another. Because there were no inns or lodging houses, the monasteries were among the few places where travelers could find refuge. There, monks fed the tired and hungry steaming bowls of broth flavored with whatever scraps of meat, fish, or vegetables were available. These humble but nourishing soups came to be called *minestre*, from the Italian word meaning "to serve."

From these simple origins came the classic soup of Italy— minestrone, which means "big soup." The name is fitting because, in addition to its vegetable base, minestrone is enriched with pasta, beans, or rice, and is often topped with grated cheese, so that it can easily be a hearty meal in itself. According to aficionados of Italian culinary history, Lombardy can lay claim to the creation of this universal favorite.

But today, every province in Italy has a soup specialty of which it is equally proud. There are the fish soups of Livorno and Viareggio, similar to the wine-poached combination in Fish Soup (page 68), delicate and succulent enough to rival the finest French bouillabaisse.

Soups are an important element in Italian cuisine, so much so that when soup is on the menu, the pasta or rice course is eliminated. You will understand why after you have sampled some of the delicious and very filling offerings in this chapter.

Chicken Stock

MAKES 10 CUPS
SERVES 12

While Italians are famous for their hearty soups, a uniquely Italian chicken soup does not exist. However, because so many soups and sauces call for a rich chicken stock base, we have developed the recipe below, which, by the way, is perfectly delicious served just as is.

1 3-pound chicken, cut up
3 quarts water
2 onions, chopped
¼ teaspoon black pepper

1 teaspoon celery seed*
1 head escarole, chopped
4 tablespoons low-sodium
  chicken bouillon

1. In Dutch oven, combine first 4 ingredients. Bring to a boil over high heat. Continue boiling 5 minutes.
2. Reduce heat to low. Add celery seed. Cover and simmer ½ hour, stirring occasionally.
3. Add escarole and bouillon, stirring to blend. Cover and simmer 20 minutes more.
4. Strain broth and pour into jars or plastic containers.
5. If refrigerated, will keep up to 1 week. If frozen, will keep indefinitely.

Per cup: 74.0 calories; 30.6 mg. sodium; 8.3 gm. carbohydrates; 5.5 gm. fat.
Per serving: 61.7 calories; 25.5 mg. sodium; 6.9 gm. carbohydrates; 4.6 gm. fat.

* Do not use celery flakes, which contain salt.

Meat Stock

Like Chicken Stock (page 64), this hearty stock forms a base for a number of dishes, and may also be enjoyed as a clear consommé.

2 pounds marrow bones
3 quarts water
2 onions, chopped
2 carrots
1 potato, peeled and diced
2 tomatoes, chopped
1 bay leaf

2 tablespoons red wine vinegar
½ teaspoon dried thyme
¼ teaspoon dried marjoram
3 tablespoons dry red wine
4 tablespoons low-sodium beef bouillon

1. In Dutch oven, combine first 8 ingredients. Bring to a boil over medium heat and continue boiling 5 minutes.
2. Reduce heat to low. Cover and simmer 2½ hours.
3. Stir in all remaining ingredients except bouillon. Cover and simmer ½ hour more.
4. Stir in bouillon. Cover and simmer ½ hour more.
5. Strain broth and pour into jars or plastic containers.
6. If refrigerated will keep up to 1 week. If frozen, will keep indefinitely.

Per cup: 95.2 calories; 36.5 mg. sodium; 12.4 gm. carbohydrates; 3.6 gm. fat.
Per serving: 79.3 calories; 30.4 mg. sodium; 10.4 gm. carbohydrates;
    2.8 gm. fat.

Arugola Soup

SERVES 4

Arugola is a nutty-tasting green plant which adds an elegant flavor to soups and salads. This marvelous southern-style soup is a great introduction to any meal, such as one featuring Flounder in Cheesy Dill Sauce (page 119).

1 tablespoon olive oil
2 cloves garlic, minced
2 bunches arugola, chopped
2 cups Chicken Stock (page 64)

Black pepper to taste
2 potatoes, parboiled,* peeled
   and diced
1 leek, chopped, including greens

1. In saucepan, heat oil over medium-low heat. Add garlic and cook 5 minutes, or until garlic is lightly browned, stirring often.
2. Add arugola and stir to blend thoroughly.
3. Add all remaining ingredients. Raise heat to high and bring to a boil.
4. Reduce heat to low. Cover and simmer 10 minutes, stirring occasionally.

Per serving: 152.7 calories; 23.7 mg. sodium; 22.7 gm. carbohydrates;
   7.2 gm. fat.

* Do not add salt to water.

Carrot Soup with Capers

SERVES 4

A simply exquisite northern-style soup. The carrots taste all the sweeter in contrast to the puckery, pungent flavor of the capers. Broiled Lamb Chops in Lemon-Parsley Sauce (page 168) is an excellent follow-up.

3 cups Chicken Stock (page 64)
¼ cup dry sherry
3 carrots, cut into ½-inch rounds
⅛ teaspoon ground nutmeg

Black pepper to taste
2 tablespoons capers*
Sprigs of fresh parsley

1. In saucepan, combine first 5 ingredients. Turn heat to high and bring to a boil.

2. Reduce heat to low. Cover and simmer ½ hour.
3. Stir in remaining ingredients. Cover and simmer 15 minutes more.

Per serving: 99.9 calories; 56.6 mg. sodium; 14.3 gm. carbohydrates; 4.3 gm. fat.

* Preserved in vinegar only.

Easter Soup   SERVES 8

This classic Italian soup originated in Naples and traditionally is served on Easter Sunday. There are now as many variations on this delicious and hearty dish as there are cities in Italy. Our version follows.

2 lamb shanks
2 quarts water
2 onions, chopped
½ cup dried parsley
¼ teaspoon fennel seed
Black pepper to taste

3 carrots, cut in 1-inch rounds
2 tablespoons low-sodium beef bouillon
2 ounces low-sodium Gouda cheese, minced
1 cup macaroni, cooked al dente*

1. In Dutch oven, combine first 2 ingredients. Bring to a boil over high heat.
2. Reduce heat to low. Add onions, parsley, fennel seed, pepper, and carrots. Cover and simmer 45 minutes.
3. Add bouillon and cheese. Cover and simmer 15 minutes more, stirring occasionally.
4. Add macaroni. Cover and simmer 5 minutes more.

Per serving: 189.0 calories; 40.8 mg. sodium; 32.9 gm. carbohydrates; 3.9 gm. fat.

* Do not add salt to water.

Fish Soup

SERVES 8

There is no more famous or tasty soup in all of Italy than *zuppa di pesce*, for the Mediterranean Sea offers a bounty of fish and shellfish from which to choose. It is a meal in itself when combined with a plate of pasta or a rice dish.

½ pound red snapper fillets, cut in 1-inch chunks
½ pound swordfish, cut in 1-inch chunks
½ cup dry white wine
1 tablespoon olive oil
2 onions, chopped
3 cloves garlic, minced
6 cups Chicken Stock (page 64)
1 can (29 ounces) unsalted plum tomatoes, chopped, including liquid

⅛ teaspoon black pepper
2 tablespoons dried parsley
1 tablespoon dried basil
¼ pound shrimp, shelled, deveined, and halved lengthwise
1 pint shucked oysters, including liquid

1. In bowl, combine first 3 ingredients. Cover and refrigerate 1 hour, turning fish occasionally.
2. In Dutch oven, heat oil over low heat. Add onions and garlic and cook 5 minutes, or until onions are golden, stirring occasionally.
3. Raise heat to high. Add stock, tomatoes, pepper, parsley, and basil. Bring to a boil.
4. Reduce heat to low. Cover and simmer 45 minutes, stirring occasionally.
5. Add snapper, swordfish, wine marinade, and shrimp. Stir to blend. Cover and simmer 10 minutes.
6. Add oysters plus liquid. Cover and simmer 5 minutes more.

Per serving: 221.8 calories; 102.2 mg. sodium; 19.0 gm. carbohydrates; 8.6 gm. fat.

Green Bean and Barley Soup SERVES 8

A mixed green salad and Stuffed Burgers (page 166) are all you need to complement this delicious and zesty soup from the northern Alto Adige region. For a different taste, replace the green beans with 3 zucchini, diced.

1 tablespoon unsalted margarine	2 tablespoons low-sodium beef
1 onion, minced	bouillon
2 cloves garlic, minced	Black pepper to taste
½ cup barley	1 carrot, diced
¼ cup dried parsley	½ pound green beans, chopped
4 cups Chicken Stock (page 64)	1 leek, chopped, including greens

1. In Dutch oven, heat margarine over low heat. Add onion and garlic and cook 5 minutes, or until onion is golden brown, stirring often.
2. Stir in barley and parsley.
3. Add stock, bouillon, pepper, and carrot. Raise heat to medium and bring to a slow boil.
4. Reduce heat to low. Cover and simmer 45 minutes, stirring occasionally.
5. Add green beans and leek. Cover and simmer 15 minutes more.

Per serving with green beans: 147.8 calories; 36.3 gm. sodium; 25.6 gm. carbohydrates; 5.4 gm. fat.
Per serving with zucchini: 151.4 calories; 35.1 mg. sodium; 26.2 gm. carbohydrates; 5.4 gm. fat.

Mushroom-Rice Soup   SERVES 4

This hearty northern-style soup makes a satisfying light meal when accompanied by the salad of your choice. Chicken and Caper Salad (page 115) or Squid Salad Vinaigrette (page 111) are just two possibilities.

1 tablespoon unsalted margarine
1 leek, chopped, including greens
Black pepper to taste
⅛ teaspoon celery seed*
⅛ teaspoon fennel seed

3 cups Meat Stock (page 65)
8 mushrooms, chopped
¼ cup low-sodium ricotta cheese
1½ cups cooked rice†

1. In Dutch oven, heat margarine over low heat. Add leek and cook 5 minutes, stirring often.
2. Stir in pepper, celery seed, fennel seed, and stock. Raise heat to high and bring to a boil. Continue boiling 5 minutes.
3. Reduce heat to low. Add mushrooms. Cover and simmer ½ hour.
4. Stir in cheese and rice. Cover and simmer 10 minutes more.

Per serving: 242.1 calories; 35.3 mg. sodium; 35.9 gm. carbohydrates;
    7.7 gm. fat.

* Do not use celery flakes, which contain salt.
† Do not add salt to water.

Oyster Soup

SERVES 4

The city of Florence, known for its beauty and priceless art, is also a city of consummate culinary skill. This dish is one delectable example. You can transform it from a soup to a main course by adding Rice with Chicken Livers (page 203) and a mixed green salad. If you are feeling extravagant, replace the oysters with the chopped meat of a 2-pound steamed lobster.

1 tablespoon unsalted margarine	1 bay leaf
1 onion, chopped	Black pepper to taste
3 tablespoons dried parsley	1 pint shucked oysters, chopped,
2 tablespoons dry sherry	liquid reserved
3 cups Chicken Stock (page 64)	¼ cup heavy cream

1. In large saucepan, heat margarine over low heat. Add onion and cook 5 minutes, or until onion is golden, stirring occasionally.
2. Stir in parsley and sherry.
3. Add stock, bay leaf, and pepper. Raise heat to high and bring to a boil.
4. Reduce heat to low. Cover and simmer ½ hour.
5. Stir in oysters plus liquid and cream. Cover and simmer 5 minutes more, stirring once.

Per serving with oysters: 209.7 calories; 98.7 mg. sodium; 15.8 gm. carbohydrates; 32.8 gm. fat.
Per serving with lobster: 205.1 calories; 156.1 mg. sodium; 13.1 gm. carbohydrates; 32.3 gm. fat.

Pea Soup with Squid   SERVES 8

In Parma and elsewhere in the north-central region, peas are a favorite vegetable. Their sweetness blends perfectly with the delicate flavor of seafood, as the dish below will prove. Follow it with Fettuccine in Wine-Cream Sauce (page 186) or Rice and Sausage (page 198).

2 tablespoons unsalted
  margarine, divided
1 onion, minced
2 cloves garlic, minced
Dash of ground nutmeg
½ teaspoon sugar
Black pepper to taste

5 cups Chicken Stock (page 64)
1 pound fresh peas, shelled, or
  1 can (15 ounces) low-sodium
  peas
½ pound squid, cleaned and
  chopped

1. In large saucepan, heat 1 tablespoon margarine over low heat. Add onion and garlic and cook 5 minutes, or until onion is golden, stirring occasionally.
2. Stir in nutmeg, sugar, and pepper, blending thoroughly.
3. Add stock. Raise heat to medium and bring to a slow boil.
4. Reduce heat to low. Cover and simmer 20 minutes, stirring occasionally.
5. Add peas and squid. Cover and simmer 10 minutes more.

Per serving with fresh peas: 153.0 calories; 22.5 mg. sodium; 16.1 gm. carbohydrates; 15.5 gm. fat.
Per serving with canned peas: 146.8 calories; 23.0 mg. sodium; 15.6 gm. carbohydrates; 15.5 gm. fat.

Bean, Pork, and Pasta Soup   SERVES 8

Naples, a city of wonderful food, is the source for our adaptation of a traditional combination of beans, pork, and pasta. If you want a spicier version, replace the pork with ½ pound Sweet and Hot Sausage (page 173).

½ pound pinto beans
2 quarts water
1 tablespoon olive oil
½ pound pork shoulder,
   trimmed and diced
3 cloves garlic, minced
1 tablespoon paprika
Dash of hot pepper flakes
½ teaspoon dried thyme

½ teaspoon dried oregano
¼ teaspoon fennel seed
6 tablespoons low-sodium beef
   bouillon
½ pound macaroni, boiled
   al dente*
¼ pound low-sodium mozzarella
   cheese, cut in strips

1. In Dutch oven, combine first 2 ingredients. Turn heat to medium and bring to a slow boil.
2. Reduce heat to low. Cover and cook 1 hour, or until beans are tender.
3. While beans are cooking, in skillet, heat oil over low heat. Add pork and garlic and cook 10 minutes, or until pork loses all pink color, stirring often.
4. Add pork to bean mixture. Stir in paprika, hot pepper flakes, thyme, oregano, fennel seed, and bouillon, blending thoroughly. Cover and simmer 20 minutes.
5. Add macaroni and cheese. Cover and simmer 5 minutes more.

Per serving with pork: 251.3 calories; 47.2 mg. sodium; 26.0 gm. carbohydrates; 9.2 gm. fat.
Per serving with sausage: 251.3 calories; 47.2 mg. sodium; 26.0 gm. carbohydrates; 9.2 gm. fat.

* Do not add salt to water.

Potato and Pork Soup   SERVES 8

A popular blend throughout the southern regions. For variety, you can use ¼ pound stewing beef, diced, in place of the pork. Mixed Vegetable Salad (page 104) is a flavorful accompaniment.

1 tablespoon olive oil
¼ pound pork shoulder, trimmed and diced
2 cloves garlic, minced
2 onions, chopped
2 tablespoons low-sodium beef bouillon

Black pepper to taste
¼ teaspoon celery seed*
4 potatoes, peeled and diced
3 cups Meat Stock (page 65)
1 tablespoon dry sherry
2 ounces low-sodium Gouda cheese, minced

1. In Dutch oven, heat oil over low heat. Add pork, garlic, and onions and cook 10 minutes, or until pork loses all pink color.
2. Stir in bouillon, pepper, and celery seed.
3. Add potatoes and stock. Raise heat to medium-low. Cover and cook ½ hour, stirring occasionally.
4. Stir in all remaining ingredients. Cover and cook 10 minutes more, stirring occasionally.

Per serving with pork: 196.3 calories; 39.4 mg. sodium; 24.5 gm. carbo-hydrates; 6.7 gm. fat.
Per serving with beef: 184.0 calories; 38.0 mg. sodium; 24.5 gm. carbo-hydrates; 7.6 gm. fat.

* Do not use celery flakes, which contain salt.

Sausage Soup

SERVES 4

There is nothing as warming and comforting as the wholesome goodness of this soup. When served with vegetables like Carrots in Cheese Sauce (page 220) or Broccoli and Leeks (page 217) it will make a most satisfying meal.

¼ pound Hot Sausage (page 171)
2 onions, chopped
4 cups water
2 potatoes, peeled and cubed
¼ cup dry red wine
Black pepper to taste

⅓ cup dried parsley
3 tablespoons low-sodium chicken bouillon
1 tablespoon low-sodium beef bouillon

1. In Dutch oven, cook sausage over medium heat 10 minutes, or until it loses all pink color, stirring often.
2. With slotted spoon, transfer sausage to bowl.
3. In sausage fat, cook onion over medium heat 5 minutes, or until onion is golden.
4. Add water, potatoes, wine, and pepper, stirring to blend. Bring to a slow boil over medium heat.
5. Reduce heat to medium-low. Stir in parsley. Cook 10 minutes, stirring occasionally.
6. Stir in all remaining ingredients, including sausage. Cook 15 minutes more, stirring occasionally.

Per serving: 237.9 calories; 59.4 mg. sodium; 31.6 gm. carbohydrates; 8.2 gm. fat.

Spinach and Cheese Soup　　SERVES 4

From the central regions comes this delicious soup. For a wonderful meal, follow it with Chicken and Mushrooms (page 141).

1 tablespoon unsalted margarine
2 onions, chopped
½ pound spinach, chopped
¼ cup dry vermouth
Dash of ground cinnamon

Black pepper to taste
3 cups Chicken Stock (page 64)
2 ounces low-sodium Swiss
　cheese, minced

1. In large saucepan, heat margarine over low heat. Add onions and cook 10 minutes, or until onions are golden, stirring occasionally.
2. Stir in spinach, vermouth, cinnamon, and pepper. Cover and simmer 10 minutes.
3. Add stock. Raise heat to high and bring to a boil.
4. Reduce heat to medium-low. Add cheese and cook, uncovered, 10 minutes more, stirring occasionally.

Per serving: 174.5 calories; 49.4 mg. sodium; 17.1 gm. carbohydrates; 12.2 gm. fat.

Tomato-Bean Soup

SERVES 8

Rich in flavor, filled with hearty produce of central Italy, this soup is delicious from the first savory spoonful to the last.

½ pound pinto beans
1 quart water
1 tablespoon olive oil
2 onions, minced
4 cloves garlic, minced
¼ teaspoon celery seed*
⅛ teaspoon black pepper
¼ cup cider vinegar

1 can (6 ounces) low-sodium
   tomato paste
2 tomatoes, chopped
1 bay leaf
2 cups Meat Stock (page 65)
½ cup fresh basil, chopped, or
   2 teaspoons dried basil

1. In Dutch oven, combine first 2 ingredients. Bring to a boil over high heat.
2. Reduce heat to low. Cover and simmer 1 hour.
3. While beans are cooking, in skillet heat oil over low heat. Add onions and garlic and cook 10 minutes, or until onions are golden, stirring occasionally.
4. Stir onion mixture into bean mixture.
5. Stir in celery seed, pepper, vinegar, tomato paste, tomatoes, and bay leaf. Cover and simmer ½ hour, stirring occasionally.
6. Add stock. Raise heat to high and bring to a boil.
7. Reduce heat to medium-low and cook 10 minutes, stirring often.
8. Add basil and cook 10 minutes more.

Per serving: 158.5 calories; 18.6 mg. sodium; 28.8 gm. carbohydrates;
   3.2 gm. fat.

* Do not use celery flakes, which contain salt.

Minestrone

SERVES 8

Minestrone—Italian vegetable soup—can be thick or sauce-like; some versions contain rice, others pasta. There are as many varieties of this soup as there are cities in Italy, and while each is unique, the one thing they have in common is vegetables, simmered together to create a savory, unforgettable blend. Our southern-style version follows.

2 tablespoons olive oil
2 onions, chopped
4 cloves garlic, minced
2 carrots, diced
6 mushrooms, chopped
Black pepper to taste
¼ teaspoon dried thyme

6 cups Chicken Stock (page 64)
3 tomatoes, chopped
¼ pound green beans, chopped
1 zucchini, diced
1 tablespoon dry red wine
2 ounces low-sodium Swiss
   cheese, minced

1. In Dutch oven, heat oil over low heat. Add onions and garlic and cook 10 minutes, or until onions are golden, stirring often.
2. Stir in carrots, mushrooms, pepper, and thyme.
3. Add stock and tomatoes. Raise heat to medium and bring to a slow boil, stirring occasionally.
4. Reduce heat to low. Cover and simmer ½ hour, stirring occasionally.
5. Add green beans. Cover and simmer 15 minutes more.
6. Add zucchini and wine, stirring to blend. Cover and simmer 5 minutes more.
7. Add cheese. Cover and simmer 10 minutes more, stirring occasionally.

Per serving: 165.2 calories; 44.1 mg. sodium; 19.9 gm. carbohydrates; 10.1 gm. fat.

Breads

The preeminence of pasta on the Italian table might make bread seem superfluous. Yet it stands to reason that cooks skilled in handling pasta and pizza dough must be equally versed in the ways of making bread. This is indeed the case with Italian bread.

From the hard-crusted loaves of Tuscany, to the flat breads that go back to the Roman days, to the almond bread of Lucania, traditionally served at Easter, the breads of Italy are as much a source of sensory pleasure as of sustenance. Once you try the recipes in this chapter, you will understand exactly what we mean.

Garlic Bread

SERVES 32

Garlic bread, the delicious and ubiquitous accompaniment to Italian meals, was invented in Rome.

1 loaf Basic Italian White Bread
(page 82), cut into 16 slices
8 cloves garlic, sliced

5 tablespoons olive oil
3 tablespoons low-sodium
chicken bouillon

1. Preheat oven to broil.
2. Place bread slices on baking sheet and toast 4 inches from heat 2 minutes, or until top is golden brown.
3. Turn bread and toast 2 minutes more, or until top is golden brown. Transfer toast to platter.
4. While toast is still hot, rub one side with garlic.
5. Drizzle oil over toast.
6. Sprinkle bouillon over toast.
7. Cut each slice in half.
8. Serve immediately.

Per serving: 101.5 calories; 3.5 mg. sodium; 15.9 gm. carbohydrates;
2.8 gm. fat.

Cheese and Sausage Biscuits

MAKES 48 BISCUITS

It will be a test of willpower if you can stop after eating only one of these delicious little breads.

1¾ cups all-purpose flour
2½ teaspoons low-sodium
baking powder
2 teaspoons dried tarragon
1 tablespoon lemon peel powder

3 tablespoons shortening
½ pound low-sodium Swiss
cheese, minced
¾ pound Sausage Napoli
(page 172)

1. Preheat oven to 425°.
2. In bowl, combine first 4 ingredients, blending thoroughly.

3. With fork, cut in shortening.
4. Add cheese and sausage, blending thoroughly.
5. Break dough into walnut-size balls and place on baking sheets, about 1 inch apart. Then bake 15 to 20 minutes, or until biscuits are golden brown.

Per biscuit: 64.0 calories; 7.8 mg. sodium; 6.5 gm. carbohydrates; 3.2 gm. fat.

Dilled Cheese Bread SERVES 36

The combination of flavors makes this melt-in-your-mouth bread irresistible.

1 package active, dry yeast
¾ teaspoon low-sodium baking powder
2 tablespoons sugar
2 teaspoons low-sodium chicken bouillon
1½ tablespoons dried dill
2½ cups all-purpose flour, divided

2 tablespoons unsalted margarine
2 onions, minced
¼ cup hot water
1 cup low-sodium cottage cheese
1 egg
½ cup low-fat milk
6 ounces low-sodium Cheddar cheese, minced

1. Preheat oven to 350°.
2. In large bowl, combine first 5 ingredients, blending thoroughly.
3. Stir in ¼ cup flour.
4. At medium speed, beat in margarine, onion, and water.
5. At high speed, beat in cottage cheese, egg, milk, cheese, and ¾ cup flour.
6. At high speed, beat in remaining flour.
7. Cover mixture and let stand in warm, dry place 2 hours, or until doubled in bulk.
8. Stir down dough. (Dough will be sticky and rubbery, almost like a batter.)
9. Divide dough into 2 equal sections. Place each section in lightly floured 5 x 9-inch baking pan.
10. Bake ½ hour, or until crust is golden brown.

Per serving: 99.7 calories; 6.7 mg. sodium; 14.4 gm. carbohydrates; 2.7 gm. fat.

Basic Italian White Bread   SERVES 48

Common to all regions, this most basic of Italian breads originated in the north. We have replaced the shortening commonly used with olive oil.

3 cups warm water, divided
3 packages active, dry yeast
4 tablespoons low-sodium
  chicken bouillon

2 tablespoons sugar
8 cups all-purpose flour, divided
1 tablespoon olive oil
1 egg, lightly beaten

1. In bowl, combine 1 cup water with yeast, bouillon, and sugar. Let stand 15 minutes, stirring once.
2. At medium speed, beat in 2 cups flour, plus the oil.
3. At medium speed, beat in 1 more cup water.
4. At medium speed, beat in 2 more cups flour.
5. At medium speed, beat in remaining cup water.
6. At medium speed, beat in remaining flour until a smooth stiff dough is formed.
7. Turn dough into lightly greased bowl. Cover and let stand in warm, dry place 3 hours, or until doubled in bulk.
8. Punch down dough. Cover and let rise again.
9. Turn dough onto lightly floured board. Divide into 3 equal sections. Knead each section 5 minutes.
10. Shape each section into a rounded loaf. Cover and let stand in warm, dry place 45 minutes.
11. Preheat oven to 350°.
12. Place loaves on lightly floured baking sheets. Brush with beaten egg and cut a slit down the center of each loaf.
13. Bake 10 minutes. Then lower heat to 325° and bake 20 minutes more, or until loaves are golden brown.

Per serving: 148.7 calories; 3.4 mg. sodium; 29.7 gm. carbohydrates;
    0.4 gm. fat.

Herbed Vegetable Bread

SERVES 48

This is a hearty, delectable bread. One slice with a bowl of Fish Soup (page 68) or Basil and Tarragon Chicken Salad (page 114) is all you need for a wonderful meal.

½ cup sugar
1 tablespoon low-sodium chicken bouillon
½ tablespoon lemon peel powder
¼ teaspoon garlic powder
1 package active, dry yeast
7½ cups all-purpose flour, divided

2½ cups hot water
½ cup shortening
1 egg
2 carrots, diced
2 onions, chopped
1 green pepper, diced
1 small zucchini, diced

1. In bowl, combine first 5 ingredients, blending thoroughly.
2. Stir in 3 cups flour. Set aside.
3. In second bowl, combine water and shortening, stirring until shortening is dissolved.
4. At medium speed, beat water mixture into flour mixture.
5. At medium speed, beat in egg and 1 cup flour.
6. At medium speed, beat in carrots, onions, green pepper, and zucchini.
7. At medium speed, gradually beat in remaining flour. (Dough will be very sticky.)
8. Turn dough onto lightly floured board and knead 5 minutes.
9. Turn dough into greased bowl. Cover and let stand in warm, dry place 3 hours, or until doubled in bulk.
10. Punch down dough. Cover and let rise again.
11. Divide dough into 3 equal sections. Place each section in 5 x 9-inch baking pan.
12. Place pans in cold oven. Turn heat to 400° and bake 15 minutes.
13. Reduce heat to 375° and bake 20 minutes more, or until crust is golden brown.

Note: This bread takes a long time to rise, so be patient.

Per serving: 168.7 calories; 5.1 mg. sodium; 30.7 gm. carbohydrates; 2.7 gm. fat.

Potato Bread

SERVES 48

This crusty, hearty bread is wonderful anytime, but is especially good with light salads, soups, or fish.

5 potatoes
6 cups water
2 packages active, dry yeast
1½ cups warm water, divided
8 cups all-purpose flour

3 tablespoons low-sodium
  chicken bouillon
2 tablespoons onion powder
½ tablespoon garlic powder
¼ teaspoon black pepper

1. In saucepan, combine first 2 ingredients. Bring to a boil over medium heat. Continue boiling 20 minutes, or until potatoes are fork tender. Drain. Let stand 20 minutes.
2. Peel potatoes and mash.
3. In bowl, combine yeast and ½ cup warm water. Let stand 10 minutes.
4. In second bowl, combine flour, bouillon, onion and garlic powders, and pepper, blending thoroughly.
5. Add yeast mixture, blending thoroughly.
6. Add potatoes and as much of remaining water as necessary to form elastic, sticky dough.
7. Turn dough onto lightly floured board and knead 5 minutes, or until dough is smooth and springy.
8. Turn dough into greased bowl, and turn to grease all over. Cover with dry cloth and let stand in warm, dry place 2 hours, or until doubled in bulk.
9. Preheat oven to 350°.
10. Punch down dough and turn onto lightly floured board.
11. Divide dough into 3 equal parts. Knead briefly.
12. Place each dough part into greased 5 x 9-inch loaf pan.
13. Bake 45 minutes, or until tops are golden brown.

Per serving: 154.6 calories; 2.3 mg. sodium; 31.4 gm. carbohydrates; 0.3 gm. fat.

Italian Flat Bread

SERVES 24

Crisp, crunchy, and delicious, this bread lends itself to any number of variations. For example, you might press 2 chopped onions into the dough before glazing with milk; or add ¼ cup unsalted crushed walnuts to Step 2; or add any herbs of your choice to Step 3. Each variation is sure to please.

1 package active, dry yeast
½ cup warm water
3 cups all-purpose flour, divided
¼ cup olive oil
¼ cup cold water

2 teaspoons onion powder
2 tablespoons low-sodium
 chicken bouillon
5 tablespoons low-fat milk

1. In bowl, combine first 2 ingredients. Let stand 10 minutes.
2. Add half the flour and knead until sticky dough is formed.
3. In second bowl, combine remaining flour, oil, water, onion powder, and bouillon, blending thoroughly.
4. Slowly knead both dough mixtures together, adding more water, if necessary, to make dough elastic and spongy.
5. Turn dough into greased bowl and turn to grease all over. Cover with damp cloth and let stand in warm, dry place 2 hours, or until doubled in bulk.
6. Preheat oven to 375°.
7. Turn dough onto lightly floured board and roll out to a large rectangle, ½ inch thick.
8. Carefully slide rectangle onto floured cookie sheet.
9. Sprinkle milk over surface.
10. Bake 25 minutes, or until golden brown on top.

Per serving plain: 131.7 calories; 3.5 mg. sodium; 22.1 gm. carbohydrates; 2.8 gm. fat.
Per serving with onions: 135.3 calories; 4.5 mg. sodium; 45.6 gm. carbohydrates; 2.8 gm. fat.
Per serving with walnuts: 141.4 calories; 3.6 mg. sodium; 22.3 gm. carbohydrates; 3.7 gm. fat.

Meat-Stuffed Flat Bread   SERVES 16

Meat-stuffed flat breads are popular both in the northern region of Bologna and in Sicily. Below is our version. If you want to be really extravagant, add 3 ounces low-sodium Swiss cheese, sliced very thin, to Step 6.

1 recipe Italian Flat Bread
  (page 85)
½ pound chopped beef
¼ cup low-sodium seasoned
  bread crumbs
3 tablespoons dry white wine
3 tablespoons low-sodium
  ketchup

¼ teaspoon dried sage
1 teaspoon dried oregano
2 tablespoons low-sodium beef
  bouillon
2 tablespoons dried parsley
Black pepper to taste

1. Follow Steps 1 through 5 for Italian Flat Bread.
2. While dough is rising, in bowl combine remaining ingredients, blending thoroughly.
3. Preheat oven to 350°.
4. Turn dough onto lightly floured board and roll out into rectangle, ¼ inch thick.
5. Cut dough in half and slide one half onto floured baking sheet.
6. Top with meat mixture, spreading to evenly cover surface.
7. Carefully slide second dough half on top of meat mixture. Crimp edges together.
8. Bake 25 minutes, or until golden brown on top.

Per serving plain: 259.0 calories; 18.5 mg. sodium; 35.9 gm. carbohydrates; 7.5 gm. fat.
Per serving with cheese: 278.0 calories; 20.1 mg. sodium; 36.0 gm. carbohydrates; 9.0 gm. fat.

Almond Bread with Aniseed   SERVES 32

Almond bread, from Lucania, is traditionally served at Easter. We have adapted the original to include the licorice-tasting aniseed.

½ cup warm water
1 package active, dry yeast
¾ cup sugar, divided
2 eggs
1 tablespoon shortening, melted

3½ cups all-purpose flour
½ cup unsalted, slivered almonds
2 tablespoons aniseed
¼ cup low-fat milk

1. In bowl, combine water and yeast. Let stand 10 minutes.
2. In second bowl, beat together ¼ cup sugar, eggs, and shortening.
3. At low speed, gradually beat in flour and remaining sugar.
4. Turn dough onto lightly floured board and knead 5 minutes, or until smooth and springy to the touch.
5. Turn dough into lightly greased bowl and let stand in warm, dry place 2 hours, or until doubled in bulk.
6. Punch down dough and divide into 2 equal sections.
7. Place each dough section into lightly floured 5 x 9-inch loaf pan.
8. Press half the almonds into top of each loaf.
9. Sprinkle half the aniseed over each loaf. Let stand 10 minutes.
10. Preheat oven to 375°.
11. Brush loaves with milk and bake ½ hour, or until loaves are golden brown.

Per serving: 124.1 calories; 5.1 mg. sodium; 24.6 gm. carbohydrates;
    2.0 gm. fat.

Cinnamon Fruit Biscuits   MAKES 24 BISCUITS

This recipe proves beyond any doubt that healthy food can taste delicious.

¼ cup dates, pitted and chopped
¼ cup golden raisins*
6 dried figs, chopped
10 dried pears, chopped
1 orange, chopped, including rind
1 lemon, chopped, including rind
2 cups water

1 cup all-purpose flour
2 tablespoons low-sodium baking powder
2½ teaspoons ground cinnamon
2 tablespoons shortening
⅓ cup low-fat milk

1. Preheat oven to 375°.
2. In saucepan, combine first 7 ingredients. Bring to a boil over medium heat.
3. Reduce heat to low. Cover and simmer 45 minutes, stirring occasionally.
4. Simmer, uncovered, 15 minutes more, or until liquid is almost absorbed.
5. While fruit is cooking, in bowl combine flour, baking powder, and cinnamon, blending thoroughly.
6. Cut in shortening. Then add milk, blending well until dough is formed.
7. Turn dough onto lightly floured board and roll into a narrow rectangle ¼ inch thick.
8. Spread fruit mixture down center of dough. Roll up from one long side to another.
9. Cut roll into slices about ½ inch thick. Place on lightly floured baking sheet and bake ½ hour, or until biscuits are golden brown.

Per biscuit: 80.2 calories; 4.3 mg. sodium; 15.4 gm. carbohydrates; 1.4 gm. fat.

* Preserved in non-sodium ingredient.

Easy Pizza Dough

SERVES 12

Pizza is synonymous with Italy—from the thick-crusted square Sicilian loaves to the round pie with which we are most familiar. The often-applied label "junk food" is undeserved, for pizza—rich in protein and fiber—is as nutritious as it is delicious. Following are an easy recipe for the pie dough and two suggested toppings.

½ cup warm water, divided
½ package active, dry yeast
1 cup all-purpose flour
½ cup wheat flour

1 tablespoon low-sodium chicken bouillon
1 tablespoon garlic powder
1 tablespoon olive oil

1. In bowl, combine ¼ cup water and yeast, stirring to dissolve. Set aside.
2. In second bowl, combine both flours, bouillon, and garlic powder, blending thoroughly.
3. Push dry ingredients to sides of bowl to form a well in the center.
4. Into well, pour yeast mixture, remaining water, and oil. Blend mixture with fork or fingers until dough is formed.
5. Transfer dough to lightly floured board and knead until smooth and springy, adding more all-purpose flour, if necessary, to prevent sticking.
6. Turn dough into lightly greased bowl, turning dough to coat all over. Cover with dry cloth and let stand in warm place until doubled in bulk.
7. Preheat oven to 425°.
8. Punch down dough. Turn onto lightly floured 12-inch baking tray and push down with hand to form a 12-inch circle, ¼ inch thick. Or divide dough in half and, using two 6-inch trays, form two 6-inch circles, each ¼ inch thick.
9. Pinch rim all around to form an edge.
10. Add pizza topping and bake 15 to 20 minutes, or until dough is golden brown and topping bubbles.

Per recipe:* 1,404.9 calories; 25.0 mg sodium; 258.9 gm. carbohydrates; 20.35 gm. fat.
Per serving:* 117.1 calories; 2.1 mg. sodium; 21.6 gm. carbohydrates; 1.7 gm. fat.

* Dough only.

Pizza with Topping I   SERVES 12

Try this topping using any of the sausage recipes in this book. You might also want to experiment with different cheeses. Whatever you select, the result is sure to be delicious.

1 recipe Easy Pizza Dough
  (page 89)
3 cups Tomato Sauce I (page
  242), divided
1 tablespoon olive oil
2 onions, chopped
½ pound Sausage Sicilian
  (page 172), sliced thin

2 green peppers, chopped
1 cup fresh basil, chopped, or
  1 tablespoon dried basil
¼ pound low-sodium Cheddar
  cheese, diced

1. Prepare Easy Pizza Dough through Step 9.
2. Spoon 2 cups tomato sauce over pizza dough. Smooth out with back of ladle. Set aside.
3. In skillet, heat oil over medium-low heat. Add onions and sauté 5 minutes, or until onions are golden, stirring often.
4. Scatter onions over pizza.
5. Add sausage, green peppers, basil, and cheese.
6. Top with remaining cup of tomato sauce.
7. Bake 15 to 20 minutes, or until dough is golden brown and topping bubbles.

Per serving: 264.2 calories; 5.0 mg. sodium; 34.6 gm. carbohydrates;
    10.9 gm. fat.

Pizza with Topping II

SERVES 12

Eight or nine sliced mushrooms, scattered over the pizza before adding the cheese, make a marvelous addition to this recipe.

1 recipe Easy Pizza Dough
  (page 89)
2 cups Tomato Sauce II
  (page 243)
1 tablespoon olive oil
2 onions, chopped

2 cloves garlic, minced
1 medium eggplant, diced
1½ tablespoons dried oregano
½ pound low-sodium
  mozzarella, sliced thin

1. Prepare Easy Pizza Dough through Step 9.
2. Spoon tomato sauce over pizza dough. Smooth out with back of ladle. Set aside.
3. In skillet, heat oil over medium-low heat. Add onions and garlic and sauté 5 minutes, or until onions are golden, stirring often.
4. Add eggplant. Reduce heat to low. Cover and simmer 10 minutes, stirring occasionally.
5. Stir in oregano.
6. Spoon eggplant mixture over pizza.
7. Top with cheese.
8. Bake 15 to 20 minutes, or until dough is golden brown and topping bubbles.

Per serving plain: 187.0 calories; 9.7 mg. sodium; 32.5 gm. carbohydrates; 4.3 gm. fat.
Per serving with mushrooms: 189.7 calories; 10.7 mg. sodium; 33.1 gm. carbohydrates; 4.3 gm. fat.

Italian Stuffing with Sausage

MAKES 6 CUPS
(enough for a 4- to 5-pound bird)

If you like stuffing, you will love this version from Italy's northern regions. The combined flavors of sausage and fruit are addictive. Try this with your Thanksgiving turkey; just double or triple the recipe as needed.

8 slices low-sodium white bread,
  toasted
4 cups boiling water
4 tablespoons low-sodium beef
  bouillon
⅛ teaspoon black pepper
4 apples, peeled, cored, and
  chopped, or 4 pears, peeled,
  cored, and chopped

8 prunes, pitted and chopped
2 teaspoons dried basil
¼ pound Hot Sausage (page
  171), diced
2 leeks, chopped, including
  greens

1. In bowl, combine first 2 ingredients, breaking toast with fork.
2. Stir in bouillon, pepper, apples, prunes, and basil, blending thoroughly. Set aside.
3. In skillet, place sausage. Turn heat to medium and sauté 2 minutes, stirring often.
4. Add leeks and sauté 2 minutes more, or until sausage loses all pink color, stirring often.
5. Stir sausage mixture into bread mixture, blending thoroughly.
6. Spoon stuffing into bird and roast according to directions. Or spoon stuffing into lightly greased 9-inch square ovenproof casserole. Cover and bake 1 hour at 350°.

With apples:
  Per cup: 323.9 calories; 53.3 mg. sodium; 56.9 gm. carbohydrates;
    7.8 gm. fat.
  Per tablespoon: 20.2 calories; 3.3 mg. sodium; 3.6 gm. carbohydrates;
    0.5 gm. fat.
With pears:
  Per cup: 329.2 calories; 54.7 mg. sodium; 57.9 gm. carbohydrates;
    7.6 gm. fat.
  Per tablespoon: 20.6 calories; 3.4 mg. sodium; 3.6 gm. carbohydrates;
    0.5 gm. fat.

Italian Stuffing with Nuts

MAKES 5 CUPS
(enough for a 4- to 5-pound bird)

The blending of sweet tastes and hot produces a distinctly southern version for stuffing lovers to enjoy.

10 slices low-sodium white
  bread, toasted
4 cups boiling water
4½ tablespoons low-sodium
  chicken bouillon
1 tablespoon olive oil
2 onions, chopped

⅓ cup unsalted, crushed walnuts
¹⁄₁₆ teaspoon ground cinnamon
½ teaspoon celery seed*
3 tablespoons dried parsley
½ tablespoon dried oregano
3 low-sodium hot cherry peppers,
  seeded and minced

1. In bowl, combine first 2 ingredients, breaking toast with fork.
2. Stir in bouillon. Set aside.
3. In skillet, heat oil over low heat. Add onions and cook 15 minutes, or until onions are lightly browned, stirring occasionally.
4. Stir onions into bread mixture.
5. Stir in all remaining ingredients, blending thoroughly.
6. Spoon stuffing into bird and roast according to directions. Or spoon into lightly greased 9-inch square ovenproof casserole. Cover and bake 1 hour at 350°.

Per cup: 313.9 calories; 42.1 mg. sodium; 45.2 gm. carbohydrates; 13.7 gm. fat.
Per tablespoon: 19.6 calories; 2.6 mg. sodium; 2.8 gm. carbohydrates;
  0.9 gm. fat.

* Do not use celery flakes, which contain salt.

Salads

As in most European countries, salads in Italy are served toward the end of a meal. There are three reasons for this custom. One is to allow the body to wind down gastronomically and digest the meal that preceded. The second is to cleanse the palate for dessert. The third, and perhaps most important reason, is because the vinegar in most salad dressings does not mix well with the wine served at meals.

Because the rich flavor of Italian cuisine comes, in great part, from the freshness of its ingredients, the components of salads vary seasonally, as well as regionally, to take advantage of home-grown produce. Paradoxically, these sun-sweet vegetables are rarely served raw. Instead, the three favorite salad preparations are *all' agro* (boiled vegetables tossed with an olive oil and lemon mixture), *al burro* (vegetables sautéed in butter), and *passati in padella* (vegetables sautéed in olive oil, often along with garlic).

The pickled and marinated mixed vegetables, so often found in antipasti, are also favorite salad alternatives in the Italian home.

For our American tastes, the salads in this chapter feature the crisp crunch and sweetness of raw vegetables. But do try them cooked in one of the three Italian fashions.

Either way, raw or cooked, when salads are topped with the distinctive Italian dressings offered in the chapter on Sauces (pages 239–59), you will be delightfully satisfied.

Braised Arugola Salad SERVES 8

If arugola is not available, 6 bunches of watercress or 4 medium endives, halved diagonally, are excellent alternates for this lovely warm salad. Serve it with Parsley Flounder in Herb Sauce (page 120) for a delicious meal.

⅔ cup boiling water
2 teaspoons low-sodium chicken bouillon
½ teaspoon sugar
1 teaspoon onion powder

Black pepper to taste
1½ tablespoons unsalted margarine
8 bunches arugola, chopped
⅛ teaspoon dried sage

1. In bowl, combine first 5 ingredients, blending thoroughly. Set aside.
2. In skillet, heat margarine over low heat. Add arugola and sage, blending thoroughly. Simmer 5 minutes, stirring often.
3. Transfer arugola mixture to bowl. Add bouillon mixture. Toss to blend.

Per serving with arugola: 37.8 calories; 8.1 mg. sodium; 3.3 gm. carbohydrates; 0.8 gm. fat.
Per serving with watercress: 35.1 calories; 29.5 mg. sodium; 1.0 gm. carbohydrates; 0.9 gm. fat.
Per serving with endive: 55.0 calories; 20.1 mg. sodium; 4.3 gm. carbohydrates; 0.7 gm. fat.

Beet Salad   SERVES 4

This sweet and tasty dish comes from the southern region of Lucania. Chicken in Parsley Wine (page 144) makes a good main course companion.

1 can (4 ounces) low-sodium
  beets, drained, liquid reserved
2 scallions, chopped, including
  greens

2 tablespoons lemon juice
2 tablespoons olive oil
1 teaspoon dried mint

1. In bowl, combine all ingredients, except beet liquid, blending thoroughly.
2. Add beet liquid. Toss to blend.

Per serving: 76.4 calories; 13.6 mg. sodium; 3.4 gm. carbohydrates; 7.4 gm. fat.

Cauliflower Salad   SERVES 8

The spicy flavor of this dish reflects its Neapolitan origins. Six cups broccoli flowerettes or 1 pound green beans, steamed,* are wonderful substitutes for the cauliflower. Serve it with Fish Soup (page 68) for an elegant meal.

¼ **pound Hot Sausage (page 171)**
2 leeks, chopped, including
  greens
¹⁄₁₆ **teaspoon ground nutmeg**
1 head cauliflower, broken into
  flowerettes and steamed*

1 head iceberg lettuce, shredded
1 cup Oil and Vinegar Dressing
  (page 254)

1. In skillet, combine first 3 ingredients. Turn heat to medium-low and cook 5 minutes, stirring often, or until sausage loses all pink color. Transfer to bowl.
2. Add cauliflower and lettuce. Toss to blend.
3. Add dressing. Toss to blend.

Per serving with cauliflower: 141.9 calories; 29.8 mg. sodium; 11.1 gm. carbohydrates; 8.5 gm. fat.
Per serving with broccoli: 146.2 calories; 31.5 mg. sodium; 11.7 gm. carbohydrates; 8.6 gm. fat.
Per serving with green beans: 136.9 calories; 22.6 mg. sodium; 10.8 gm. carbohydrates; 8.5 gm. fat.

* Do not add salt to water.

Christmas Salad
SERVES 4

Although traditionally served on Christmas Eve, this salad from the central region of Abruzzi can be relished year round. As a contrast to the fruit, serve it with delectable London Broil Vinaigrette (page 161).

2 oranges, peeled and sliced thin
Black pepper to taste
2 tablespoons olive oil

12 large leaves romaine lettuce, shredded

1. On platter, arrange orange slices. Season with pepper and olive oil. Let stand ½ hour.
2. Top oranges with shredded lettuce.

Per serving: 116.5 calories; 3.3 mg. sodium; 13.1 gm. carbohydrates; 7.7 gm. fat.

Braised Endive Salad
SERVES 4

Milan inspired this elegant first course. Wine-Baked Trout (page 129) is a delicious follow-up.

1 tablespoon unsalted margarine
4 small endives
½ cup water
2 teaspoons low-sodium chicken bouillon

Black pepper to taste
1 tablespoon dry vermouth

1. In skillet, heat margarine over low heat. Add endives, turning to coat all over.
2. Add all remaining ingredients. Cover and simmer 15 minutes, turning endives occasionally.

Per serving: 60.7 calories; 19.2 mg. sodium; 5.9 gm. carbohydrates; 3.5 gm. fat.

Fennel Salad

SERVES 4

Delicious and crisply refreshing. For an extra treat, garnish with 1 orange, peeled and chopped. Honey-Vinegar Baked Chicken (page 150) is the perfect accompaniment. Pork Chops in Raspberry Sauce (page 169) is another excellent choice.

6 cups water
1 large fennel, sliced, tops removed
¼ cup olive oil
½ cup boiling water

2 teaspoons low-sodium chicken bouillon
2 tablespoons lemon juice
Black pepper to taste

1. In saucepan, bring water to a boil over high heat. Add fennel and boil 5 minutes. Drain. Transfer to bowl.
2. In second bowl, combine all remaining ingredients, blending thoroughly. Pour over fennel. Toss to blend.
3. Serve hot or chilled.

Per serving plain: 152.2 calories; 2.6 mg. sodium; 5.1 gm. carbohydrates; 15.8 gm. fat.
Per serving with orange: 176.7 calories; 3.0 mg. sodium; 11.2 gm. carbohydrates; 15.9 gm. fat.

Green Bean and Carrot Salad

SERVES 4

This dish from Abruzzi is nothing short of marvelous, and goes well with Simple Broiled Trout (page 128).

¼ pound green beans, steamed*
1 large carrot, grated
1 tablespoon lemon juice

¾ cup Cucumber Dressing (page 259)

1. In bowl, combine first 3 ingredients. Toss to blend.
2. Add dressing. Toss to blend. Cover and refrigerate ½ hour to allow flavors to blend.

Per serving: 77.6 calories; 24.4 mg. sodium; 6.9 gm. carbohydrates; 4.3 gm. fat.

* Do not add salt to water.

Italian Potato Salad SERVES 8

A superb rival to your favorite potato salad. For variety, add ¼ pound green beans, steamed,* or 1 can (8 ounces) low-sodium beets, chopped, including liquid.

4 large potatoes, parboiled,*   **1 tablespoon dried parsley**
   peeled and cubed   **1 teaspoon dried mint**
1 cup Mustard-Garlic Sauce
   (page 256)

In bowl, combine all ingredients, blending thoroughly. Cover and refrigerate at least 4 hours to allow flavors to blend.

Per serving plain: 163.5 calories; 3.3 mg. sodium; 3.9 gm. carbohydrates; 5.7 gm. fat.
Per serving with green beans: 168.1 calories; 4.3 mg. sodium; 4.9 gm. carbohydrates; 5.7 gm. fat.
Per serving with beets: 172.6 calories; 16.4 mg. sodium; 6.1 gm. carbohydrates; 5.7 gm. fat.

* Do not add salt to water.

Potato and Green Bean Salad   SERVES 8

This southern dish is yet another variation on the ever-popular potato salad. Try this with Parsley Beef in Brandy (page 163).

4 large red potatoes, boiled* and
  diced
1 pound green beans, steamed*

¼ cup sour cream
¾ cup Italian Vinaigrette
  (page 254)

1. In bowl, combine first 2 ingredients. Toss to blend.
2. In second bowl, combine all remaining ingredients, blending thoroughly.
3. Pour sour cream mixture over vegetables. Toss to blend.
4. Serve warm or chilled.

Per serving: 138.2 calories; 9.4 mg. sodium; 17.5 gm. carbohydrates;
    7.8 gm. fat.

* Do not add salt to water.

Italian Coleslaw   SERVES 12

A marvelous variation on one of America's favorites. Braised Pork (page 169) is a hearty and tasty companion.

¼ pound Sausage Sicilian
  (page 172)
1 head cabbage, shredded
2 carrots, shredded
1 green pepper, minced

1⅓ cups Herbed Mayonnaise
  Dressing (page 257)
½ teaspoon sugar
4 halves low-sodium sweet
  peppers, chopped

1. In skillet, fry sausage over medium heat 5 minutes, or until pork loses all pink color. Set aside.
2. In bowl, combine cabbage, carrots, and green papper. Toss to blend.
3. In second bowl, combine dressing and sugar, blending thoroughly.

4. Add dressing, sausage, and sweet peppers to cabbage mixture. Toss to blend. Cover and refrigerate at least 4 hours to allow flavors to blend.

Per serving: 122.1 calories; 42.7 mg. sodium; 12.8 gm. carbohydrates;
6.8 gm. fat.

Mixed Salad Surprise
SERVES 8

The tart flavors of this salad complement fish dishes like Salmon, Eggplant, and Capers (page 122) or Baked Snapper (page 123).

2 cups chopped watercress
3 cups chopped arugola
¼ cup lemon juice
Black pepper to taste
2 oranges, peeled and chopped
2 ounces low-sodium Cheddar
cheese, minced

4 scallions, chopped, including
greens
1 cup Oil and Vinegar Dressing
(page 254)

1. In bowl, combine first 4 ingredients, blending thoroughly.
2. Add oranges, cheese, and scallions, blending thoroughly.
3. Add dressing. Toss to blend.

Per serving: 135.1 calories; 40.0 mg. sodium; 10.9 gm. carbohydrates;
8.9 gm. fat.

Mixed Vegetable Salad   SERVES 8

For a deliciously different taste, substitute ¾ cup Herbed Mayonnaise Dressing (page 257) for the Italian Vinaigrette. For your main course, we suggest Meat Loaf with Cream (page 162).

2 zucchini, julienned
2 carrots, julienned
1 can (8 ounces) low-sodium beets, chopped, liquid reserved
2 red peppers, sliced thin
3 tomatoes, chopped

1 small Bermuda onion, sliced in rings
½ head cabbage, shredded
¾ cup Italian Vinaigrette (page 254)

1. In bowl, combine all ingredients, except dressing. Toss to blend.
2. Add dressing. Toss to blend.

Per serving with Italian Vinaigrette: 115.6 calories; 50.6 mg. sodium;
     20.2 gm. carbohydrates; 4.9 gm. fat.
Per serving with Herbed Mayonnaise Dressing: 125.4 calories;
     52.7 mg. sodium; 22.0 gm. carbohydrates; 4.6 gm. fat.

Salad Roma   SERVES 4

Whichever dressing you choose, you are sure to relish the contrasting flavors of this salad. Champagne Chicken with Herbs (page 139) is a perfect entrée.

1 head romaine lettuce, shredded
1 tomato, chopped
¼ cucumber, chopped
¼ green pepper, chopped
2 radishes, sliced
3 scallions, chopped, including greens

1 low-sodium sweet pepper half, chopped
1 tablespoon capers* (optional)
⅔ cup Creamy Garlic Dressing (page 256), or Wine-Caper Sauce (page 251)

1. In bowl, combine all ingredients, except the last, blending thoroughly.

2. Add dressing or sauce. Toss to blend.

Per serving with Creamy Garlic Dressing: 147.0 calories; 38.7 mg. sodium;
    13.4 gm. carbohydrates; 9.7 gm. fat.
Per serving with Wine Caper Sauce: 92.9 calories; 36.9 mg. sodium;
    15.2 gm. carbohydrates; 1.4 gm. fat.

* Preserved in vinegar only.

Roast Peppers and Beet Salad   SERVES 8

This wonderful contrast in textures and tastes goes well with
Rosemary Chicken and Green Peppercorns (page 153).

**2 green peppers,
    halved lengthwise and seeded
2 red peppers,
    halved lengthwise and seeded
1 cup Oil and Vinegar Dressing
    (page 254)**

**1 can (8 ounces) low-sodium
    beets, drained and diced
16 cherry tomatoes, halved
4 scallions, chopped, including
    greens
1 head iceberg lettuce, chopped**

1. Preheat oven to broil.
2. On baking sheet, place green and red peppers, cut side down.
   Broil 6 inches from heat 5 minutes, or until skins start to
   blacken. Transfer to platter.
3. Slice peppers. Transfer to bowl.
4. Add all remaining ingredients. Toss to blend.

Per serving: 112.7 calories; 39.8 mg. sodium; 13.8 gm. carbohydrates;
    6.5 gm. fat.

Tomato and Mozzarella Salad   SERVES 4

One of the simplest yet most delicious dishes from the southern regions. Chicken with Lemon Sauce (page 143) is a natural main-course dish. Or you might choose Veal with Artichokes and Mushrooms (page 180).

½ cup Oil and Vinegar Dressing (page 254), divided
3 tomatoes, sliced
1 cup fresh basil, chopped, or
  1 tablespoon dried basil

3 ounces low-sodium mozzarella cheese, sliced very thin

1. On platter, pour half the dressing. Top with tomato slices.
2. Sprinkle basil over tomatoes.
3. Top tomatoes with cheese.
4. Pour remaining dressing over all.

Per serving: 97.9 calories; 6.2 mg. sodium; 6.0 gm. carbohydrates; 7.1 gm. fat.

Stuffed Tomato Salad   SERVES 4

This delicious treat comes from the southernmost tip of Italy. For an enjoyable variation try 1 cup cooked chicken, cubed, or ¼ pound shrimp, shelled, deveined, and chopped, instead of the oysters in Step 3. This salad makes a wholly satisfying light lunch when accompanied by Mushroom-Rice Soup (page 70).

4 tomatoes
1 teaspoon olive oil
1 onion, minced
2 cloves garlic, minced
1 pint oysters, shucked and
  chopped, including liquid

1 teaspoon dried basil
1 teaspoon red wine vinegar
2 teaspoons capers*
⅓ cup Herbed Mayonnaise
  Dressing (page 257)

1. Cut ½ inch off tops of tomatoes. Scoop out pulp and reserve in bowl.
2. In skillet, heat oil over low heat. Add onion and garlic. Cook 5 minutes, or until onion is wilted, stirring occasionally.

3. Add oysters, including liquid, basil, vinegar, and capers. Cover and simmer 5 minutes, stirring occasionally.
4. Transfer oyster mixture to bowl. Add tomato pulp and dressing, blending thoroughly.
5. Stuff tomatoes with oyster mixture and refrigerate ½ hour to allow flavors to blend.

Per serving with oysters: 159.2 calories; 73.6 mg. sodium; 18.3 gm. carbohydrates; 6.8 gm. fat.
Per serving with chicken: 145.9 calories; 30.9 mg. sodium; 15.4 gm. carbohydrates; 7.0 gm. fat.
Per serving with shrimp: 128.7 calories; 51.0 mg. sodium; 15.8 gm. carbohydrates; 5.5 gm. fat.

* Preserved in vinegar only.

Zucchini, Tomato, and Sardine Salad

SERVES 4

For an extra-special treat, replace the sardines in Step 1 with the chopped meat of a steamed* 1-pound lobster, 1 cup cooked chicken, cubed, or 1 cup cooked pork, cubed. Serve with Spinach and Cheese Soup (page 76) for a memorable light meal.

1 zucchini, julienned
2 tomatoes, chopped
1 can (3⅜ ounces) low-sodium sardines, chopped
1 teaspoon dried dill

½ cup Honey-Vinegar Dressing (page 255)
½ head romaine lettuce, chopped
1 lemon, cut in wedges

1. In bowl, combine first 4 ingredients, blending thoroughly.
2. Add dressing, blending thoroughly. Cover and refrigerate ½ hour to allow flavors to blend.
3. Divide lettuce among 4 plates. Top with zucchini mixture.
4. Garnish with lemon wedges.

Per serving with sardines: 104.4 calories; 42.3 mg. sodium; 11.2 gm. carbohydrates; 3.5 gm. fat.
Per serving with lobster: 74.2 calories; 69.0 mg. sodium; 11.3 gm. carbohydrates; 0.9 gm. fat.
Per serving with chicken: 91.4 calories; 28.9 mg. sodium; 11.2 gm. carbohydrates; 2.1 gm. fat.
Per serving with pork: 117.9 calories; 29.0 mg. sodium; 11.2 gm. carbohydrates; 4.5 gm. fat.

* Do not add salt to water.

Lobster Salad in Brandied Mayonnaise

SERVES 4

This exquisite northern-style main dish is perfect with Rice in Wine-Caper Sauce (page 201) or Potatoes Baked in Pungent Basil Sauce (page 208).

1 tablespoon green peppercorns,* ground
⅓ cup boiling water
2 teaspoons low-sodium chicken bouillon
1 teaspoon low-sodium Dijon mustard
¹⁄₁₆ teaspoon celery seed†
1 tablespoon dried parsley
2 tablespoons brandy
⅓ cup cider vinegar

⅓ cup low-sodium mayonnaise
1 2-pound lobster, steamed,‡ meat removed and chopped
1 head iceberg lettuce, shredded
½ cucumber, chopped
2 halves low-sodium sweet peppers, chopped
4 low-sodium butter pickles, diced
2 tomatoes, chopped
1 lemon, cut in wedges

1. In bowl, combine first 4 ingredients, blending thoroughly.
2. Stir in celery seed and parsley. Set aside.
3. In second bowl, combine brandy, vinegar, and mayonnaise, blending thoroughly.
4. Stir mayonnaise mixture into bouillon mixture, blending thoroughly.
5. In third bowl, combine all remaining ingredients, except mayonnaise mixture. Toss to blend.
6. Add mayonnaise mixture. Toss to blend.
7. Garnish with lemon wedges.

Per serving: 197.7 calories; 102.0 mg. sodium; 14.6 gm. carbohydrates; 16.5 gm. fat.

* Preserved in vinegar only.
† Do not use celery flakes, which contain salt.
‡ Do not add salt to water.

Shrimp and Potato Salad   SERVES 8

Along the Mediterranean coast, you can find exotic and tasty combinations like the one below. For variety and an elegant touch, add 2 tablespoons unsalted, chopped walnuts or 4 dried figs, chopped, to Step 1.

4 potatoes, parboiled,* peeled
   and cubed
½ tablespoon green
   peppercorns,† ground
2 tablespoons lemon juice
3 cups broccoli flowerettes,
   steamed*
1 pound shrimp,
   shelled, deveined, and halved
   lengthwise

2 tablespoons dry vermouth
¼ cup orange juice
1 cup Herbed Mayonnaise
   Dressing (page 257)
1 head iceberg lettuce, chopped
16 cherry tomatoes, halved

1. In bowl, combine first 5 ingredients. Toss to blend.
2. In second bowl, combine vermouth, orange juice, and dressing, blending thoroughly.
3. Pour vermouth mixture over shrimp mixture. Toss to blend. Cover and refrigerate ½ hour to allow flavors to blend.
4. Divide lettuce among 8 plates. Top with shrimp mixture.
5. Garnish with cherry tomatoes.

Per serving plain: 217.0 calories; 99.9 mg. sodium; 25.2 gm. carbohydrates;
   7.0 gm. fat.
Per serving with walnuts: 240.3 calories; 99.9 mg. sodium; 25.8 gm. carbohydrates; 9.8 gm. fat.
Per serving with figs: 230.1 calories; 101.1 mg. sodium; 28.5 gm. carbohydrates; 7.0 gm. fat.

* Do not add salt to water.
† Preserved in vinegar only.

Squid and Shrimp Salad

SERVES 4

The waters of the Adriatic and the Mediterranean abound in seafood. This southern-style dish is just one of many tasty ways it is used. Macaroni and Spinach (page 189) makes a nice accompaniment.

1 head romaine lettuce, chopped
1 green pepper, chopped
4 radishes, minced
1 carrot, shredded
½ pound squid, cleaned and
  cut in ½-inch rings
¼ pound small shrimp,
  shelled, deveined, and halved
  lengthwise

1 cup boiling water
2 teaspoons low-sodium chicken
  bouillon
1 cup Italian Vinaigrette
  (page 254)
8 cherry tomatoes, halved

1. In bowl, combine first 4 ingredients. Toss to blend.
2. In saucepan, combine squid, shrimp, water, and bouillon. Turn heat to low. Cover and simmer 5 minutes. Drain, reserving half the liquid.
3. Add squid and shrimp to lettuce mixture. Toss to blend.
4. In second bowl, combine reserved bouillon mixture and vinaigrette, blending thoroughly. Pour over seafood mixture. Toss to blend.
5. Garnish with cherry tomato halves.

Per serving: 247.1 calories; 76.0 mg. sodium; 16.9 gm. carbohydrates; 13.7 gm. fat.

Squid Salad Vinaigrette

SERVES 8

One of the most popular Italian specialties, squid (or calamari) salad is a dish you are sure to enjoy. To complete your meal, serve it with Hot Sauce Shells (page 191).

1¼ pounds squid, cleaned and chopped
3 tablespoons cider vinegar
2 cups cold water
¼ cup olive oil
½ cup boiling water
¼ cup lemon juice
3 tablespoons red wine vinegar
1 teaspoon celery seed*
⅛ teaspoon hot pepper flakes

1 tablespoon dried parsley
1 teaspoon dried basil
⅛ teaspoon dried thyme
2 tablespoons green peppercorns,† crushed
1 head romaine lettuce, chopped
16 cherry tomatoes, halved
4 scallions, chopped, including greens

1. In saucepan, combine first 3 ingredients. Turn heat to medium and bring to a slow boil. Continue boiling 3 minutes. Drain. Set aside.
2. In bowl, combine oil, boiling water, lemon juice, red wine vinegar, celery seed, hot pepper flakes, parsley, basil, thyme, and peppercorns, blending thoroughly. Set aside.
3. In second bowl, combine lettuce, tomatoes, scallions, and squid. Toss to blend.
4. Add dressing from Step 2. Toss to blend.

Per serving: 151.6 calories; 8.5 mg. sodium; 7.3 gm. carbohydrates; 8.4 gm. fat.

* Do not use celery flakes, which contain salt.
† Preserved in vinegar only.

Tuna Salad SERVES 4

This southern-style dish will quickly become one of your favorites. For a refreshing change, eliminate the oil and vinegar mixture in Step 2, and substitute ¾ cup Piquant Mayonnaise (page 258) without sardines. To complete your meal, try Basil Rice and Leeks (page 198).

1 head romaine lettuce, shredded
⅓ cup chopped Bermuda onion
1 can (6½ ounces) low-sodium
    tuna, chopped, including
    liquid
2 halves low-sodium sweet
    peppers, chopped

1 cucumber, seeded and chopped
2 tablespoons olive oil
¼ cup boiling water
¼ teaspoon garlic powder
Black pepper to taste
2 tablespoons red wine vinegar

1. In bowl, combine first 5 ingredients. Toss to blend. Set aside.
2. In second bowl, combine all remaining ingredients, except tuna mixture, blending thoroughly. Let cool 15 minutes.
3. Pour oil and vinegar mixture over tuna mixture. Toss to blend.

Per serving with oil and vinegar: 184.9 calories; 60.6 mg. sodium;
    13.2 gm. carbohydrates; 8.4 gm. fat.
Per serving with Piquant Mayonnaise: 198.1 calories; 64.1 mg. sodium;
    13.4 gm. carbohydrates; 9.2 gm. fat.

Pasta and Tuna Salad

SERVES 8

This sumptuous salad from the south will be just as good if you replace the tuna with chunks of meat from 4 half chicken breasts, poached.*

1 tablespoon olive oil
6 cloves garlic, minced
1 onion, minced
2 cans (13 ounces) low-sodium tuna, including liquid
3 tomatoes, chopped
2 teaspoons low-sodium Worcestershire sauce
¾ pound spaghetti, boiled al dente*

1½ cups boiling water
2½ tablespoons low-sodium chicken bouillon
¼ cup fresh, chopped parsley, or 2 tablespoons dried parsley
½ cup fresh, chopped basil, or 1 tablespoon dried basil
Black pepper to taste
¼ cup heavy cream
1 head romaine lettuce, shredded

1. In skillet, heat oil over low heat. Add garlic and onion and cook 10 minutes, or until garlic is lightly browned, stirring often. Set aside.
2. In bowl, combine tuna, tomatoes, Worcestershire sauce, and spaghetti. Toss to blend.
3. Add garlic and onion mixture. Toss to blend. Set aside.
4. In second bowl, combine water, bouillon, parsley, basil, pepper, and cream, blending thoroughly.
5. Pour bouillon mixture over tuna mixture. Toss to blend.
6. Divide lettuce among 8 plates. Top with tuna mixture.

Per serving with tuna: 202.0 calories; 31.8 mg. sodium; 28.4 gm. carbohydrates; 6.5 gm. fat.
Per serving with chicken: 232.0 calories; 44.9 mg. sodium; 28.4 gm. carbohydrates; 6.4 gm. fat.

* Do not add salt to water.

Basil and Tarragon Chicken Salad

SERVES 8

A pleasingly refreshing salad. For a totally different taste treat, replace the chicken with ¾ pound swordfish, poached,* and cut into 1-inch chunks, or 1 pound leftover pork, cubed. To complete your meal, serve with Carrot Soup with Capers (page 66), or Stuffed Baked Potatoes (page 211).

¼ cup low-sodium mayonnaise
½ cup plain yogurt
¼ cup lemon juice
1 teaspoon dried basil
1 teaspoon dried tarragon
1 tablespoon low-sodium Dijon mustard
¼ cup dry white wine
Black pepper to taste

4 cups cooked, cubed chicken
¼ cup unsalted, slivered almonds
6 scallions, chopped, including greens
¼ pound green beans, steamed* and chopped
4 radishes, sliced
1 head iceberg lettuce, chopped

1. In bowl, combine first 8 ingredients, blending thoroughly. Set aside.
2. In second bowl, combine chicken, almonds, scallions, green beans, and radishes. Toss to blend.
3. Pour mayonnaise mixture over chicken mixture. Toss to blend.
4. Divide lettuce among 8 plates. Top with chicken mixture.

Per serving with chicken: 177.7 calories; 58.2 mg. sodium; 6.7 gm. carbohydrates; 12.0 gm. fat.
Per serving with swordfish: 141.9 calories; 18.4 mg. sodium; 6.7 gm. carbohydrates; 10.2 gm. fat.
Per serving with pork: 230.7 calories; 58.4 mg. sodium; 6.7 gm. carbohydrates; 16.7 gm. fat.

* Do not add salt to water.

Chicken and Caper Salad

SERVES 8

This superb northern-style dish is sure to please even the fussiest eater. Serve with Fettuccine in Wine-Cream Sauce (page 186).

1 3-pound chicken
2 quarts water
3 tablespoons low-sodium mayonnaise
⅓ cup lemon juice
2 teaspoons dried dill
2 teaspoons dried basil
Black pepper to taste

1 small onion, minced
1 green pepper, chopped fine
1 jar (3½ ounces) capers,* including liquid
1 head romaine lettuce, torn into pieces
4 tomatoes, cut into thin wedges

1. In Dutch oven, place first 2 ingredients. Turn heat to high and bring to a boil. Reduce heat to low. Cover and simmer 45 minutes. Drain. Transfer chicken to platter. Let cool 20 minutes.
2. Discard chicken skin. Slice chicken and chop coarsely. Set aside.
3. In bowl, combine mayonnaise, lemon juice, dill, basil, and black pepper, blending thoroughly.
4. Add onion, green pepper, capers, including liquid, and chicken, blending thoroughly. Cover and refrigerate at least 1 hour to allow flavors to blend.
5. Divide lettuce among 8 plates. Top with chicken mixture.
6. Garnish with tomato wedges.

Per serving: 206.1 calories; 74.1 mg. sodium; 10.6 gm. carbohydrates; 9.8 gm. fat.

* Preserved in vinegar only.

Fish and Shellfish

The slim, elegant, boat-shaped peninsula that is Italy is surrounded by some of the richest waters of the continent. On the east coast is the Adriatic; on the west, the Mediterranean; throughout Italy, lakes dot the terrain from north to south. Together, the lakes and sea yield an endless bounty of fish and seafood, all of which find their way to the Italian table. *Gamberi* (shrimp), *scampi* (prawns), *calamari* (squid), *pesce spada* (swordfish), and *spigola* (bass) are but a few of the many sea delicacies available.

Every region of Italy takes pride in its fish specialties. Lake Barda, near Venice, is famous for its trout. The Marches, on the Adriatic Coast, and Tuscany, in the north, boast delectable fish soups. Sicily offers an unforgettable Lobster fra Diablo. All these dishes are undeniably superb, but what truly distinguishes Italian fish cookery from that of any other country are the sauces.

Graced with an unmistakably Italian blend of herbs and spices, these sauces range from the simplest olive oil preparations to a seemingly infinite variety of wine-, tomato-, or cream-based creations. Amazingly, these heartily flavored sauces do not overwhelm or mask the taste of the fish. Rather, each sauce enhances the fish it adorns. See for yourself when you enjoy Flounder in Cheesy Dill Sauce (page 119), Salmon in Basil-Cream Sauce (page 121), Shrimp in Spicy Tomato Sauce (page 135), and the many other uniquely Italian fish dishes in this chapter.

Baked Cod Venezia SERVES 4

Venice, the romantic city of canals, is the inspiration for this tasty dish. If you wish, you can substitute an equal amount of haddock for the cod. Spiced Apple Relish (page 61), Salad Roma (page 104), and Potatoes Baked in Pungent Basil Sauce (page 208) are delightful accompaniments.

1 pound cod fillets
¼ cup lemon juice
1 teaspoon olive oil
2 cloves garlic, minced
2 teaspoons low-sodium chicken bouillon

Black pepper to taste
6 mushrooms, sliced
1 carrot, cut in ¼-inch rounds
2 teaspoons dried mint
¾ cup water

1. Preheat oven to 350°.
2. In 9-inch square casserole, combine first 2 ingredients. Let stand 10 minutes, turning fillets once.
3. In skillet, heat oil over low heat. Add garlic and cook 5 minutes, or until garlic is lightly browned, stirring often.
4. Spoon garlic over cod. Then season cod with bouillon and pepper.
5. Scatter mushrooms, carrot, and mint around fish. Then pour water around fish.
6. Cover and bake 20 minutes, or until fish flakes easily.

Per serving with cod: 133.4 calories; 97.3 mg. sodium; 6.6 gm. carbohydrates; 2.5 gm. fat.
Per serving with haddock: 134.5 calories; 87.0 mg. sodium; 6.6 gm. carbohydrates; 2.3 gm. fat.

Flounder in Cheesy Dill Sauce SERVES 8

Southern, light, lovely, and delicious. Some good accompaniments include Minestrone (page 78) and Rice and Sausage (page 198).

1 cup low-sodium ricotta cheese
2 teaspoons low-sodium chicken bouillon
6 scallions, chopped, including greens
1½ tablespoons dried dill

2 tablespoons olive oil, divided
1½ pounds flounder fillets, divided
12 mushrooms, sliced thick
2 tablespoons lemon juice
2 lemons, cut in wedges

1. In bowl, combine first 4 ingredients, blending thoroughly. Cover and refrigerate overnight to allow flavors to blend.
2. Preheat oven to 425°.
3. In skillet, heat half the oil over low heat. Add half the flounder. Raise heat to medium-low and cook flounder 3 minutes. Turn and cook 3 minutes more. Transfer flounder to 9-inch square casserole.
4. Spoon half the cheese mixture over flounder.
5. Repeat Step 3 with remaining oil and flounder.
6. To skillet, add mushrooms and lemon juice. Cover and cook 5 minutes.
7. Spoon mushrooms over fish. Top with remaining cheese mixture, and bake 15 minutes, or until cheese is bubbly.
8. Garnish with lemon wedges.

Per serving: 164.2 calories; 74.4 mg. sodium; 3.6 gm. carbohydrates; 8.7 gm. fat.

Parsley Flounder in Herb Sauce

SERVES 8

Sweet, elegant, and surprisingly light for a southern-style dish. You may substitute an equal amount of cod or salmon fillets for the flounder and have equally delicious results. Serve with Eggplant with Mushrooms (page 224) and pasta.

8 small flounder fillets
Black pepper to taste
2 cups fresh parsley, chopped, or
   8 teaspoons dried parsley
8 teaspoons low-sodium chicken
   bouillon

1½ cups water
½ cup dry white wine
¼ cup lemon juice
4 teaspoons paprika
2½ cups Herb Sauce (page 249)

1. Preheat oven to 325°.
2. Place fillets on flat surface. Sprinkle each fillet with pepper.
3. Put an equal portion of parsley in the center of each fillet. Then sprinkle a teaspoon of bouillon over each filet.
4. Roll up fillets and skewer with toothpicks. Place, seam side down, on 9 x 13-inch casserole.
5. Pour water, wine, and lemon juice around fillets. Then sprinkle fillets with paprika.
6. Bake, uncovered, 20 minutes.
7. Spoon sauce over all. Cover and bake 10 minutes more.

Per serving with flounder: 245.4 calories; 115.9 mg. sodium; 7.8 gm. carbohydrates; 12.0 gm. fat.
Per serving with cod: 244.3 calories; 106.7 mg. sodium; 7.8 gm. carbohydrates; 11.5 gm. fat.
Per serving with salmon: 403.1 calories; 99.9 mg. sodium; 7.8 gm. carbohydrates; 26.4 gm. fat.

Salmon in Basil-Cream Sauce

SERVES 8

The meaty flavor of swordfish is an admirable stand-in for the salmon in this sophisticated northern dish. Shrimp and Potato Salad (page 109) is the only accompaniment you need.

1½ pounds salmon fillets
¼ cup dry sherry
2 tablespoons lemon juice
1 tablespoon unsalted margarine
2 leeks, chopped, including greens

Black pepper to taste
1 cup fresh basil, loosely packed, chopped, or 1 tablespoon dried basil
⅓ cup heavy cream

1. In 9-inch square casserole, place salmon. Pour sherry and lemon juice over all. Let stand 10 minutes.
2. In skillet, heat margarine over low heat. Add leeks and cook 2 minutes, stirring often.
3. To skillet, add salmon and marinade plus pepper. Cover and simmer 10 minutes, turning salmon once.
4. Add basil and cream. Cover and simmer 10 minutes more, or until salmon flakes easily.

Per serving with salmon: 257.9 calories; 60.3 mg. sodium; 4.8 gm. carbohydrates; 16.7 gm. fat.
Per serving with swordfish: 173.0 calories; 5.5 mg. sodium; 4.8 gm. carbohydrates; 8.6 gm. fat.

Salmon, Eggplant, and Capers   SERVES 8

Risotto (page 197) and a mixed green salad with Cucumber Dressing (page 259) will enhance this sumptuous southern dish.

1 tablespoon olive oil
2 onions, chopped
2 cloves garlic, minced
2 cans (14½ ounces) low-sodium
  salmon, including liquid
¼ teaspoon dried rosemary
⅛ teaspoon dried thyme
1 large eggplant, peeled and
  diced

1 tablespoon dried basil
2 tablespoons dried parsley
2 tablespoons capers*
½ cup dry red wine
Black pepper to taste
2 teaspoons low-sodium beef
  bouillon

1. In large skillet, heat oil over low heat. Add onions and garlic and cook 10 minutes, or until onions are lightly browned, stirring often.
2. Add salmon, including liquid, rosemary, and thyme. Stir to blend.
3. Add all remaining ingredients, except bouillon, blending thoroughly. Cover and simmer 40 minutes, stirring occasionally.
4. Stir in bouillon. Cover and simmer 5 minutes more.

Per serving: 151.3 calories; 46.9 mg. sodium; 13.4 gm. carbohydrates;
    5.5 gm. fat.

* Preserved in vinegar only.

Baked Snapper

SERVES 8

French overtones mark this dish of the northern regions. Good accompaniments include Piquant Mayonnaise (page 258), Sweet-and-Sour Zucchini (page 238), and boiled brown rice.

¼ cup cider vinegar
2 tablespoons dry sherry
½ teaspoon orange peel powder

2 pounds red snapper fillets
1 cup fresh basil, chopped, or
  2 teaspoons dried basil

1. In shallow baking dish, combine first 4 ingredients. Cover and refrigerate at least 2 hours, turning fish occasionally.
2. Preheat oven to broil.
3. Broil 6 inches from heat 4 minutes.
4. Turn fish and broil 4 minutes more.
5. Turn off oven. To baking dish, add basil.
6. Cover baking dish and let rest in oven 10 minutes more, or until fish flakes easily.

Per serving: 110.3 calories; 77.3 mg. sodium; 0.6 gm. carbohydrates; 1.0 gm. fat.

Snapper Stuffed with Seafood

SERVES 8

Variations on stuffed fish abound in southern Italy. The tempting recipe below is Sicilian in origin. Serve with Braised Endive Salad (page 99) and Broccoli and Pine Nuts (page 218).

1 pint oysters, shucked
¼ pound shrimp,
   shelled, deveined, and halved
   lengthwise
¼ cup low-sodium seasoned
   bread crumbs
¼ teaspoon dried oregano
⅛ teaspoon dried marjoram
1 tablespoon dried parsley
⅛ teaspoon dried sage

Black pepper to taste
½ cup lemon juice, divided
1 2-pound red snapper, cleaned,
   head and tail intact
2 cloves garlic, sliced
2 teaspoons low-sodium chicken
   bouillon
¼ cup dry vermouth
1 cup water
2 carrots, julienned

1. In bowl, combine first 8 ingredients plus 2 tablespoons lemon juice. Stir to blend thoroughly. Set aside.
2. Line a baking dish with aluminum foil. Lay fish on foil and make several gashes along the top of the fish.
3. In gashes, insert garlic slices.
4. Preheat oven to 450°.
5. Stuff fish with oysters and shrimp mixture.
6. Pour remaining lemon juice over fish. Then sprinkle bouillon on top of fish.
7. Pour vermouth and water around fish.
8. Scatter carrots around fish.
9. Cover baking dish with another strip of aluminum foil. Then bake fish ½ hour.
10. Puncture foil cover and bake 10 minutes more.
11. Remove fish from oven and let stand 5 minutes before serving.

Per serving: 155.5 calories; 136.3 mg. sodium; 10.3 gm. carbohydrates;
   2.3 gm. fat.

Squid with
Bread Crumb Topping

SERVES 4

Nowhere are squid so deliciously prepared as in Italy. From the province of Puglia on the Adriatic Sea comes this adaptation of a baked squid dish which more than proves the point. Peas with Sweet Peppers (page 229) is a nice accent.

2 cups Chicken Stock (page 64)
1 teaspoon low-sodium beef
   bouillon
⅛ teaspoon garlic powder
⅛ teaspoon black pepper
¼ teaspoon dried marjoram
2 tablespoons dried parsley
2 tablespoons unsalted margarine

⅓ cup low-sodium seasoned
   bread crumbs
1 teaspoon dried basil
¾ pound squid, cleaned and
   chopped
¼ cup lemon juice
¼ cup dry vermouth

1. In saucepan, combine first 6 ingredients. Turn heat to medium and bring to a slow boil, stirring occasionally. Continue boiling 10 minutes.
2. While soup is heating, in skillet heat margarine over low heat. Add bread crumbs and basil. Cook 5 minutes, stirring often.
3. To saucepan, add squid and lemon juice, stirring to blend.
4. Raise heat to high. Add vermouth and cook 3 minutes.
5. Pour squid mixture into serving dish. Top with bread crumb mixture.

Per serving: 234.8 calories; 29.5 mg. sodium; 17.9 gm. carbohydrates;
   10.2 gm. fat.

Swordfish and Sweet Peppers

SERVES 8

One taste of this southern dish will win you over. Serve it with Mixed Salad Surprise (page 103) and Rice in Wine (page 199).

4 low-sodium sweet pepper halves	2 onions, minced
1½ pounds swordfish steak	4 cloves garlic, minced
½ cup dry white wine	1 cup chopped fresh basil, or
Black pepper to taste	½ tablespoon dried basil
1 tablespoon olive oil	2 lemons cut in wedges

1. In 9-inch square ovenproof casserole, combine first 4 ingredients. Cover and refrigerate at least 4 hours, turning fish occasionally.
2. While fish is marinating, in skillet, heat oil over low heat. Add onions and garlic and cook 5 minutes, or until onions are wilted.
3. Preheat oven to broil.
4. Spoon onion mixture around fish and broil 6 inches from heat 7 minutes.
5. Turn fish. Spoon basil around fish and broil 5 minutes more.
6. Garnish with lemon wedges.

Per serving: 160.3 calories; 16.8 mg. sodium; 10.2 gm. carbohydrates; 5.5 gm. fat.

Swordfish in Pepper-Wine Sauce

SERVES 8

This dish of the Alto Adige region reflects the influence of neighboring Austria and Germany. It is just as tasty made with an equal amount of cod or salmon steaks. Serve with Buttery Green Beans with Mushrooms (page 227) and Creamy Garlic Potatoes (page 206).

½ cup dry white wine
¼ cup lemon juice
2 tablespoons low-sodium mustard
2 tablespoons boiling water

1½ tablespoons low-sodium beef bouillon
¼ teaspoon black pepper
1½ pounds swordfish steaks
1 tablespoon unsalted margarine

1. In bowl, combine first 3 ingredients, stirring until mustard is completely blended.
2. In second bowl, combine water, bouillon, and pepper, blending thoroughly.
3. Preheat oven to broil.
4. Place swordfish on shallow baking dish. Pour wine mixture over all.
5. Broil swordfish 6 inches from heat 7 minutes.
6. Turn swordfish. Spoon on bouillon mixture and broil 5 minutes more.
7. Dot swordfish with margarine and broil 2 minutes more, or until fish flakes easily.

Per serving with swordfish: 141.2 calories; 6.9 mg. sodium; 2.5 gm. carbohydrates; 5.7 gm. fat.
Per serving with cod: 106.9 calories; 66.9 mg. sodium; 2.5 gm. carbohydrates; 2.5 gm. fat.
Per serving with salmon: 226.0 calories; 61.8 mg. sodium; 2.5 gm. carbohydrates; 13.7 gm. fat.

Simple Broiled Trout   SERVES 4

The lakes in the northern province of Lombardy, Lake Como among them, are stocked with trout which require only the slightest touch of seasonings. Try this dish with Salad Roma (page 104) and Vermicelli with Oysters (page 195).

4 teaspoons low-sodium chicken bouillon	2 1-pound lake trout, heads and tails intact
Black pepper to taste	¼ cup lemon juice
1 teaspoon dried oregano	1 tablespoon unsalted margarine
1 tablespoon dried basil	

1. In bowl, combine first 4 ingredients, blending thoroughly.
2. Preheat oven to broil.
3. On broiler pan, place trout. Pour lemon juice over all. Then sprinkle bouillon mixture over all.
4. Broil 6 inches from heat 5 minutes.
5. Turn trout and broil 5 minutes more.
6. Dot with margarine.

Per serving: 315.8 calories; 5.6 mg. sodium; 3.1 gm. carbohydrates; 19.9 gm. fat.

Wine-Baked Trout   SERVES 4

This delicate dish is decidedly northern. Serve with Lemon-Mint Artichokes (page 214) and Basil Rice and Leeks (page 198) for a stylish and very tasty meal.

1 2-pound lake trout, cleaned, head and tail intact	¼ teaspoon dried sage
	¼ teaspoon dried rosemary
2 cloves garlic, sliced thin	1 tablespoon unsalted margarine
1 onion, sliced thin	½ cup water
2 tablespoons dried parsley	⅓ cup dry vermouth
½ teaspoon dried basil	1 lemon, cut in wedges

1. Preheat over to 375°.
2. Place trout on lightly greased shallow baking dish. Cut several slits in the body of the fish.
3. Insert garlic slices in slits. Scatter onion around fish.
4. In bowl, combine parsley, basil, sage, and rosemary. Sprinkle mixture over fish.
5. Dot top of fish with margarine.
6. Pour water and vermouth around fish.
7. Cover fish with aluminum foil and bake 40 minutes.
8. Remove fish from oven and let stand 5 minutes before serving.
9. Garnish with lemon wedges.

Per serving: 329.6 calories; 8.2 mg. sodium; 7.5 gm. carbohydrates; 19.0 gm. fat.

Tuna Sautéed in Wine SERVES 8

Tuna has never tasted as good as it does in this Sicilian specialty which derives its succulent flavor from a combination of wine, vinegar, and sugar. Swordfish would be a wonderful substitute; Squash with Orange-Nut Stuffing (page 237) and Risotto (page 197) are the perfect accompaniments.

2 pounds tuna steaks
¼ cup all-purpose flour
2 tablespoons olive oil, divided
3 onions, sliced thin
Black pepper to taste
2 teaspoons low-sodium beef
  bouillon

⅓ cup dry white wine
1/16 teaspoon ground nutmeg
3 tablespoons red wine vinegar
1 teaspoon sugar
⅛ teaspoon dried marjoram

1. In plastic bag, combine first 2 ingredients. Shake to coat tuna with flour. Set aside.
2. In skillet, heat 1 tablespoon oil over low heat. Add onions and black pepper. Cook 10 minutes, or until onions are lightly browned, stirring often.
3. Push onions to sides of skillet. To well created in center, add remaining tablespoon oil. Add tuna steaks.
4. Raise heat to medium-high and cook tuna for 3 minutes.
5. Turn tuna. Add remaining ingredients. Cover and cook 3 minutes more, or until fish flakes easily.

Per serving with tuna: 255.1 calories; 50.0 mg. sodium; 14.5 gm. carbohydrates; 11.1 gm. fat.
Per serving with swordfish: 224.2 calories; 7.8 mg. sodium; 14.5 gm. carbohydrates; 8.6 gm. fat.

Tuna, Cheese, and Tomato Bake

SERVES 8

Wonderfully Italian, in the style of Rome and Naples, this dish needs only a salad or soup accompaniment. Roast Peppers and Beet Salad (page 105) and Green Bean and Barley Soup (page 69) are two possibilities.

½ **pound macaroni, cooked al dente***
1 **tablespoon dried basil**
1 **teaspoon dried oregano**
⅟₁₆ **teaspoon ground nutmeg**
3 **leeks, chopped, including greens**
2 **cups boiling water**

2 **tablespoons low-sodium chicken bouillon**
⅟₁₆ **teaspoon hot pepper flakes**
2 **cans (13 ounces) low-sodium tuna, including liquid**
4 **tomatoes, sliced**
⅓ **pound low-sodium mozzarella, sliced thin**

1. Preheat oven to 350°.
2. In 9-inch square ovenproof casserole, combine first 5 ingredients, blending thoroughly.
3. In bowl, combine water, bouillon, and hot pepper flakes, blending thoroughly. Set aside.
4. To casserole, add tuna plus its liquid, breaking up tuna with fork. Toss to blend thoroughly.
5. Add bouillon mixture.
6. Top mixture first with tomatoes, then with cheese. Cover and bake 20 minutes. Uncover and bake 10 minutes more.

Per serving: 207.8 calories; 23.2 mg. sodium; 32.9 gm. carbohydrates; 2.2 gm. fat.

* Do not add salt to water.

Lobster in Creamy Wine Sauce   SERVES 8

The Mediterranean is rich in seafood; this dish, traditionally made with langoustine, is one tempting example of the regional use of shellfish. For variety, you may replace the lobster with 1½ pounds shrimp, shelled, deveined, tails intact. Serve over pasta, accompanied by Mixed Vegetable Salad (page 104).

1 teaspoon unsalted margarine	2½ cups Wine-Cream Sauce
8 mushrooms, sliced	(page 246)
Black pepper to taste	2 teaspoons dried parsley
¼ cup dry vermouth	2 1-pound lobsters, steamed*
½ cup water	

1. In skillet, heat margarine. Add mushrooms and pepper and cook 2 minutes, stirring often.
2. Add all remaining ingredients, except lobster, stirring to blend thoroughly. Cover and simmer 15 minutes, stirring occasionally.
3. Add lobsters in the shell. Cover and simmer 5 minutes more.

Per serving with lobster: 134.7 calories; 91.9 mg. sodium; 7.4 gm. carbohydrates; 7.0 gm. fat.
Per serving with shrimp: 186.7 calories; 151.9 mg. sodium; 8.5 gm. carbohydrates; 7.2 gm. fat.

* Do not add salt to water.

Broiled Oysters

SERVES 4

From the island of Sardinia comes the inspiration for this succulent dish. Serve with Fennel Salad (page 100) and Spice-Broiled Tomatoes (page 235) for a meal fit for an Italian princess.

2 pints oysters, shucked,
  including liquid
¼ cup lemon juice
¾ cup boiling water
2 teaspoons low-sodium chicken
  bouillon

1 teaspoon paprika
¼ cup chopped parsley
2 teaspoons olive oil
1 onion, minced
2 cloves garlic, minced

1. Preheat oven to broil.
2. In bowl, combine first 2 ingredients. Set aside.
3. In second bowl, combine water, bouillon, paprika, and parsley.
4. In shallow baking dish, combine oyster and bouillon mixtures. Broil 8 inches from heat 3 minutes.
5. While oysters are broiling, in skillet heat oil over medium heat. Add onion and garlic and sauté 2 minutes, or until onions are golden.
6. Transfer oysters to platter. Spoon onion mixture over all.

Per serving: 168.5 calories; 137.7 mg. sodium; 15.2 gm. carbohydrates; 6.2 gm. fat.

Deviled Shrimp   SERVES 8

This is a marvelous dish which any of the southern provinces
would be proud to claim as its own. For two spectacular variations, replace the shrimp with an equal amount of swordfish or
red snapper, cut in 1-inch chunks. Just remember, if you use either
of these substitutes, add it in Step 3. Whichever you choose, serve
over pasta or boiled white rice and balance with the refreshing
taste of mixed greens with Herbed Mayonnaise Dressing (page
257).

1½ pounds shrimp,
 shelled, deveined, tails intact
½ cup dry red wine
Dash of cayenne pepper
1 tablespoon olive oil
3 cloves garlic, minced
6 tomatoes, chopped

¾ teaspoon dried basil
¼ teaspoon dried oregano
2 teaspoons low-sodium beef
 bouillon
1/16 teaspoon hot pepper flakes
2 tablespoons brandy

1. In bowl, combine first 3 ingredients. Set aside.
2. In skillet, heat oil over medium-low heat. Add garlic and cook
   5 minutes, or until garlic is lightly browned.
3. To skillet, add tomatoes, basil, oregano, bouillon, and hot
   pepper flakes, blending thoroughly. Reduce heat to low. Cover
   and simmer 10 minutes, stirring occasionally.
4. Add shrimp mixture. Cover and simmer 5 minutes more, or
   until shrimp turn pink all over.
5. Raise heat to high. Add brandy and flame. Serve immediately.

Per serving with shrimp: 148.2 calories; 127.0 mg. sodium; 8.2 gm. carbohy-
    drates; 3.0 gm. fat.
Per serving with swordfish: 171.3 calories; 7.0 mg. sodium; 7.0 gm. carbohy-
    drates; 5.8 gm. fat.
Per serving with red snapper: 149.9 calories; 64.4 mg. sodium; 7.0 gm. carbo-
    hydrates; 13.8 gm. fat.

Shrimp in Spicy Tomato Sauce SERVES 8

Southern and typically hot, this dish is sure to become one of your special favorites. Zucchini, Tomato, and Sardine Salad (page 107) and pasta are excellent accompaniments.

1½ pounds medium shrimp,
  shelled, deveined, tails intact
1 tablespoon paprika
3 tablespoons dry sherry
1½ tablespoons olive oil, divided
2 onions, minced

6 cloves garlic, minced
1½ tablespoons dried parsley
4 tomatoes, chopped
3 tablespoons lemon juice
½ teaspoon sugar

1. In bowl, combine first 3 ingredients. Toss to blend. Set aside.
2. In skillet, heat 1 tablespoon oil over medium-low heat. Add onions and garlic and cook 5 minutes, or until onions are golden, stirring often.
3. Add remaining oil and parsley, blending thoroughly. Cook 2 minutes more, stirring often.
4. Add tomatoes, lemon juice, and sugar, stirring to blend. Reduce heat to low. Cover and simmer 15 minutes.
5. Add shrimp mixture, stirring to blend thoroughly. Cover and cook 3 minutes more, or until shrimp turn pink all over.

Per serving: 143.7 calories; 127.6 mg. sodium; 12.5 gm. carbohydrates;
  3.8 gm. fat.

Shrimp, Zucchini, and Peppers in Wine Cream

SERVES 8

This southern-style dish is sure to please the eye as well as the palate. Serve it over pasta accompanied by Braised Arugola Salad (page 96) for a delightful meal. The chopped meat of a steamed 3-pound lobster would make an elegant substitute for the shrimp.

1 tablespoon olive oil
1 onion, minced
4 cloves garlic, minced
1/4 cup crushed, unsalted almonds
1/16 teaspoon hot pepper flakes
1 cup boiling water
1 tablespoon low-sodium beef bouillon

1/2 cup dry vermouth
1/8 teaspoon ground nutmeg
2 zucchini, julienned
2 red peppers, sliced thin
1 1/2 pounds shrimp, shelled, deveined, and halved lengthwise
2 tablespoons heavy cream

1. In skillet, heat oil over low heat. Add onion and garlic and cook 5 minutes, stirring occasionally.
2. Add almonds and hot pepper flakes and cook 2 minutes more.
3. Stir in water and bouillon, blending thoroughly.
4. Add vermouth and nutmeg, stirring to blend.
5. Add zucchini and red peppers. Cover and simmer 15 minutes.
6. Add shrimp, stirring to blend well. Cover and simmer 5 minutes more, or until shrimp are pink all over.
7. Stir in cream.

Per serving with shrimp: 202.3 calories; 141.0 mg. sodium; 13.1 gm. carbohydrates; 8.4 gm. fat.
Per serving with lobster: 163.3 calories; 136.0 mg. sodium; 12.0 gm. carbohydrates; 8.5 gm. fat.

Poultry

Although Italians have adopted the American preference for turkey as holiday fare, generally speaking, in the Italian home, poultry appears neither as often nor in as many ways as do fish and meat.

The most popular poultry dish is also the simplest—chicken, lightly seasoned with herbs, spices, and lemon, then grilled, broiled, or roasted. Variations on this theme are found in every region in Italy. One of our favorites is Chicken with Lemon Sauce (page 143).

Chicken in Parsley Wine (page 144) is a perfect example of the northern tradition. Here chicken is slowly simmered or poached in wine, flavored with the barest hint of seasonings, until it literally falls off the bone. As you might expect, the southern-style dishes are more robust. The flavor of herbs and spices is more pronounced, and a variety of vegetables, one of which is usually tomatoes, are frequently incorporated to produce a hearty, thoroughly satisfying casserole dish. This chapter offers several of these one-dish meals, including Chicken and Artichokes (page 140) and Chicken Stew Roma (page 148).

When all is said and done, the secret of poultry recipes in Italy is that they are as uncomplicated and easy to make as they are tasty.

Braised Chicken with Applesauce

SERVES 4

We have taken the liberty of substituting margarine for olive oil in this Sicilian dish to give the chicken a lighter, sweeter flavor. It is luscious with Asparagus Vinaigrette (page 216) and Mashed Potatoes with Pork Bits (page 207).

1 tablespoon unsalted margarine
4 half chicken breasts, skinned
2 onions, sliced
1/16 teaspoon hot pepper flakes
1/2 teaspoon dried rosemary

1/2 cup dry red wine
1/2 cup unsweetened apple sauce
1 tablespoon dried parsley
2 teaspoons dried basil

1. In skillet, melt margarine over low heat. Add chicken and sauté 10 minutes.
2. Turn chicken. Add onions and sauté 10 minutes more.
3. Add hot pepper flakes, rosemary, and wine. Cover and simmer 15 minutes.
4. Add all remaining ingredients, stirring to blend thoroughly. Cover and simmer 15 minutes more.

Per serving: 170.0 calories; 59.8 mg. sodium; 14.5 gm. carbohydrates; 5.5 gm. fat.

Champagne Chicken with Herbs

SERVES 4

This is a remarkably tasty dish, worthy of its French origins. Braised Endive Salad (page 99), pasta with one cup of Bechamel Sauce (page 240), and Lemon-Mint Artichokes (page 214) are three of many possible accompaniments.

4 half chicken breasts, skinned
1 cup champagne (or dry white wine)
½ cup lemon juice
4 bay leaves
1½ teaspoons garlic powder

1 tablespoon dried basil
1 teaspoon dried thyme
½ teaspoon ground nutmeg
2 teaspoons low-sodium chicken bouillon
2 tablespoons unsalted margarine

1. In 9-inch square ovenproof casserole, place all ingredients, except margarine. Let stand 1 hour, turning chicken occasionally.
2. Preheat oven to 350°.
3. Into saucepan, pour ½ cup of the marinade. Reserve remainder.
4. Cover casserole and bake 40 minutes.
5. Turn chicken. Bake, uncovered, 10 minutes more.
6. To saucepan, add margarine. Turn heat to medium-low and cook 5 minutes, or until margarine is melted, stirring occasionally.
7. Transfer chicken to individual plates. Pour reserved marinade over all. Then pour margarine sauce over all.

Per serving: 225.7 calories; 56.6 mg. sodium; 5.6 gm. carbohydrates; 8.7 gm. fat.

Chicken and Artichokes

SERVES 8

Artichokes are a favorite Italian vegetable, and they certainly do this dish proud. You can find this savory combination in many parts of Italy—in Naples, Rome, Bologna, Milan, or Florence.

2 onions, sliced
6 cloves garlic, minced, divided
2 carrots, julienned
8 half chicken breasts, skinned
  and boned
Black pepper to taste
¼ teaspoon dried sage
4 tablespoons low-sodium beef
  bouillon

4 teaspoons dried basil
1½ cups water
16 frozen artichoke hearts
¼ cup lemon juice
4 ounces low-sodium mozzarella
  cheese, sliced thin

1. Preheat oven to 350°.
2. In 9 x 13-inch casserole, place onions and garlic. Top with carrots.
3. Lay chicken breasts on top of vegetables. Season with pepper, sage, bouillon, and basil.
4. Pour water around chicken. Cover and bake 40 minutes.
5. Scatter artichoke hearts around chicken.
6. Pour lemon juice around chicken.
7. Place cheese slices over chicken. Bake, uncovered, 15 minutes more.

Per serving: 189.2 calories; 94.6 mg. sodium; 14.7 gm. carbohydrates; 4.6 gm. fat.

Chicken and Mushrooms   SERVES 8

Although this elegant northern dish has French accents, the cheese gives it its distinctively Italian flavor. Rice Primavera (page 202) is an excellent accompaniment.

2 tablespoons unsalted
   margarine, divided
8 half chicken breasts, skinned
   and boned
Black pepper to taste
8 mushrooms, sliced
2 tablespoons brandy
2 cups boiling water

2½ tablespoons low-sodium
   chicken bouillon
2 leeks, chopped, including
   greens
⅛ teaspoon fennel seed
1 tablespoon dried parsley
3 tablespoons low-sodium ricotta
   cheese

1. In large skillet, heat margarine over low heat. Add chicken. Raise heat to medium and cook 5 minutes.
2. Turn chicken. Cook 5 minutes more.
3. Sprinkle pepper over chicken. Scatter mushrooms around chicken.
4. Pour brandy over all. Flame.
5. Add all remaining ingredients, except cheese.
6. Reduce heat to low. Cover and cook ½ hour, turning chicken once.
7. Stir in cheese. Cover and cook 10 minutes more.

Per serving: 190.6 calories; 60.4 mg. sodium; 6.9 gm. carbohydrates;
   7.2 gm. fat.

Chicken and Sausage

SERVES 8

So Italian, so Sicilian, and so delicious. This recipe is sure to become a standard in your Italian repertoire. Two serving suggestions are Spinach and Cheese Soup (page 76) or Fettuccine in Wine-Cream Sauce (page 186).

¼ **pound Hot Sausage (page 171)**
3 **cloves garlic, minced**
6 **half chicken breasts, skinned, boned, and cut in 2-inch chunks**
1 **tablespoon low-sodium chicken bouillon**

1½ **cups water**
4 **carrots, julienned**
½ **cup dry red (or white) wine**
2 **teaspoons dried oregano**
3 **green peppers, sliced**

1. In large skillet, cook sausage and garlic over medium heat, 5 minutes, or until sausage loses all pink color, stirring often.
2. Add chicken and cook 10 minutes, turning chicken once.
3. Add all remaining ingredients, stirring to blend.
4. Reduce heat to low. Cover and cook ½ hour, stirring occasionally.

Per serving: 180.8 calories; 83.1 mg. sodium; 11.1 gm. carbohydrates; 5.3 gm. fat.

Chicken with Lemon Sauce   SERVES 4

An Italian classic, this northern dish is typical of the Alto Adige region, bordering Yugoslavia. Try it with Christmas Salad (page 99) and Basil Rice and Leeks (page 198).

**4 half chicken breasts, skinned,
   boned, and pounded flat**
¼ teaspoon dried rosemary
¼ teaspoon dried basil
⅟₁₆ teaspoon hot pepper flakes
**2 tablespoons unsalted
   margarine, divided**

8 mushrooms, chopped
1 egg yolk
¼ cup lemon juice
2 tablespoons dry white wine

1. On platter, combine first 4 ingredients. Let stand 15 minutes, turning chicken once.
2. In skillet, heat 1 tablespoon margarine over low heat. Add chicken. Cover and cook 10 minutes.
3. Turn chicken. Cover and cook 10 minutes more.
4. Add remaining margarine and mushrooms. Cover and cook ½ hour, turning chicken occasionally.
5. While chicken is cooking, in saucepan, combine egg yolk and lemon juice. Turn heat to low and cook 5 minutes, stirring often.
6. Stir in wine and cook sauce 2 minutes more.
7. Pour lemon sauce over chicken. Serve immediately.

Per serving: 194.6 calories; 69.6 mg. sodium; 2.7 gm. carbohydrates;
   9.2 gm. fat.

Chicken in Parsley Wine   SERVES 4

Grace your table with this lovely chicken dish from the Piedmont region. Serve it with 1 cup Tomato-Plum Relish (page 62), Broccoli in Sherry Garlic (page 218), and boiled potatoes.

4 half chicken breasts
2 cloves garlic, minced
1/8 teaspoon dried sage
Black pepper to taste
1 1/2 tablespoons unsalted
    margarine
1/2 cup water

2 teaspoons low-sodium chicken
    bouillon
1/4 cup dry white wine
1 tablespoon dried parsley
2 leeks, chopped, including
    greens

1. In skillet, place chicken skin side down. Turn heat to medium and cook 10 minutes, or until skin is browned.
2. Turn chicken. Add garlic and cook 5 minutes more.
3. Season chicken with sage and pepper.
4. Add margarine and cook 10 minutes more, turning chicken once.
5. Add remaining ingredients and cook 10 minutes more.
6. Reduce heat to low. Cover and simmer 5 minutes more.

Per serving: 213.4 calories; 59.9 mg. sodium; 11.0 gm. carbohydrates;
    7.5 gm. fat.

Chicken in Wine

SERVES 4

Whether you use white wine or red, this dish is marvelous. Serve it with Fennel Salad (page 180), Green Beans with Orange Slices (page 228), and pasta with 1½ cups Mustard-Tomato Sauce (page 246).

¼ teaspoon garlic powder
½ teaspoon lemon peel powder
Black pepper to taste
4 half chicken breasts, skinned
1 tablespoon olive oil
1 teaspoon unsalted margarine
8 mushrooms, chopped

2 teaspoons all-purpose flour
1 teaspoon dried oregano
½ cup dry white (or red) wine
½ cup water
2 teaspoons low-sodium chicken bouillon

1. On platter, combine first 4 ingredients. Let stand 10 minutes, turning chicken once.
2. In skillet, heat oil over medium-low heat. Add chicken and cook 10 minutes.
3. Turn chicken and cook 10 minutes more.
4. Add margarine and mushrooms. Cook 5 minutes more, stirring occasionally.
5. Stir in flour, blending thoroughly.
6. Raise heat to medium. Add remaining ingredients and cook 5 minutes.
7. Reduce heat to low. Turn chicken. Cover and cook 10 minutes more.

Per serving: 200.1 calories; 58.4 mg. sodium; 5.3 gm. carbohydrates; 7.6 gm. fat.

Chicken in Wine-Tomato Sauce   SERVES 4

Variations on this wonderful southern dish can be found in kitchens from Rome to Palermo. Carrots in Orange Wine (page 220) and Mashed Potatoes with Pork Bits (page 207) are two possible accompaniments.

4 chicken breasts
1 onion, chopped fine
⅛ teaspoon ground cinnamon
1½ teaspoons dried sage
1 teaspoon dried thyme
1 tablespoon dried basil
2 tablespoons low-sodium beef
  bouillon

2 cups water
2 cups Tomato Sauce II
  (page 243)
¼ cup dry white wine
2 tablespoons dry sherry

1. In Dutch oven, place chicken skin side down. Turn heat to medium and cook 15 minutes, or until skin is browned.
2. Turn chicken. Add onion and cook 10 minutes more, stirring onion occasionally.
3. Add cinnamon, sage, thyme, basil, bouillon, and water. Raise heat to high and bring to a boil.
4. Reduce heat to low. Stir in tomato sauce and wine. Cover and simmer ½ hour.
5. Stir in sherry. Cover and simmer 5 minutes more.

Per serving: 214.4 calories; 75.2 mg. sodium; 19.4 gm. carbohydrates;
  5.2 gm. fat.

Chicken Milano   SERVES 4

This dish is as elegant as the city for which it is named. Braised Spinach (page 233) and boiled white rice with 1½ cups Mushroom-Cheese Sauce (page 241) or 1¾ cups Pungent Basil Sauce (page 248) will make a very tasty meal.

4 half chicken breasts
2 onions, chopped
2 cloves garlic, minced
3 tablespoons white vinegar
2 tablespoons low-sodium Dijon
 mustard

1 cup boiling water
1 tablespoon low-sodium chicken
 bouillon
3 tomatoes, chopped
Black pepper to taste
2 tablespoons dried parsley

1. In skillet, place chicken, skin side down. Turn heat to medium and cook 10 minutes.
2. Add onions and garlic. Cook 10 minutes more, or until skin is browned, stirring onions occasionally.
3. Turn chicken. Add vinegar and cook 5 minutes more.
4. Stir in remaining ingredients, blending thoroughly.
5. Reduce heat to low. Cover and simmer ½ hour, stirring occasionally.

Per serving: 187.8 calories; 68.1 mg. sodium; 19.3 gm. carbohydrates; 4.2 gm. fat.

Chicken Stew Roma · SERVES 8

This dish raises the word "stew" to new culinary heights. It needs no accompaniment other than rice or pasta, for example, spaghetti with Wine-Caper Sauce (page 251).

1 3-pound chicken, cut into serving pieces	2 tablespoons dried basil
1 large onion, chopped	⅛ teaspoon black pepper
2 cloves garlic, minced	3 tomatoes, chopped
1 cup water	1 teaspoon dried rosemary
1 teaspoon sugar	1 small eggplant; cubed
2 bay leaves	2 green peppers, sliced
3 tablespoons dried parsley	¼ cup dry vermouth
	8 mushrooms, sliced

1. In Dutch oven, combine first 3 ingredients. Turn heat to medium and cook 15 minutes, stirring often.
2. Stir in all remaining ingredients, blending thoroughly.
3. Reduce heat to low. Cover and simmer 45 minutes, stirring occasionally.

Per serving: 194.7 calories; 77.0 mg. sodium; 15.6 gm. carbohydrates; 5.7 gm. fat.

Chicken Tetrazzini

SERVES 12

This universally popular northern Italian dish is one of the most elegant ways to turn leftover chicken into a classic delight. Tuscany can claim credit for its creation. Serve with a mixed green salad with 2½ cups Italian Vinaigrette (page 254).

1 tablespoon unsalted margarine
2 onions, chopped
12 mushrooms, sliced
1 tablespoon all-purpose flour
¼ cup dry white wine
6 cups cooked chicken, cubed
1 pound macaroni, cooked
  al dente*

3 cups Chicken Stock (page 64)
⅟₁₆ teaspoon ground nutmeg
4 ounces low-sodium Swiss
  cheese, minced
3 tablespoons heavy cream

1. In skillet, heat margarine over low heat. Add onions and cook 15 minutes, or until onions are golden brown, stirring often.
2. Stir in mushrooms and cook 5 minutes, stirring often.
3. Stir in flour, blending thoroughly. Transfer mixture to 9-inch square ovenproof casserole.
4. Stir in all remaining ingredients, except cream, blending thoroughly.
5. Preheat oven to 350°.
6. Cover casserole and bake ½ hour.
7. Stir in cream, blending thoroughly. Cover and bake 5 minutes more.

Per serving: 252.5 calories; 28.2 mg. sodium; 36.0 gm. carbohydrates; 7.7 gm. fat.

* Do not add salt to water.

Honey-Vinegar Baked Chicken SERVES 4

One bite of this spicy, saucy, tender chicken will have you singing its praises. Serve with Peas with Sweet Peppers (page 229) and plain boiled potatoes for a delicious meal.

4 half chicken breasts, skinned
   and boned
1½ cups water

2 onions, sliced
2 cups Honey-Vinegar Dressing
   (page 255), divided

1. Preheat oven to 350°.
2. In 9-inch square ovenproof casserole, place chicken. Add water and onions.
3. Spoon 1 cup dressing over chicken. Cover and bake 20 minutes.
4. Turn chicken. Spoon on remaining dressing. Bake, uncovered, 20 minutes more.

Per serving: 186.4 calories; 60.5 mg. sodium; 26.1 gm. carbohydrates;
   2.5 gm. fat.

Lemon-Basil Chicken SERVES 8

Every bite of this fantastic northern-style dish will tantalize your taste buds. Rice Primavera (page 202) is a good companion.

6 tablespoons all-purpose flour
¼ teaspoon black pepper
4 tablespoons low-sodium
   chicken bouillon
2 tablespoons paprika
8 half chicken breasts, skinned,
   boned, and pounded thin

1½ tablespoons olive oil
1½ tablespoons unsalted
   margarine
⅓ cup lemon juice
1 cup fresh basil, chopped, or
   2 tablespoons dried basil

1. In bowl, combine first 4 ingredients, blending thoroughly.
2. In plastic bag, combine spice mixture and chicken. Shake to coat chicken. Set aside.
3. In large skillet, heat oil over medium-low heat. Add chicken and cook 15 minutes.

4. Turn chicken. Add margarine and cook 20 minutes more.
5. Raise heat to medium. Add lemon juice and basil.
6. Turn chicken and cook 5 minutes more.

Per serving: 221.2 calories; 58.2 mg. sodium; 11.7 gm. carbohydrates;
   7.4 gm. fat.

Mustard Chicken   SERVES 8

Slavic and German influences are evident in this central Italian dish. It is a distinctive taste treat and goes perfectly with Cabbage and Capers (page 219) and boiled potatoes.

8 chicken breasts
2 cups water
2 cups dry white (or red) wine
6 tablespoons sour cream
4 teaspoons low-sodium Dijon
   mustard

1⅓ cups water
1 tablespoon low-sodium chicken
   bouillon
2 teaspoons dried basil
1 onion, minced
3 tablespoons heavy cream

1. In Dutch oven, place chicken, skin side down. Turn heat to high and sauté 10 minutes, or until skin is browned.
2. Reduce heat to medium. Turn chicken and cook 10 minutes more.
3. Add all remaining ingredients, except cream, stirring to blend.
4. Reduce heat to low. Cover and simmer 45 minutes, stirring occasionally.
5. Stir in cream. Cover and simmer 5 minutes more.

Per serving: 229.5 calories; 61.4 mg. sodium; 6.2 gm. carbohydrates;
   9.0 gm. fat.

Roast Stuffed
Chicken Italiano

SERVES 8

This recipe is sure to please. The nut stuffing is northern in origin; the sausage stuffing, southern. Both are extraordinary. If you use the nut stuffing, serve the dish with Buttery Green Beans with Mushrooms (page 227) or Mixed Salad Surprise (page 103). If sausage stuffing is your choice, you might choose Squash with Orange-Nut Stuffing (page 237) or Roast Peppers and Beet Salad (page 97) as companions.

1 4-pound chicken
4 teaspoons dried sage
2 teaspoons low-sodium chicken
  bouillon
2 cloves garlic, sliced

4 cups Italian Stuffing with Nuts
  (page 93) or Italian Stuffing
  with Sausage* (page 92)
⅓ cup lemon juice
2 cups water

1. On platter, place chicken, breast side up. With knife, lift the skin away from the breasts. Rub sage and bouillon over the breasts. Then lower the skin to cover all.
2. With knife, gash chicken. In gashes, insert garlic slices.
3. Spoon stuffing into chicken. Then tie legs together.
4. Preheat oven to 375°.
5. Place chicken on rack in roasting pan. Pour lemon juice over all.
6. Pour water into pan.
7. Roast chicken 25 minutes, or until skin turns golden brown.
8. Reduce heat to 350° and roast 45 minutes more, or until juices run clear when chicken is pierced between drumstick and breast, basting occasionally with pan juices.

Per serving with Italian Stuffing with Nuts:
    338.9 calories; 102.3 mg. sodium; 23.9 gm. carbohydrates; 14.1 gm. fat.
Per serving with Italian Stuffing with Sausage:
    343.9 calories; 107.9 mg. sodium; 29.8 gm. carbohydrates; 11.2 gm. fat.

* Use apples.

Rosemary Chicken with Green Peppercorns

SERVES 8

This memorable and elegant dish with northern touches is just as delicious if you replace the chicken with 1½ pounds of swordfish. Baked Polenta with Tomatoes and Eggplant (page 205) is a delicious way to complete your meal.

8 half chicken breasts, skinned and boned
6 cloves garlic, minced
¾ cup lemon juice
¾ cup orange juice
1½ tablespoons dried rosemary

2 teaspoons green peppercorns*
1½ tablespoons low-sodium chicken bouillon
2 tablespoons brandy (or dry white wine)

1. In skillet, place chicken, skin side down. Turn heat to high and sauté 10 minutes, or until skin is browned.
2. Turn chicken. Add garlic and sauté 5 minutes more, stirring garlic occasionally.
3. Reduce heat to medium-low. Add lemon juice, orange juice, and rosemary. Cover and cook 5 minutes.
4. While chicken is cooking, in blender, grind peppercorns to a rough blend. Add to skillet.
5. Stir in bouillon. Reduce heat to low. Cover and simmer ½ hour.
6. Stir in brandy. Cover and simmer 5 minutes more.

Per serving with chicken: 238.3 calories; 56.4 mg. sodium; 7.0 gm. carbohydrates; 1.8 gm. fat.
Per serving with swordfish: 229.5 calories; 6.4 mg. sodium; 7.0 gm. carbohydrates; 4.1 gm. fat.

* Preserved in vinegar only.

Simple Italian Chicken

SERVES 4

The "simple" in the name of this dish really means classic. And like all things classic, this recipe is sure to be a favorite for years to come. Tomato and Mozzarella Salad (page 106) and Basil Rice and Leeks (page 198) are two possible companions.

4 half chicken breasts
1 onion, chopped
2 teaspoons olive oil
2 cloves garlic, minced
4 tomatoes, chopped

2 tablespoons lemon juice
2 tablespoons dry red wine
Black pepper to taste
1½ tablespoons dried parsley
⅛ teaspoon dried marjoram

1. In skillet, place chicken, skin side down. Turn heat to medium and cook chicken 10 minutes, or until skin is browned.
2. Turn chicken. Add onion and cook 5 minutes more.
3. Add oil and garlic and cook 5 minutes, or until garlic is lightly browned.
4. Reduce heat to low. Add remaining ingredients. Cover and simmer 1 hour, or until chicken is fork tender.

Per serving: 188.2 calories; 60.7 mg. sodium; 14.1 gm. carbohydrates; 5.3 gm. fat.

Chicken Picante

SERVES 8

Two different vinegars and sugar combine to give you one of the most memorable meals you will ever enjoy. This is especially good served with Basil-Crumbed Cauliflower (page 221) and Fettuccine in Wine-Cream Sauce (page 186).

3 tablespoons olive oil, divided
8 half chicken breasts, skinned and boned
2 onions, diced
¼ cup cider vinegar
¼ cup red wine vinegar

¼ cup sugar
Black pepper to taste
2 teaspoons low-sodium chicken bouillon
¼ teaspoon dried thyme
3 cups water

1. In skillet, heat 2 tablespoons oil over medium heat. Add chicken and sauté 15 minutes, or until browned, turning often.
2. While chicken is cooking, in small skillet, heat remaining oil over medium-low heat. Add onions and cook 5 minutes, or until onions are golden.
3. Spoon onions over chicken. Add remaining ingredients.
4. Reduce heat to low. Cover and simmer ½ hour, or until chicken is fork tender, turning chicken occasionally.

Per serving: 202.1 calories; 55.2 mg. sodium; 13.3 gm. carbohydrates; 8.3 gm. fat.

Marinated Rock Cornish Hens   SERVES 8

Although this northern dish is traditionally made with pigeons, the slightly gamey yet sweet Rock Cornish hens are more to our taste. Sweet-and-Sour Zucchini (page 238) and Stuffed Baked Potatoes (page 211) will complete an unforgettable meal.

4 Rock Cornish hens, halved lengthwise
½ cup cider vinegar
3 cloves garlic, chopped
3 tablespoons capers*
4 cloves
⅛ teaspoon hot pepper flakes
½ cup lemon juice

1 tablespoon olive oil
2 onions, chopped
1 cup water
2½ tablespoons low-sodium beef bouillon
⅛ teaspoon dried thyme
¼ teaspoon dried sage

1. In 9 x 13-inch ovenproof casserole, place hens, cut side down. Pour vinegar over all. Cover and refrigerate 1 hour.
2. In blender, combine garlic, capers, and cloves. Grind to a coarse consistency. Scatter around hens.
3. In bowl, combine hot pepper flakes and lemon juice. Set aside.
4. In skillet, heat oil over low heat. Add onions and cook 10 minutes, or until onions are golden, stirring often.
5. Add onions to casserole.
6. Pour lemon juice mixture over all.
7. Add remaining ingredients. Let stand 10 minutes.
8. Preheat oven to 350°.
9. Cover casserole and bake ½ hour.
10. Uncover and bake 15 minutes more, basting hens occasionally with pan juices.

Per serving: 166.1 calories; 65.8 mg. sodium; 9.7 gm. carbohydrates; 5.3 gm. fat.

* Preserved in vinegar only.

Rock Cornish Hens and Beans   SERVES 8

The delicate flavor of Cornish hens is beautifully blended with the robust taste of beans in this Tuscan dish. You will need only a green salad with Oil and Vinegar Dressing (page 254) to complete your meal.

**4 Rock Cornish hens, halved
    lengthwise**
¼ cup lemon juice
1 cup orange juice

3 green peppers, sliced
**1 recipe Beans and Tomatoes
    (page 212)**

1. In 9 x 13-inch casserole, place hens, cut side down. Pour lemon juice and orange juice over all. Cover and refrigerate 1 hour.
2. Preheat oven to 350°.
3. Scatter peppers around hens.
4. Spoon beans and tomatoes around hens. Cover and bake 1 hour.

Per serving: 369.5 calories; 86.1 mg. sodium; 50.2 gm. carbohydrates;
    6.9 gm. fat.

Meat

Although lamb is a particular favorite of the southern regions, it is popular throughout Italy, and is frequently the featured dish at specific occasions and holidays. It is usually seasoned simply, often with garlic, rosemary, and a little olive oil, and then roasted or grilled to succulent, juicy, and pink perfection. Roast Leg of Lamb (page 170) is one example.

Then there is veal which Italian chefs from north to south prepare in every fashion imaginable: grilled, roasted, sautéed, breaded, with sauce or without. A splash of wine, lemon juice, or vinegar plus a sprinkling of herbs and spices are often the final touches. That the results are well worth the effort will be evident when you try two of our adaptations, Veal and Mushroom Stew (page 177) and Veal with Braised Watercress (page 181).

Of course, pork is the one meat no Italian home would be without, for pork is the key ingredient in every Italian sausage, be it mild, sweet, hot, or pungent. Sweet and Hot Sausage (page 173) and Sausage Napoli (page 172) are just two of the selections in this chapter. Like lamb and veal, pork is often roasted or grilled. In fact, the quintessential Italian sandwich consists of slices of pork wedged between thick slabs of bread.

If we have left beef for last, there is good reason. It is the one kind of meat with which Italian cooks are not as familiar because cattle are not raised in Italy and so beef is a rarity.

However, in deference to American tastes, Italian chefs in the United States have become skilled in creating beef dishes which are prominently featured on the menus of Italian restaurants. Beef baked in a parsley, lemon, and brandy sauce is particularly noteworthy, and our version appears on page 163 of this chapter.

In recognition of our own eating habits, this chapter has as many recipes for beef as for veal and pork, while lamb selections are fewer. Whatever the balance, we are sure you will agree that the Italian touch makes any meat very special indeed.

Italian Beef Stew

SERVES 8

This full-bodied, flavorful dish from the northern Piedmont region is reminiscent of France's boeuf bourguignon, which was probably its inspiration. One bite, however, marks it as distinctly Italian. Serve it with Asparagus Vinaigrette (page 216) and Risotto (page 197).

2 cups dry red wine
4 cloves garlic, minced
1 onion, minced
2 carrots, chopped
1 tablespoon green peppercorns*
4 cloves
1 stick cinnamon

½ teaspoon dried sage
¼ teaspoon dried thyme
2 pounds London broil
2 tablespoons all-purpose flour
2 cups Meat Stock (page 65), divided

1. In Dutch oven, combine first 9 ingredients. Turn heat to medium-low and cook 10 minutes.
2. Add London broil. Reduce heat to low. Cover and simmer 1 hour, turning meat occasionally.
3. In bowl, combine flour and ½ cup stock, stirring until flour is dissolved. Add to Dutch oven, stirring to blend.
4. Stir in remaining stock. Cover and simmer 1 hour more, or until meat is fork tender.
5. Discard cloves and cinnamon.

Per serving: 324.5 calories; 99.2 mg. sodium; 14.2 gm. carbohydrates; 9.2 gm. fat.

* Preserved in vinegar only.

London Broil Vinaigrette   SERVES 8

Neapolitan flavor and flair dress up this easy-to-prepare dish. Set
it off with Spice-Broiled Tomatoes (page 235) and Shells with
Mushroom-Cheese Sauce (page 191) for a delightful meal.

2 pounds London broil   **2 tablespoons capers***
1 cup Italian Vinaigrette   **1 tablespoon unsalted margarine**
** (page 254)**   **Black pepper to taste**
½ cup water

1. In 9-inch square ovenproof casserole, combine first 4 ingredients. Cover and refrigerate overnight, turning meat occasionally.
2. Preheat oven to broil.
3. Broil meat 4 inches from heat 8 minutes.
4. Turn meat and broil 8 minutes more.
5. Dot meat with margarine. Season with pepper.

Per serving: 285.4 calories; 76.2 mg. sodium; 1.4 gm. carbohydrates;
    16.9 gm. fat.

* Preserved in vinegar only.

Meat Loaf with Cream   SERVES 8

From the southern tip of Italy comes one of the most sophisticated meat loaves you will ever savor. Add Braised Arugola Salad (page 96) plus Creamy Garlic Potatoes (page 206). If you prefer, you can replace the beef with 1½ pounds ground veal.

1½ pounds chopped beef
¼ teaspoon black pepper
2 teaspoons garlic powder
1 tablespoon low-sodium beef bouillon
2 teaspoons low-sodium chicken bouillon

¼ cup low-sodium seasoned bread crumbs
¼ cup heavy cream
3 tablespoons dark raisins*

1. Preheat oven to 350°.
2. In bowl, combine first 5 ingredients, blending thoroughly.
3. Stir in bread crumbs and cream, blending thoroughly.
4. Stir in raisins.
5. Transfer mixture to 9-inch square ovenproof casserole and form into loaf. Bake 1 hour, or until brown crust forms on top.

Per serving with beef: 316.3 calories; 51.6 mg. sodium; 9.2 gm. carbohydrates; 21.0 gm. fat.
Per serving with veal: 204.8 calories; 88.4 mg. sodium; 9.2 gm. carbohydrates; 24.2 gm. fat.

* Preserved in non-sodium ingredient.

Parsley Beef in Brandy SERVES 8

The flair of French haute cuisine inspired this elegant dish of northern Italy. Two perfect accompaniments are Tomato-Plum Relish (page 62) and Creamy Garlic Potatoes (page 206).

1½ pounds London broil, gashed
6 cloves garlic, sliced
20 black peppercorns, crushed
⅓ cup lemon juice

¼ cup brandy
⅓ cup dried parsley
2 tablespoons unsalted margarine

1. Preheat oven to 325°.
2. Place London broil in 9-inch square ovenproof casserole. Insert garlic slices in gashes. Sprinkle crushed peppercorns over meat.
3. Pour lemon juice and brandy around meat. Cover and bake 1½ hours, turning meat occasionally.
4. Sprinkle parsley over all. Bake, uncovered, 20 minutes more.
5. Dot meat with margarine. Bake, uncovered, 5 minutes more.

Per serving: 242.2 calories; 61.7 mg. sodium; 3.2 gm. carbohydrates;
8.6 gm. fat.

Pot Roast Bologna

SERVES 8

This dish of the north-central region exhibits Germanic accents. All you need to complete your meal is Potato and Green Bean Salad (page 102) served on a bed of mixed greens.

1 tablespoon green peppercorns*
3 cloves garlic, sliced
1 2-pound bottom round roast, gashed
¼ cup all-purpose flour
1½ cups water, divided
2 carrots, chopped
2 onions, chopped
½ teaspoon dried sage
1 tablespoon paprika
½ cup dry vermouth
Black pepper to taste
2 tablespoons low-sodium beef bouillon
2 teaspoons dried basil
⅛ teaspoon dried marjoram

1. Preheat oven to 350°.
2. Insert peppercorns and garlic slices into gashes in roast. Dust all over with flour.
3. In Dutch oven, place roast. Turn heat to high and sear all over. Transfer to 9 x 13-inch ovenproof casserole.
4. Pour water around meat. Scatter carrots and onions all around.
5. Season meat with sage and paprika. Cover and bake ½ hour.
6. Turn meat. Add all remaining ingredients. Cover and bake 1 hour more, or until meat is fork tender, turning meat occasionally.

Per serving: 302.1 calories; 96.8 mg. sodium; 15.7 gm. carbohydrates; 14.9 gm. fat.

* Preserved in vinegar only.

Steak and Cheese
SERVES 8

Both north and south would place this flavorful dish high on their list. Accent it with Fennel in Cream Sauce (pages 226–27) and a plate of fettuccine.

2 pounds London broil
¼ cup cider vinegar
¼ cup lemon juice
¼ cup dry red wine
Black pepper to taste
4 teaspoons dried basil

2 teaspoons dried oregano
2 teaspoons garlic powder
1 tablespoon low-sodium beef bouillon
3 ounces low-sodium Cheddar cheese, cut into 8 thin slices

1. In 9-inch square ovenproof casserole, combine first 4 ingredients. Cover and refrigerate overnight, turning meat occasionally.
2. In bowl, combine pepper, basil, oregano, garlic powder, and bouillon, blending thoroughly. Rub mixture on meat. Let stand 20 minutes.
3. Preheat oven to broil.
4. Turn meat and broil 4 inches from heat 7 minutes.
5. Turn meat and broil 7 minutes more.
6. Remove meat from oven and make 8 diagonal slices halfway down the meat. Insert cheese into slices in meat.
7. Return to broiler for 2 minutes more.

Per serving: 276.4 calories; 80.2 mg. sodium; 2.2 gm. carbohydrates; 11.4 gm. fat.

Stuffed Burgers SERVES 8

This northern-style dish would be just as good if you substituted an equal amount of ground lamb for the beef. Either way, Tomato-Bean Soup (page 77) or Mixed Salad Surprise (page 103) and Hot Sauce Shells (page 191) are tasty side dish choices.

1¼ pounds chopped beef
⅛ teaspoon hot pepper flakes
2½ tablespoons low-sodium beef bouillon
¼ cup low-sodium ketchup
¼ cup low-sodium seasoned bread crumbs

3 ounces low-sodium Cheddar cheese, minced
⅓ cup boiling water
1 tablespoon low-sodium Dijon mustard
¼ cup brandy

1. In bowl, combine first 5 ingredients, blending thoroughly.
2. Stir in cheese. Set aside.
3. In second bowl, combine water and mustard, stirring until mustard is completely dissolved.
4. Stir mustard mixture into beef mixture, blending thoroughly.
5. Stir in brandy.
6. Form mixture into 8 patties and place on baking sheet. Let stand 5 minutes.
7. Preheat oven to broil.
8. Broil patties 4 inches from heat 5 minutes.
9. Turn patties and broil 5 minutes more.

Per serving with beef: 307.3 calories; 48.4 mg. sodium; 5.9 gm. carbohydrates; 19.2 gm. fat.
Per serving with lamb: 243.8 calories; 68.4 mg. sodium; 5.9 gm. carbohydrates; 10.9 gm. fat.

Tender Meatballs

SERVES 8

For a spicy variation, add ⅛ teaspoon hot pepper flakes and ¾ teaspoon dried sage to the recipe below. Or substitute an equal amount of ground veal or pork plus ½ teaspoon dried rosemary for the beef. Any way at all, these meatballs will do any sauce proud.

1¼ pounds ground beef
1 tablespoon garlic powder
2 tablespoons dried basil
4 tablespoons low-sodium beef
  bouillon

1 tablespoon paprika
2 teaspoons dried oregano
⅓ cup low-sodium seasoned
  bread crumbs
⅓ cup low-sodium ketchup

1. In bowl, combine first 6 ingredients, blending thoroughly.
2. Stir in remaining ingredients, blending thoroughly.
3. Form mixture into walnut-size meatballs.
4. In Dutch oven, place meatballs. Turn heat to medium and sauté 10 minutes, or until browned all over, turning occasionally.
5. Drain fat from Dutch oven. Add 6 cups of your favorite sauce. Reduce heat to low. Cover and simmer 1 hour.

Per serving with beef: 247.4 calories; 53.9 mg. sodium; 7.0 gm. carbohydrates; 15.6 gm. fat.
Per serving with veal: 154.6 calories; 84.6 mg. sodium; 7.0 gm. carbohydrates; 6.7 gm. fat.
Per serving with pork: 224.6 calories; 70.3 mg. sodium; 7.0 gm. carbohydrates; 11.2 gm. fat.

Broiled Lamb Chops in Lemon-Parsley Sauce

SERVES 4

This northern dish is so easy to make, and, oh, so delicious. Braised Endive Salad (page 99) and Vermicelli and Oysters (page 195) are just two of many possible accompaniments. For a tasty variation, replace the lamb chops with pork chops.

1 tablespoon unsalted margarine, divided
4 cloves garlic, minced
¼ cup lemon juice
½ cup dried parsley

4 rib lamb chops
Black pepper to taste
1 tablespoon low-sodium beef bouillon, divided

1. In skillet, heat 1 teaspoon margarine over low heat. Add garlic and cook 5 minutes, or until garlic is golden brown. Set aside.
2. In bowl, combine lemon juice and parsley. Set aside.
3. Preheat oven to broil.
4. On shallow baking sheet, place lamb chops. Season with pepper and half the bouillon. Broil 6 inches from heat 7 minutes.
5. Turn lamb chops. Season with remaining bouillon and broil 7 minutes more. Transfer chops to platter.
6. While lamb chops are broiling, to skillet, add lemon juice mixture to garlic. Turn heat to medium-low and bring to a slow boil.
7. Add remaining margarine and cook until margarine is completely melted.
8. Pour lemon sauce over lamb chops.

Per serving with lamb: 320.8 calories; 108.0 mg. sodium; 7.2 gm. carbohydrates; 17.6 gm. fat.
Per serving with pork: 343.7 calories; 102.3 mg. sodium; 7.2 gm. carbohydrates; 20.2 gm. fat.

Lamb Chops in Raspberry Sauce

SERVES 4

This northern dish is very special, and every bite will delight your taste buds. For variety, try 4 pork chops or 4 half chicken breasts instead of the lamb chops. Rice Primavera (page 202) is an excellent accompaniment for all three options.

4 rib lamb chops
1½ tablespoons low-sodium chicken bouillon

1 cup Raspberry Sauce (page 253)

1. Preheat oven to broil.
2. In shallow baking dish, place lamb chops. Season with bouillon and broil 6 inches from heat 8 minutes.
3. Turn lamb chops and broil 4 minutes more.
4. Pour sauce over all and broil 2 minutes more.

Per serving with lamb: 308.4 calories; 93.4 mg. sodium; 6.6 gm. carbohydrates; 16.1 gm. fat.

Per serving with pork: 342.7 calories; 87.7 mg. sodium; 6.6 gm. cabohydrates; 18.5 gm. fat.

Per serving with chicken: 162.4 calories; 57.7 mg. sodium; 6.6 gm. carbohydrates; 4.7 gm. fat.

Roast Leg of Lamb   SERVES 8

This tender, succulent dish is worthy of every Roman holiday and goes with every dish. One notable suggestion is Rice-Stuffed Peppers (page 231).

1 4-pound leg of lamb, gashed	**½ cup dry white wine**
4 cloves garlic, sliced	**2 teaspoons dried rosemary**
½ cup lemon juice	**2 teaspoons dried tarragon**
½ cup red wine vinegar	**1 teaspoon ground cinnamon**

1. Preheat oven to 400°.
2. On rack in roasting pan, place lamb. Insert garlic slices in gashes. Bake 20 minutes.
3. While lamb is baking, in bowl, combine all remaining ingredients, blending thoroughly.
4. Reduce heat to 350° and bake 1½ hours more, or until lamb is barely pink, basting occasionally with lemon juice mixture.

Per serving: 241.8 calories; 88.2 mg. sodium; 3.6 gm. carbohydrates; 8.8 gm. fat.

Hot Sausage

MAKES 2 POUNDS

Sausage is a staple of Italian cuisine and every region has its own specialty. However, there are some general preparation tips which apply for every sausage recipe. First, sausage meat should have a small amount of fat to keep it moist and bound together. Second, the meat should be ground coarse rather than fine, so that it is not too mushy. Last, traditional casings should not and need not be used—should not because they are packed in salt to preserve freshness; need not because the plastic wrap method we use is not only salt-free but easier. The recipes which follow are typical of those found throughout Italy.

2 pounds pork shoulder, cubed
3 tablespoons low-sodium beef
  bouillon
1 tablespoon fennel seed
2 teaspoons dried oregano

2 tablespoons paprika
½ teaspoon hot pepper flakes
¼ cup dry red wine
Plastic wrap

1. In bowl, combine all ingredients, blending thoroughly. Let stand 20 minutes to allow flavors to blend.
2. In blender, grind mixture a little at a time. Grind a second time and stir thoroughly.
3. Form mixture into rolls or patties. Seal in plastic wrap and freeze up to 6 months.
Note: Before use, allow sausage to thaw slightly to facilitate slicing and removal of plastic wrap.

Per recipe: 2,441.4 calories; 732.8 mg. sodium; 20.4 gm. carbohydrates;
  139.8 gm. fat.
Per pound: 1,220.7 calories; 361.4 mg. sodium; 10.2 gm. carbohydrates;
  69.9 gm. fat.

Sausage Napoli
MAKES 2 POUNDS

A touch of spice, a taste of sweet, this sausage is delectable with pasta, rice, and eggs.

1 pound veal shoulder, cubed
1 pound stewing beef, cubed
3 tablespoons low-sodium beef
  bouillon
2 tablespoons dried basil
¼ teaspoon black pepper
¼ teaspoon dried sage

⅛ teaspoon ground nutmeg
1 tablespoon dried parsley
¹⁄₁₆ teaspoon ground cinnamon
2 tablespoons water
2 tablespoons dry sherry
Plastic wrap

Follow Steps 1 through 3 for Hot Sausage (page 171).

Per recipe: 2,012.0 calories; 783.3 mg. sodium; 20.4 gm. carbohydrates;
    125.2 gm. fat.
Per pound: 1,006.0 calories; 392.8 mg. sodium; 10.2 gm. carbohydrates;
    62.6 gm. fat.

Sausage Sicilian
MAKES 2 POUNDS

This is our version of the spicy sausage that adds its spark to pizza.

2 pounds pork shoulder, cubed
5 tablespoons low-sodium
  chicken bouillon
½ teaspoon hot pepper flakes

10 cloves garlic, minced
⅛ teaspoon allspice powder
¼ cup cider vinegar
Plastic wrap

Follow Steps 1 through 3 for Hot Sausage (page 171).

Per recipe: 2,606.8 calories; 733.0 mg. sodium; 55.2 gm. carbohydrates;
    145.9 gm. fat.
Per pound: 1,303.4 calories; 316.5 mg. sodium; 27.6 gm. carbohydrates;
    73.0 gm. fat.

Sweet and Hot Sausage   MAKES 2 POUNDS

The herbs and spices in this blend give it a northern flair.

2 pounds pork shoulder, cubed
½ teaspoon hot pepper flakes
1/16 teaspoon allspice powder
1/16 teaspoon ground cinnamon
1/16 teaspoon clove powder

1/16 teaspoon ground nutmeg
2 tablespoons water
2 tablespoons dry vermouth
Plastic wrap

Follow Steps 1 through 3 for Hot Sausage (page 171).

Per recipe: 2,255.1 calories; 641.4 mg. sodium; 1.2 gm. carbohydrates;
    130.8 gm. fat.
Per pound: 1,127.6 calories; 320.7 mg. sodium; 0.6 gm. carbohydrates;
    65.4 gm. fat.

Braised Pork   SERVES 12

The Roman version of the Italian favorite roast pork follows.

2½-pound pork roast
10 cloves garlic, sliced
10 cloves
½ teaspoon black pepper
4 onions, sliced
1 teaspoon fennel seed

½ teaspoon celery seed*
3 cups water
2 tablespoons low-sodium beef
    bouillon
¼ cup red wine vinegar

1. Gash pork all over. Insert garlic slices and cloves in gashes.
   Sprinkle all over with pepper.
2. In Dutch oven, sear pork on all sides over high heat.
3. Add onions, fennel seed, celery seed, and water. Reduce heat
   to low. Cover and simmer 1½ hours, turning pork occasionally.
4. Add remaining ingredients, stirring to blend. Cover and simmer
   ½ hour more, or until pork is fork tender.

Per serving: 277.6 calories; 76.9 mg. sodium; 9.7 gm. carbohydrates;
    14.1 gm. fat.

* Do not use celery flakes, which contain salt.

Italian Pork and Beans   SERVES 8

The central region of Tuscany supplies the inspiration for this succulent dish which can challenge the best Boston has to offer. Serve with a mixed green salad with Oil and Vinegar Dressing (page 254).

2 quarts water	**2 tablespoons unsalted margarine**
2 cups navy beans	**½ pound pork shoulder, trimmed**
1 can (29 ounces) low-sodium	**and cubed**
tomato puree	**1 teaspoon low-sodium beef**
Black pepper to taste	**bouillon**
Pinch of clove powder	**2 tablespoons peach brandy**
¹⁄₁₆ teaspoon fennel seed	

1. In Dutch oven, combine first 2 ingredients. Bring to a boil over medium heat.
2. Reduce heat to low and cook 1½ hours, or until beans are tender and liquid is almost absorbed.
3. Stir in tomato puree, pepper, clove powder, and fennel seed. Cover and simmer 10 minutes more, stirring occasionally.
4. While beans are cooking, in skillet, heat margarine over low heat. Add pork. Raise heat to medium and cook until pork loses all pink color, stirring often.
5. Stir pork and all remaining ingredients into bean mixture. Cover and cook 20 minutes more, stirring occasionally.

Per serving: 294.3 calories; 36.2 mg. sodium; 35.7 gm. carbohydrates; 8.0 gm. fat.

Sausage, Peppers, and Eggs   SERVES 4

Eggs never tasted as good as they do with the spicy goodness of Sausage Napoli (page 171) to enhance them. This makes a beautiful lunch when accompanied by Asparagus in Spicy Cheese Sauce (page 216).

¼ pound Sausage Napoli
  (page 172)
1 tablespoon unsalted margarine
1 onion, minced
2 green peppers, chopped

4 eggs, lightly beaten
2 teaspoons low-sodium chicken
  bouillon
Black pepper to taste
½ teaspoon dried oregano

1. In skillet, cook sausage over medium heat until pork loses all pink color. Transfer to platter.
2. To skillet, add margarine. Reduce heat to medium-low. Add onion and green peppers and cook 5 minutes, stirring often.
3. While onion and peppers are cooking, in bowl beat together all remaining ingredients, except sausage.
4. To skillet, add egg mixture. Raise heat to medium and cook 2 minutes, stirring often.
5. Add sausage and cook 3 minutes more, or until eggs are firm but soft, stirring often.

Per serving: 208.5 calories; 98.4 mg. sodium; 11.8 gm. carbohydrates;
    15.8 gm. fat.

Veal Como

SERVES 4

We have the province of Lombardy to thank for this delicately seasoned veal specialty. Salad Roma (pages 104–105) and Fettuccine in Parsley-Cream Sauce (page 185) complete the meal.

1 egg, lightly beaten
¼ cup low-fat milk
⅛ teaspoon black pepper
½ teaspoon dried oregano
1 tablespoon low-sodium chicken bouillon
½ cup low-sodium seasoned bread crumbs

2 tablespoons dried parsley
4 veal scallops
1 tablespoon olive oil
1 teaspoon unsalted margarine
1 lemon, cut in wedges

1. In bowl, beat together first 5 ingredients. Set aside.
2. In second bowl, combine bread crumbs and parsley, blending thoroughly.
3. Dip veal first in egg mixture, then in crumb mixture. Set on rack to drain.
4. In skillet, heat oil and margarine over medium-low heat. Add veal and cook 10 minutes, or until bottom is golden brown.
5. Turn veal and cook 10 minutes more, or until bottom is golden brown. Drain on paper towels.
6. Garnish with lemon wedges.

Per serving: 338.1 calories; 141.2 mg. sodium; 17.3 gm. carbohydrates; 15.6 gm. fat.

Veal and Mushroom Stew   SERVES 8

That most romantic city, Venice, inspired this delicious veal stew. Some tasty accompaniments include Cauliflower Salad (page 98), Squash Melt (page 236), and Potato Fritters (page 209).

1½ pounds stewing veal, cut in
    1-inch chunks
1 teaspoon celery seed*
1 teaspoon dried tarragon
Black pepper to taste
¼ cup lemon juice
2 tablespoons unsalted
    margarine, divided

1 onion, minced
8 mushrooms, sliced
2 teaspoons all-purpose flour
1 cup water
¼ cup dry sherry
2 tablespoons low-sodium
    ketchup

1. In 9-inch square ovenproof casserole, combine first 5 ingredients. Cover and marinate at least 4 hours, turning veal occasionally.
2. In Dutch oven, heat margarine over low heat. Add onions and mushrooms and cook until onions are wilted, stirring occasionally.
3. Stir in flour, blending thoroughly.
4. Stir in water, blending thoroughly.
5. To Dutch oven, add veal and marinade. Cover and cook 1 hour, stirring occasionally.
6. Stir in sherry and ketchup. Raise heat to medium-low. Cover and cook ½ hour more, or until veal is fork tender.

Per serving: 246.7 calories; 82.4 mg. sodium; 4.9 gm. carbohydrates;
    17.5 gm. fat.

* Do not use celery flakes, which contain salt.

Veal Marsala with Peppers and Mushrooms

SERVES 8

This traditional and much loved southern Italian dish is so delectable you will keep asking for more. Try this specialty with Spinach and Cheese Soup (page 76). For variety, substitute 8 half chicken breasts, skinned and boned, for the veal, and increase the cooking time to 5 minutes per side.

¼ cup all-purpose flour
⅟₁₆ teaspoon black pepper
1 teaspoon lemon peel powder
8 veal scallops (4 ounces each)
2 tablespoons unsalted
   margarine, divided
1 onion, minced
¼ teaspoon dried sage

1 teaspoon paprika
4 tomatoes, chopped
2 green peppers, chopped
3 tablespoons dried parsley
½ cup Marsala (or dry red) wine
8 mushrooms, sliced
½ cup fresh basil, chopped, or
   1 teaspoon dried basil

1. In bag, combine first 3 ingredients. Shake to blend. Add scallops and shake to coat. Set aside.
2. In large skillet, melt 1 tablespoon margarine over low heat. Add veal and onion. Raise heat to medium-low and cook 3 minutes, or until veal is lightly browned on bottom.
3. Add remaining margarine. Turn veal and cook 3 minutes more, or until browned on bottom.
4. Add all remaining ingredients, except basil. Cook 5 minutes, stirring occasionally.
5. Stir in basil. Cover and cook 10 minutes more.

Per serving with veal: 280.7 calories; 118.9 mg. sodium; 15.3 gm. carbohydrates; 12.3 gm. fat.
Per serving with chicken: 212.4 calories; 66.0 mg. sodium; 15.3 gm. carbohydrates; 5.6 gm. fat.

Veal Scallops and Leeks in Lemon-Basil Sauce

SERVES 8

This is a variation of the famous veal piccata, which all regions claim as their own. Eight chicken cutlets (cooked 5 minutes per side) can be substituted for the veal. Spaghetti with Mock White Clam Sauce (page 245) and Carrots in Cheese Sauce (page 220), are two possible accompaniments.

¼ cup dry sherry
2 teaspoons red wine vinegar
½ cup lemon juice
½ cup chopped basil, or
   3 tablespoons dried basil
8 veal scallops, pounded thin

1 tablespoon olive oil
1 teaspoon unsalted margarine
3 leeks, chopped, including
   greens
Black pepper to taste
2 lemons, cut in wedges

1. In 9 x 13-inch ovenproof casserole, combine first 4 ingredients, stirring to blend. Add veal. Cover and let stand ½ hour, turning occasionally.
2. Remove veal to platter, reserving marinade.
3. In large skillet, heat oil and margarine over low heat.
4. Add veal. Raise heat to medium and sauté 2 minutes.
5. Turn veal. Add leeks, pepper, and half the marinade. Sauté 2 minutes more.
6. With slotted spoon, remove veal and leeks to warm platter.
7. To skillet, add remaining marinade. Raise heat to high and cook 1 minute more, scraping all particles from bottom and sides of skillet.
8. Pour sauce over veal.
9. Garnish with lemon wedges.

Per serving with veal: 234.1 calories; 106.2 mg. sodium; 7.5 gm. carbohydrates; 11.6 gm. fat.
Per serving with chicken: 165.8 calories; 53.3 mg. sodium; 7.5 gm. carbohydrates; 9.0 gm. fat.

Veal with Artichokes and Mushrooms

SERVES 4

A complete meal, perfect for every important occasion, compliments of the Piedmont region. Rice in Wine-Caper Sauce (page 201) is a worthy companion.

2 cups water
8 frozen artichoke hearts
1 tablespoon unsalted margarine
4 veal scallops
Black pepper to taste
8 mushrooms, chopped
½ cup dry white wine

½ cup boiling water
1 tablespoon low-sodium beef bouillon
1 teaspoon dried basil
2 teaspoons dried parsley
Dash of ground nutmeg

1. In Dutch oven, bring water to a boil over high heat. Add artichoke hearts and cook 5 minutes. Drain. Set aside.
2. In skillet, heat margarine over medium heat. Add veal. Season with pepper and cook 3 minutes.
3. Turn veal. Add mushrooms and cook 3 minutes more.
4. Place artichoke hearts around veal. Pour wine over all. Reduce heat to low. Cover and simmer 3 minutes.
5. While veal mixture is cooking, in bowl, combine all remaining ingredients, blending thoroughly.
6. To skillet, add bouillon mixture. Raise heat to high. Cook, uncovered, 2 minutes more.

Per serving: 257.6 calories; 131.0 mg. sodium; 5.9 gm. carbohydrates; 12.8 gm. fat.

Veal with Braised Watercress   SERVES 4

This Sicilian-inspired dish is both simple and elegant and will be equally delicious if you replace the veal with 4 half chicken breasts, or 1 pound flounder fillets. Carrots in Orange Wine (page 220) and Basil Rice and Leeks (page 198) will add the crowning touch.

1 tablespoon olive oil
4 veal scallops (4 ounces each),
   pounded thin
1½ tablespoons low-sodium
   chicken bouillon, divided
2 ounces low-sodium mozzarella
   cheese, sliced thin

½ tablespoon unsalted margarine
1 cup chopped watercress
2 tablespoons dark raisins*
½ teaspoon sugar
3 tablespoons dry vermouth
   (or cassis)

1. In skillet, heat oil over medium-low heat. Add veal. Season with half the bouillon. Cook 3 minutes.
2. Turn veal. Season with remaining bouillon and cook 3 minutes more. Transfer veal to 9-inch square ovenproof casserole.
3. Place mozzarella on top of veal. Set aside.
4. Preheat oven to 375°.
5. In skillet, heat margarine over low heat. Add watercress. Cover and simmer 5 minutes, stirring occasionally.
6. Stir in raisins and sugar, blending thoroughly.
7. Spoon watercress mixture on top of veal.
8. Spoon vermouth over all. Cover and bake 15 minutes.

Per serving with veal: 301.0 calories; 142.6 mg. sodium; 9.4 gm. carbohydrates; 15.9 gm. fat.
Per serving with chicken: 232.7 calories; 123.2 mg. sodium; 9.4 gm. carbohydrates; 9.2 gm. fat.
Per serving with flounder: 213.0 calories; 162.4 mg. sodium; 9.4 gm. carbohydrates; 7.8 gm. fat.

* Preserved in non-sodium ingredient.

Pasta, Rice, Polenta, and Beans

Pasta is truly the national dish of Italy. Once enjoyed primarily in the southern regions, in the last few decades, pasta has become a favorite with northerners as well. Although in the north, pasta is made with eggs and is reserved primarily for special occasions, in the south, this daily fare calls for the traditional flour-and-water combination.

Folklore once claimed that Marco Polo brought pasta to Italy from China on one of his explorations. Others say that it was a Neapolitan creation. Today the popular belief is that Sicilian chefs adapted the recipe from the unleavened flat bread brought to their shores by Arab settlers. Whatever its origin, no one will deny the culinary pleasures that pasta provides.

Pasta comes in many shapes and sizes. As you might suppose, the thin strands of spaghetti, vermicelli, and linguine are the most delicate in flavor and texture. The tube varieties, including rigatoni, ziti, and macaroni, plus the broad, flat noodles and lasagna are heartier. Stuffed pastas, like ravioli, cannelloni, tortellini, and agnolotti, are the richest-tasting of all.

Northerners exhibit a more eclectic palate than their southern countrymen. Thus, while rice is generally preferred to pasta, northerners also enjoy potatoes, beans, gnocchi, and polenta.

Beans became favorites when Spanish explorers brought them from the Americas in the sixteenth century, and gave them as an offering to Pope Clement VII. He, in turn, gave them to friends in Tuscany. Although they are savored throughout the north, beans are especially suited to the basic peasant food found in the mountainous Tuscan region.

The Spanish also brought corn back from the New World and forever changed the Venetian staple, polenta, from wheat-based to corn-based. Mushlike polenta is quite versatile: once baked, it is equally good hot, cold, toasted, fried, or plain, with sauce or without. One recipe you should try is Baked Polenta with Tomato and Eggplant (page 205).

Potatoes and gnocchi are less common fare. The latter, made with semolina, are small dumplings served either in soups or as a side dish, generally baked in a rich, creamy sauce.

As for rice, Venetian sailors brought it from China at the end of the fifteenth century. It became popular immediately, but was hard to obtain before it began to thrive in the moist lowlands of Verona. Consequently, rice for some time was a precious, very expensive commodity, reserved for the sick or the rich, who used it for sweet desserts.

Today, of course, rice is abundantly available, but it is no less prized than it once was. Rice is often added to the national soup, minestrone. The most popular rice dish is risotto, in which the rice is cooked in a well-seasoned aromatic broth. Our version can be found on page 197 of this chapter.

Pasta, rice, polenta, and beans—prepared in the Italian fashion, they are as delicious as they are good for you.

Fettuccine in Parsley-Cream Sauce

SERVES 4

A terrific variation on the internationally popular Fettuccine Alfredo, this goes well with Sausage, Peppers, and Eggs (page 175).

2 teaspoons unsalted margarine,
    divided
6 mushrooms, chopped
2 cups Chicken Stock (page 64)

3 tablespoons dried parsley
¼ cup heavy cream
⅓ pound fettuccine, boiled
    al dente*

1. In skillet, heat 1 teaspoon margarine over low heat. Add mushrooms and sauté 3 minutes, stirring often.
2. Add stock and parsley. Cover and simmer 20 minutes.
3. Stir in cream and cook 5 minutes more, stirring often.
4. In bowl, combine fettuccine and remaining margarine. Toss to blend.
5. Pour cream sauce over all.

Per serving: 253.1 calories; 29.1 mg. sodium; 35.0 gm. carbohydrates; 10.6 gm. fat.

* Do not add salt to water.

Fettuccine in
Wine-Cream Sauce
SERVES 8

Fettuccine is marvelous with sauces that cling to its flat surface, giving a delicious taste with every bite. Try this recipe with Baked Snapper (page 123).

2½ cups Wine-Cream Sauce   1 tablespoon dried parsley
   (page 246)
8 ounces fettuccine, cooked
   al dente*

1. In saucepan, combine all ingredients. Turn heat to low. Cover and simmer 5 minutes.
2. Transfer to bowl. Toss to blend.

Per serving: 198.8 calories; 30.9 mg. sodium; 27.8 gm. carbohydrates; 6.3 gm. fat.

* Do not add salt to water.

Seafood Fettuccine

SERVES 8

When a dish like this one is so full of savory goodness, all you need to make your meal complete is a salad or vegetable. Mixed Vegetable Salad (page 104) and Broccoli and Pine Nuts (page 218) are just two suggestions.

1 tablespoon olive oil
1 onion, minced
3 cloves garlic, minced
12 mushrooms, sliced thick
½ pound cod fillets, cut into 1-inch chunks
1½ cups boiling water, divided
2 tablespoons low-sodium beef bouillon
Black pepper to taste
2 tablespoons dry sherry

½ pound squid, cleaned and cut into 1-inch chunks
½ pound shrimp, shelled, deveined, and halved lengthwise
¾ pound fettuccine, boiled al dente*
1 cup fresh basil, chopped, or 1½ tablespoons dried basil
2 lemons, cut in wedges

1. In skillet, heat oil over low heat. Add onion and garlic and sauté 5 minutes.
2. Add mushrooms and sauté 5 minutes more, stirring occasionally.
3. Add cod and ½ cup water. Cover and simmer 10 minutes. Set aside.
4. In saucepan, combine remaining water, bouillon, pepper, sherry, squid, and shrimp. Turn heat to low. Cover and simmer 5 minutes.
5. Add cod mixture, stirring to blend. Cover and simmer 5 minutes more.
6. Transfer seafood mixture to bowl. Add fettuccine and basil. Toss to blend.
7. Garnish with lemon wedges.

Per serving: 274.8 calories; 73.7 mg. sodium; 39.1 gm. carbohydrates; 3.7 gm. fat.

* Do not add salt to water.

Chicken-and-Oyster Lasagna Rolls

SERVES 8

You will enjoy this southern-style dish time and again. For variety, replace the oysters with ¼ pound shrimp, shelled, deveined, and chopped. Lemon-Mint Artichokes (page 214) is a good accompaniment.

1 tablespoon olive oil
2 onions, minced
2 cloves garlic, minced
3 half chicken breasts, skinned, boned, and cubed
½ pint oysters, shucked and chopped, liquid reserved
4 ounces low-sodium Cheddar cheese, minced

6 scallions, chopped, including greens
Black pepper to taste
2 teaspoons dried oregano
2 cans (16 ounces) low-sodium tomato sauce, divided
1 cup dry red wine, divided
8 lasagna noodles, cooked al dente,* and stretched on waxed paper to cool

1. Preheat oven to 325°.
2. In skillet, heat oil over low heat. Add onions and garlic and cook 10 minutes, or until garlic is lightly browned.
3. Add chicken. Raise heat to medium-low and cook 5 minutes, or until chicken turns white all over, stirring constantly.
4. Transfer chicken mixture to bowl. Stir in oysters, cheese, scallions, pepper, and oregano, blending thoroughly.
5. On bottom of 9-inch square ovenproof casserole, pour half the tomato sauce and half the wine, stirring to blend.
6. Place equal portions of chicken mixture near end of lasagna noodles. Roll up noodles and transfer, seam side down, to casserole.
7. Pour remaining tomato sauce and wine over all. Pour on reserved oyster liquid. Cover and bake 15 minutes. Uncover and bake 10 minutes more.

Per serving with oysters: 288.6 calories; 61.6 mg. sodium; 31.7 gm. carbohydrates; 8.6 gm. fat.
Per serving with shrimp: 273.3 calories; 50.3 mg. sodium; 30.4 gm. carbohydrates; 7.9 gm. fat.

* Do not add salt to water.

Macaroni
and Spinach

SERVES 4

Easy-to-prepare and sure-to-please, try this northern dish with Veal Como (page 176).

3 cups water
¼ pound spinach, chopped
¼ teaspoon orange peel powder
Dash of clove powder

⅓ pound macaroni, boiled
  al dente*
2 tablespoons low-sodium
  chicken bouillon

1. In saucepan, bring water to a boil over medium heat. Add spinach and boil 5 minutes. Drain. Transfer to bowl.
2. Add orange peel and clove powders and macaroni. Toss to blend.
3. Add bouillon. Toss to blend.

Per serving: 175.0 calories; 28.6 mg. sodium; 32.9 gm. carbohydrates;
  2.0 gm. fat.

* Do not add salt to water.

Baked Noodles, Sausage, and Vegetables

SERVES 12

A most filling and satisfying delight from central Italy. Serve it with Christmas Salad (page 99) or Mixed Vegetable Salad (page 104) to complete your meal.

1 tablespoon unsalted margarine
½ pound noodles, cooked
   al dente*
½ pound Sausage Napoli
   (page 172)
2 onions, chopped
2 cloves garlic, minced
1 cup low-fat milk
2 eggs
½ cup low-sodium ricotta cheese

½ cup low-sodium Swiss cheese,
   shredded
⅟₁₆ teaspoon ground cinnamon
1 teaspoon dried basil
1 tablespoon low-sodium chicken
   bouillon
Black pepper to taste
2 tomatoes, chopped
12 mushrooms, chopped

1. Preheat oven to 350°.
2. In 8-inch square ovenproof casserole, spread margarine over bottom and sides. Add noodles.
3. In skillet, sauté sausage, onions, and garlic over medium-low heat 10 minutes, or until sausage loses all pink color. Transfer to warm platter. Chop sausage. Set aside.
4. In bowl, heat together milk, eggs, and both cheeses. Stir in sausage mixture and remaining ingredients.
5. Spoon egg mixture on top of noodles.
6. Bake for ½ hour, or until toothpick inserted in center comes out clean.

Per serving: 212.3 calories; 48.5 mg. sodium; 22.2 gm. carbohydrates;
   8.9 gm. fat.

* Do not add salt to water.

Shells with
Mushroom-Cheese Sauce

SERVES 8

The combination of ricotta cheese and watercress makes this southern-style dish very special. It is a good accompaniment to London Broil Vinaigrette (page 161).

2½ cups Mushroom-Cheese Sauce (page 241)

8 ounces pasta shells, cooked al dente*

1. Prepare Mushroom-Cheese Sauce through Step 5.
2. In bowl, combine sauce and shells. Toss to blend. Serve immediately.

Per serving: 171.8 calories; 14.0 mg. sodium; 28.5 gm. carbohydrates; 3.7 gm. fat.

* Do not add salt to water.

Hot Sauce Shells

SERVES 8

A spicy, flavor-filled Sicilian dish that does well with Chicken and Mushrooms (page 141). For variety, add ⅓ pound leftover cubed pork to Step 1.

2 cups Hot Sauce (page 250)
1 green pepper, chopped

8 ounces pasta shells, boiled al dente*

1. In saucepan, combine first 2 ingredients. Turn heat to low. Cover and simmer ½ hour, stirring occasionally.
2. Add pasta. Raise heat to medium-low. Cover and cook 5 minutes more.

Per serving plain: 136.7 calories; 9.2 mg. sodium; 30.0 gm. carbohydrates; 0.7 gm. fat.
Per serving with pork: 183.2 calories; 22.6 mg. sodium; 30.0 gm. carbohydrates; 3.4 gm. fat.

* Do not add salt to water.

Spaghetti and Pork with Vegetables

SERVES 8

This southern-style meal is just as delicious when you replace the pork with 4 chicken breasts, skinned, boned, and cubed. Either version is wonderful with Carrot Soup with Capers (page 66).

1 pound pork, trimmed and cubed	2 yellow squash, cubed
3 cloves garlic, minced	2 tablespoons dry red wine
1 tablespoon olive oil	2 cups water
3 onions, chopped	3 tablespoons low-sodium chicken bouillon
2 green peppers, chopped	⅔ pound spaghetti, boiled al dente*
2 tomatoes, chopped	

1. In Dutch oven, brown pork and garlic over medium heat 5 minutes, stirring often.
2. Push pork mixture to sides of pot. To well created in center, add oil and onions.
3. Reduce heat to low and cook 10 minutes, stirring occasionally.
4. Add peppers, tomatoes, squash, wine, and water. Cover and simmer 20 minutes.
5. Stir in bouillon. Cover and simmer 10 minutes more.
6. Transfer vegetable mixture to bowl. Add spaghetti. Toss to blend.

Per serving with pork: 295.7 calories; 58.7 mg. sodium; 31.2 gm. carbohydrates; 12.1 gm. fat.
Per serving with chicken: 266.3 calories; 68.7 mg. sodium; 31.2 gm. carbohydrates; 6.4 gm. fat.

* Do not add salt to water.

Spaghetti and Shrimp in Tomato Sauce

SERVES 8

This is a very popular recipe from the Alto Adige region. Serve with Carrots in Cheese Sauce (page 220).

2 tablespoons unsalted margarine
16 mushrooms, chopped
2 green peppers, diced
5 cups Tomato Sauce I (page 242)
¼ cup dry red wine

2 tablespoons dried parsley
1½ pounds shrimp, shelled and
** deveined, tails intact**
½ pound spaghetti, cooked
** al dente***

1. In Dutch oven, heat margarine over low heat. Add mushrooms and peppers and cook 5 minutes.
2. Add tomato sauce, wine, and parsley. Cover and cook ½ hour, stirring occasionally.
3. Add shrimp and cook 10 minutes more. Transfer mixture to bowl.
4. Add spaghetti. Toss to blend.

Per serving: 256.6 calories; 143.8 mg. sodium; 32.2 gm. carbohydrates; 5.7 gm. fat.

* Do not add salt to water.

Spaghetti in
Spicy Green Sauce

SERVES 4

A beautiful appetizer or side dish which you can turn into a main course by adding 1 can (6½ ounces) low-sodium tuna to Step 1. If you use tuna, Braised Spinach (page 233) is an excellent side-dish choice. Otherwise, try Lobster Salad in Brandied Mayonnaise (page 108).

1½ cups Spicy Green Sauce
   (page 247)
⅟₁₆ teaspoon ground nutmeg
⅓ pound spaghetti, cooked
   al dente*

3 scallions, chopped, including
   greens

1. In bowl, combine first 2 ingredients, blending thoroughly.
2. Add spaghetti. Toss to blend.
3. Add scallions. Toss to blend.

Per serving plain: 229.9 calories; 12.3 mg. sodium; 30.4 gm. carbohydrates;
   9.5 gm. fat.
Per serving with tuna: 280.1 calories; 36.0 mg. sodium; 30.4 gm. carbohydrates; 9.9 gm. fat.

* Do not add salt to water.

Vermicelli and Oysters

SERVES 4

A lovely treat from the northern waterways near Venice. Serve with Salad Roma (page 104).

1 pint oysters, shucked and
  chopped, including liquid
¼ cup lemon juice
Black pepper to taste
2 cups boiling water
2½ tablespoons low-sodium
  chicken bouillon

4 mushrooms, chopped
¼ pound green beans, cut into
  1-inch pieces
1 teaspoon dried basil
¼ pound vermicelli, cooked
  al dente*

1. In bowl, combine first 3 ingredients. Cover and let stand 15 minutes.
2. In saucepan, combine water, bouillon, mushrooms, and green beans. Turn heat to medium and cook 5 minutes.
3. Add oyster mixture and basil. Reduce heat to low. Cover and simmer 5 minutes. Transfer mixture to bowl.
4. Add vermicelli. Toss to blend.

Per serving: 210.2 calories; 76.8 mg. sodium; 32.0 gm. carbohydrates;
  3.8 gm. fat.

* Do not add salt to water.

Vermicelli and Squid in Garlic Sauce

SERVES 8

The coastal areas of the central region lay claim to this tempting dish. Serve it with Spice-Broiled Tomatoes (page 235).

1 cup Chicken Stock (page 64)
1 tablespoon olive oil
1 teaspoon unsalted margarine
8 cloves garlic, minced
1¼ pounds squid, cleaned and chopped
2 teaspoons lemon juice

3 tablespoons dried parsley
Black pepper to taste
¾ pound vermicelli, cooked al dente*
1½ tablespoons low-sodium chicken bouillon

1. In saucepan, heat stock over low heat.
2. While stock is cooking, in skillet, heat oil and margarine over medium-low heat. Add garlic and sauté 10 minutes, or until garlic is lightly browned.
3. To garlic, add stock, squid, lemon juice, parsley, and pepper. Reduce heat to low. Cover and simmer 10 minutes.
4. Transfer squid mixture to bowl. Add vermicelli. Toss to blend.
5. Add bouillon. Toss to blend.

Per serving: 267.0 calories; 11.4 mg. sodium; 38.2 gm. carbohydrates; 4.8 gm. fat.

* Do not add salt to water.

Risotto SERVES 8

This classic Italian dish is the perfect way to prepare white rice. For an elegant variation, add 3 ounces low-sodium Swiss cheese, minced, after the rice is cooked. Cover and let stand 5 minutes. Then toss to blend thoroughly. This dish will complement any meal.

2 teaspoons olive oil
1 onion, minced
2 cloves garlic, minced
1½ cups rice
2¾ cups Chicken Stock
   (page 64)

¼ cup dry vermouth
1 tablespoon low-sodium chicken
   bouillon
1 strand saffron
2 tablespoons unsalted margarine
2 teaspoons dried parsley

1. In saucepan, heat oil over low heat. Add onion and garlic and cook 10 minutes, or until garlic is lightly browned.
2. Add rice and cook 5 minutes more, stirring occasionally.
3. Add stock, vermouth, bouillon, and saffron. Turn heat to high and bring to a boil.
4. Reduce heat to low. Cover and simmer 20 minutes, or until liquid is absorbed.
5. Transfer rice to bowl. Add margarine and parsley. Toss to blend.

Per serving plain: 199.6 calories; 17.2 mg. sodium; 32.9 gm. carbohydrates; 6.6 gm. fat.
Per serving with cheese: 237.6 calories; 20.4 mg. sodium; 33.1 gm. carbohydrates; 9.7 gm. fat.

Basil Rice and Leeks SERVES 4

This exquisitely simple dish is excellent with Italian Beef Stew (page 160).

1¾ cups water
2 tablespoons low-sodium
   chicken bouillon
Black pepper to taste

⅔ cup white rice
1 leek, chopped, including greens
½ cup fresh basil, chopped, or
   2 teaspoons dried basil

1. In saucepan, combine first 3 ingredients. Bring to a boil over high heat, stirring occasionally.
2. Reduce heat to low. Add rice and leek. Cover and simmer 10 minutes.
3. Add basil. Cover and simmer 10 minutes more, or until liquid is absorbed.

Per serving: 149.3 calories; 10.7 mg. sodium; 30.0 gm. carbohydrates;
   1.7 gm. fat.

Rice and Sausage SERVES 8

This makes an absolutely wonderful meal. Serve with Buttery Green Beans with Mushrooms (page 227) to make it complete.

2½ cups Meat Stock (page 65)
1¼ cups white rice
½ pound Sausage Napoli
   (page 172)

1 green pepper, chopped

1. In saucepan, bring stock to a boil over high heat.
2. Reduce heat to low. Add rice. Cover and simmer 10 minutes.
3. While rice is cooking, in skillet, cook sausage over medium heat 5 minutes, or until all pink color is gone, stirring often.
4. To skillet, add pepper, stirring to blend. Reduce heat to low. Cover and simmer 5 minutes, stirring occasionally.

5. Add sausage mixture to rice. Do not stir. Cover and simmer 10 minutes more, or until liquid is absorbed.
6. Transfer mixture to bowl. Toss to blend.

Per serving: 195.4 calories; 40.6 mg. sodium; 27.3 gm. carbohydrates;
    5.2 gm. fat.

Rice in Wine

SERVES 8

A subtly tasty dish like those of the north-central region of Emilia-Romagna. Perfect with Deviled Shrimp (page 134) or Stuffed Lamb Burgers (page 166).

2 tablespoons unsalted
  margarine, divided
2 onions, chopped
1¼ cups white rice
2 tablespoons low-sodium
  chicken bouillon

3 tablespoons dried parsley
2 cups boiling water
½ cup dry white wine

1. In saucepan, heat margarine over low heat. Add onions and cook 10 minutes, or until onions are golden, stirring occasionally.
2. Add rice, bouillon, and parsley. Cook 10 minutes more, stirring occasionally.
3. Add water and wine. Raise heat to high and bring to a boil.
4. Reduce heat to low. Cover and simmer 20 minutes, or until liquid is absorbed.

Per serving: 161.8 calories; 11.6 mg. sodium; 29.1 gm. carbohydrates;
    3.9 gm. fat.

Rice, Cabbage, and Sweet Peppers

SERVES 4

An exceptionally tasty dish from the southern region of Lucania. Broiled Pork Chops in Lemon-Parsley Sauce (page 168) is only one of many possible accompaniments.

1 teaspoon olive oil
2 cloves garlic, minced
1/16 teaspoon hot pepper flakes
1 cup Mustard-Tomato Sauce (page 246)
1/4 cup dry white wine

1 cup water
2 cups chopped cabbage
2/3 cup rice
2 low-sodium sweet pepper halves, chopped
1/16 teaspoon ground nutmeg

1. In saucepan, heat oil over low heat. Add garlic and hot pepper flakes and cook 5 minutes.
2. Add sauce, wine, and water. Turn heat to medium and bring to a slow boil.
3. Add cabbage, rice, sweet peppers, and nutmeg. Reduce heat to low. Cover and simmer 25 minutes, or until liquid is absorbed.

Per serving: 198.2 calories; 30.4 mg. sodium; 40.2 gm. carbohydrates; 1.8 gm. fat.

Rice in Spicy Green Sauce

SERVES 4

A pungent, savory dish you will enjoy with any main course. One suggestion is Simple Broiled Trout (page 128).

3/4 cup water
2/3 cup Spicy Green Sauce (page 247)
1 leek, chopped, including greens

1 tablespoon low-sodium beef bouillon
2/3 cup white rice

1. In saucepan, combine first 2 ingredients. Turn heat to medium and bring to a slow boil.

2. Add leek, bouillon, and rice. Reduce heat to low. Cover and simmer 15 minutes, or until liquid is absorbed.

Per serving: 175.0 calories; 16.2 mg. sodium; 28.9 gm. carbohydrates;
     5.0 gm. fat.

Rice in Wine-Caper Sauce   SERVES 4

Braised Chicken with Applesauce (page 138) and Veal with Artichokes and Mushrooms (page 180) are two of the many possible accompaniments for this tasty dish.

1½ cups Wine-Caper Sauce   **4 tomatoes, chopped**
   (page 251)
⅔ cup white rice

1. In saucepan, prepare sauce through Step 2.
2. Add rice and tomatoes. Do not stir.
3. Reduce heat to low. Cover and simmer 15 minutes, or until liquid is absorbed.

Per serving: 164.8 calories; 17.1 mg. sodium; 31.4 gm. carbohydrates;
     1.9 gm. fat.

Rice Primavera

SERVES 8

The recipe below is only one of countless vegetable combinations you might consider. Try this one; then try your own. The more vivid your imagination, the better the results. Serve with Rosemary Chicken with Green Peppercorns (page 153).

4 cups Chicken Stock (page 64)
1 tablespoon unsalted margarine
2 onions, chopped
Black pepper to taste
1½ cups white rice
½ teaspoon celery seed*

1 carrot, diced
¼ pound green beans, chopped
2 tomatoes, chopped
2 teaspoons dried basil
½ pound fresh shelled peas
1 zucchini, diced

1. In saucepan, bring stock to a slow boil over medium-low heat. Reduce heat to low and simmer 10 minutes.
2. In second saucepan, heat margarine over low heat. Add onions and pepper and cook 5 minutes, or until onion is wilted.
3. Add rice, celery seed, and carrot, stirring to blend.
4. Add 1 cup stock. Raise heat to medium and cook 5 minutes.
5. Add green beans, tomatoes, basil, and 2 more cups stock. Cook 10 minutes more, stirring occasionally.
6. Add all remaining ingredients. Cook 20 minutes more, or until liquid is absorbed, stirring often.

Per serving: 148.3 calories; 28.3 mg. sodium; 43.9 gm. carbohydrates; 4.6 gm. fat.

* Do not use celery flakes, which contain salt.

Rice with Chicken Livers   SERVES 4

This dish from the northernmost regions of Italy needs only a salad, like Shrimp-Stuffed Tomato Salad (page 106), to make the meal complete.

2 cups Chicken Stock (page 64)
   or Meat Stock (page 65)
¼ cup dry vermouth
1 cup white rice
1 tablespoon unsalted margarine

¼ pound chicken livers
¹⁄₁₆ teaspoon hot pepper flakes
½ teaspoon dried sage
1 teaspoon dried parsley

1. In saucepan, bring stock to a boil over medium heat.
2. Add vermouth and bring to a second boil.
3. Reduce heat to low. Add rice. Cover and simmer 20 minutes, or until liquid is absorbed.
4. While rice is cooking, in skillet, heat margarine over low heat. Add chicken livers and cook 5 minutes, stirring occasionally.
5. Stir in hot pepper flakes, sage, and parsley. Cook 10 minutes more, stirring occasionally.
6. Transfer liver mixture to bowl. Chop coarsely.
7. Add rice. Toss to blend.

Per serving with Chicken Stock:
   267.9 calories; 39.2 mg. sodium; 40.1 gm. carbohydrates; 6.9 gm. fat.
Per serving with Meat Stock:
   278.5 calories; 42.2 mg. sodium; 42.2 gm. carbohydrates; 5.9 gm. fat.

Rice with Tomatoes and Cheese

SERVES 8

A traditional southern-style dish that is simply delicious. Try it with Tuna Sautéed in Wine (page 130).

1 tablespoon olive oil
2 onions, minced
2 cloves garlic, minced
1¼ cups white rice
2¾ cups water
2 teaspoons dried basil

1 teaspoon dried rosemary
⅛ teaspoon black pepper
3 tomatoes, chopped
3 ounces low-sodium Cheddar
cheese, diced

1. In saucepan, heat oil over low heat. Add onions and garlic and cook 10 minutes, or until garlic is lightly browned.
2. Add rice and cook 5 minutes more, stirring occasionally.
3. Add water, basil, rosemary, and pepper. Raise heat to high and bring to a boil.
4. Reduce heat to low. Add all remaining ingredients. Cover and simmer 15 minutes, or until liquid is absorbed.

Per serving: 181.9 calories; 8.3 mg. sodium; 30.1 gm. carbohydrates;
5.6 gm. fat.

Baked Polenta with Tomatoes and Eggplant

SERVES 8

The versatile, hearty, and tasty cornmeal dish known as polenta originated in the region between Venice and Milan, and is associated with Northern Italian cuisine. Whether it is served plain, topped with margarine or cheese, or cooked with meat, poultry, or vegetables, polenta is thoroughly delightful.

2 quarts water
2 cups cornmeal*
1 tablespoon olive oil
1 small eggplant, peeled and
  diced

2 tomatoes, chopped
1 can (8 ounces) low-sodium
  tomato sauce
Black pepper to taste

1. In large saucepan, bring water to a boil over high heat.
2. Reduce heat to medium-low and stir in cornmeal, a little at a time. Continue stirring constantly for 20 minutes, or until polenta begins to form a crust on the sides of the pan and mixture is set.
3. With knife, loosen polenta from sides of pan and turn onto warm platter.
4. In skillet, heat oil over low heat. Add eggplant. Cover and cook 20 minutes more, stirring occasionally.
5. Add all remaining ingredients, except polenta, stirring to blend. Cover and cook 20 minutes more.
6. Preheat oven to 350°.
7. Slice polenta horizontally. In 9-inch square ovenproof casserole, place one layer of polenta. Cover with half the tomato-eggplant mixture.
8. Repeat Step 7 with remaining polenta and tomato-eggplant mixture.
9. Bake, uncovered, 15 minutes.

Per serving: 251.9 calories; 4.5 mg. sodium; 49.5 gm. carbohydrates;
    6.8 gm. fat.

* Do not use self-rising cornmeal, which contains salt.

Creamy Garlic Potatoes   SERVES 8

This dish from the northern regions is a perfect accompaniment to any meal. Try it with Swordfish and Sweet Peppers (page 126) for a memorable meal.

2 tablespoons unsalted
  margarine, divided
2 cloves garlic, minced
6 potatoes, boiled,* peeled, and
  mashed
1 tablespoon low-sodium chicken
  bouillon

⅓ cup low-fat milk
2 scallions, minced, including
  greens
Black pepper to taste

1. In skillet, heat 1 teaspoon margarine over low heat. Add garlic and cook 10 minutes, or until garlic is lightly browned, stirring often. Transfer to bowl.
2. Add potatoes, bouillon, milk, scallions, and pepper, blending thoroughly.
3. Add remaining margarine, blending thoroughly.

Per serving: 121.1 calories; 11.1 mg. sodium; 20.4 gm. carbohydrates;
    4.0 gm. fat.

* Do not add salt to water.

Mashed Potatoes with Pork Bits

SERVES 4

The German influence can be found in this tangy dish from the north. Serve with Chicken in Parsley Wine (page 144) for a lovely meal.

2 potatoes, parboiled,* peeled,
  and mashed
2 teaspoons dried basil
1 tablespoon low-sodium chicken
  bouillon
Dash of hot pepper flakes
2 tablespoons unsalted
  margarine, divided

1 onion, minced
2 cloves garlic, minced
¼ pound pork shoulder,
  trimmed and diced
⅛ teaspoon dried marjoram
½ tablespoon low-sodium Dijon
  mustard

1. In bowl, combine first 4 ingredients, blending thoroughly. Set aside.
2. In skillet, heat 1 tablespoon margarine over medium-low heat. Add onion, garlic, and pork and cook 10 minutes, or until pork loses all pink color, stirring often.
3. Preheat oven to 350°.
4. Stir pork mixture, marjoram, and mustard into potato mixture, blending thoroughly.
5. Grease a 4-inch soufflé dish with remaining margarine. Cover and bake 20 minutes.

Per serving: 206.4 calories; 30.6 mg. sodium; 19.9 gm. carbohydrates;
  7.3 gm. fat.

* Do not add salt to water.

Potatoes Baked in Pungent Basil Sauce

SERVES 4

This dish will add a spicy accent to any meal. Chicken in Wine (page 144) and Broiled Oysters (page 133) are two entrée suggestions.

**2 cups Pungent Basil Sauce
  (page 248), divided
3 potatoes, parboiled,* peeled,
  and sliced**

1 tablespoon paprika

1. Preheat oven to 350°.
2. Into 6-inch square ovenproof casserole, pour 1 cup sauce.
3. Add potato slices. Sprinkle with paprika.
4. Pour remaining sauce over all. Cover and bake ½ hour.

Per serving: 130.4 calories; 18.8 mg. sodium; 32.8 gm. carbohydrates;
    1.7 gm. fat.

* Do not add salt to water.

Potato Fritters

SERVES 8

An extra-special treat, especially good with seafood, such as Shrimp, Zucchini, and Peppers in Wine Cream (page 136).

5 potatoes, parboiled,* peeled, and mashed
3 tablespoons unsalted margarine
2 onions, minced
Dash of ground nutmeg
½ teaspoon dried dill
½ teaspoon dried oregano
⅛ teaspoon garlic powder
1½ tablespoons low-sodium chicken bouillon
Black pepper to taste
1 egg
1 cup vegetable oil

1. In bowl, combine potatoes and 2 tablespoons margarine, blending thoroughly. Set aside.
2. In skillet, heat remaining margarine over low heat. Add onions and cook over low heat 10 minutes, or until onions are golden.
3. Stir onions, nutmeg, dill, oregano, garlic powder, bouillon, and pepper into potatoes, blending thoroughly.
4. Beat egg into potato mixture.
5. Take small, walnut-size pieces of potato mixture and roll into balls.
6. In skillet, heat oil over medium-high heat. When oil starts to crackle around the edges, add half the potato balls. Sauté until browned all over.
7. With slotted spoon, transfer balls to paper towels. Drain.
8. Repeat Steps 6 and 7 with remaining potato balls.

Per serving: 152.9 calories; 16.0 mg. sodium; 21.4 gm. carbohydrates; 8.0 gm. fat.

* Do not add salt to water.

Potato Gnocchi with Mustard-Tomato Sauce

SERVES 8

From the northern regions comes Italy's version of dumplings. Gnocchi are wonderful served with cheese, margarine, or any number of sauces. This particular version is especially good with Chicken and Caper Salad (page 115).

5 potatoes, boiled* and peeled
¾ cup all-purpose flour
2 tablespoons low-sodium
  chicken bouillon

4 quarts water
3 cups Mustard-Tomato Sauce
  (page 246)
⅛ teaspoon ground nutmeg

1. In bowl, mash potatoes with fork.
2. Stir in flour, a little at a time. Then stir in bouillon.
3. Knead mixture until a smooth and slightly sticky dough is formed.
4. Shape dough into thin rolls and cut in 1-inch lengths.
5. Roll each piece onto a fork or cheese grater to create ridges on one side. Make a depression on the other side with your thumb. Set aside.
6. In Dutch oven, bring water to a boil. With slotted spoon, add half the gnocchi and boil 3 minutes, or until gnocchi float to the surface. Transfer to bowl.
7. Repeat Step 6 with remaining gnocchi.
8. While gnocchi are cooking, in saucepan, combine sauce and nutmeg. Turn heat to medium-low and cook 20 minutes, stirring occasionally.
9. Pour sauce over gnocchi and serve immediately.

Per serving: 216.2 calories; 11.4 mg. sodium; 46.1 gm. carbohydrates; 1.7 gm. fat.

* Do not add salt to water.

Stuffed Baked Potatoes　　　SERVES 8

This decidedly Italian version of the popular stuffed potato is delicious with Pot Roast Bologna (page 164).

4 large potatoes
3 tablespoons unsalted margarine
¼ teaspoon celery seed*
⅛ teaspoon dried thyme
⅛ teaspoon dried oregano
½ teaspoon onion powder
1½ tablespoons low-sodium
　chicken bouillon

Black pepper to taste
2 leeks, minced, including greens
4 halves low-sodium sweet
　peppers, chopped
2 tablespoons paprika

1. Preheat oven to 350°.
2. Cut a lengthwise slit in potatoes. Place on baking sheet and bake 1 hour. Transfer to platter.
3. Halve potatoes lengthwise. Scoop out potatoes, being careful to leave shells intact.
4. In bowl, combine potatoes and all remaining ingredients, except paprika and potato shells, blending thoroughly.
5. Spoon potato mixture into shells. Place on baking sheet.
6. Sprinkle paprika over all. Bake 10 minutes, or until potatoes are lightly browned on top.

Per serving: 137.1 calories; 20.0 mg. sodium; 20.9 gm. carbohydrates;
　5.7 gm. fat.

* Do not use celery flakes, which contain salt.

Beans and Tomatoes SERVES 8

This hearty dish from Emilia-Romagna and Tuscany can trace its origins to neighboring France. It is an excellent accompaniment for Salmon, Eggplant, and Capers (page 122).

2 cups navy beans	½ tablespoon dried oregano
6 cups water	2 bay leaves
1 tablespoon unsalted margarine	1 can (6 ounces) low-sodium
3 onions, minced	tomato paste
4 cloves garlic, minced	3 tomatoes, chopped
Black pepper to taste	2 tablespoons low-sodium beef
¼ teaspoon dried sage	bouillon

1. In Dutch oven, combine first 2 ingredients. Bring to a boil over high heat.
2. Reduce heat to low. Cover and simmer 2 hours, or until beans are fork tender.
3. While beans are cooking, in skillet, heat margarine over low heat. Add onions, garlic, and pepper. Cover and simmer 15 minutes, stirring occasionally.
4. Stir onion mixture into bean mixture.
5. Stir in all remaining ingredients. Cover and simmer 45 minutes more, stirring occasionally.

Per serving: 224.5 calories; 24.6 mg. sodium; 42.8 gm. carbohydrates;
    4.2 gm. fat.

Vegetables

Although not indigenous to Italy alone, certain vegetables come immediately to mind when we think of Italian cuisine. Eggplant, zucchini, artichokes, mushrooms, peppers, and, of course, tomatoes head the list. But the truth is that most vegetables thrive in the rich Italian soil. What is more, Italians so prize their vegetables that they often serve them as separate courses, to be enjoyed by themselves, rather than as accents to a main dish.

To assure the finest results, Italian cooks follow four rules in vegetable selection. First, they use only those vegetables in season. Second, they reject anything imperfect. Bruised and overgrown vegetables never make it to the Italian table. Third, they personally choose their vegetables daily to guarantee freshness. Fourth, they prefer the smallest specimens, believing them to be the sweetest. This deliberate care in selection is reflected in the exquisite taste of each and every vegetable dish.

We have applied the same careful attention to the development of the recipes in this chapter, and we believe you will find them to be faithful and flavorful replicas of the classic vegetable dishes served in Italian homes.

Lemon-Mint Artichokes   SERVES 4

Artichokes, though not unique to Italy, are a staple of the cuisine. They are served plain, marinated, stuffed, and fried, and are delicious enough to be considered a delicacy, as the recipe below and the two which follow tastily demonstrate. This recipe can be served as a first course with any fish or chicken dish.

4 artichokes	**½ cup lemon juice**
2 quarts water	**2 tablespoons dried mint**

1. Cut ¾ inch off the top of the artichoke. With scissors, cut tips off lower leaves. Then cut ¼ inch off the stem.
2. Separate leaves and, with fingers, carefully remove the prickly, purple-tinged leaves at the center, along with the fuzzy choke underneath.
3. In saucepan, stand artichokes. (Saucepan should be small enough to keep artichokes from falling.)
4. Add all remaining ingredients. Turn heat to medium. Cover saucepan and cook ½ hour, or until artichokes are fork-tender.

Per serving: 140.9 calories; 12.5 mg. sodium; 32.5 gm. carbohydrates; 0.6 gm. fat.

Stuffed Artichokes

SERVES 4

Stuffed artichokes are so good and so filling, they are a meal unto themselves. They are also versatile. In this Sicilian dish, you can replace the sardines with ½ can (3¼ ounces) low-sodium tuna with equally good results.

4 artichokes
1 can (3⅜ ounces) low-sodium sardines
2 tablespoons capers*
3 tablespoons dried parsley
¼ cup low-sodium seasoned bread crumbs

2 tablespoons low-sodium ketchup
1 tablespoon red wine vinegar
1 teaspoon dried oregano
2 cups water
¼ cup lemon juice

1. Prepare artichokes by following Steps 1 and 2 for Lemon-Mint Artichokes (page 214).
2. Preheat oven to 350°.
3. In bowl, combine sardines, capers, parsley, bread crumbs, ketchup, vinegar, and oregano, blending thoroughly.
4. Stuff sardine mixture into center of artichokes.
5. In deep 1-quart ovenproof casserole, stand artichokes.
6. Add water and lemon juice. Cover and bake 1 hour.

Per serving with sardines: 241.2 calories; 57.9 mg. sodium; 39.9 gm. carbohy-drates; 4.2 gm. fat.
Per serving with tuna: 212.0 calories; 37.4 mg. sodium; 39.9 gm. carbohy-drates; 1.3 gm. fat.

* Preserved in vinegar only.

Asparagus in Spicy Cheese Sauce

SERVES 4

This dish is a worthy accompaniment to any meat, fish, or chicken entrée.

12 stalks asparagus, blanched*
1½ cups Herb Sauce (page 249)

1 ounce low-sodium Swiss cheese, minced

1. Preheat oven to 375°.
2. In 6-inch square ovenproof casserole, place asparagus.
3. Spoon sauce and cheese over all. Cover and bake 10 minutes.

Per serving: 200.7 calories; 21.2 mg. sodium; 13.9 gm. carbohydrates; 14.3 gm. fat.

* Do not add salt to water.

Asparagus Vinaigrette

SERVES 4

Once you have tried this classic dish, experiment with other Italian sauces, such as ½ cup Cucumber Dressing (page 259), Herbed Mayonnaise Dressing (page 257), or Honey-Vinegar Dressing (page 255).

12 stalks asparagus, steamed*

½ cup Italian Vinaigrette (page 254)

1. Divide asparagus among 4 plates. Let stand 10 minutes.
2. Spoon vinaigrette over all.

Per serving with Italian Vinaigrette:
 98.6 calories; 4.6 mg. sodium; 10.1 gm. carbohydrates; 6.2 gm. fat.
Per serving with Cucumber Dressing:
 82.8 calories; 4.1 mg. sodium; 10.2 gm. carbohydrates; 3.1 gm. fat.
Per serving with Herbed Mayonnaise Dressing:
 111.6 calories; 7.5 mg. sodium; 12.5 gm. carbohydrates; 5.9 gm. fat.
Per serving with Honey-Vinegar Dressing:
 58.4 calories; 4.5 mg. sodium; 12.7 gm. carbohydrates; 0.3 gm. fat.

* Do not add salt to water.

Broccoli and Leeks   SERVES 8

This northern-style dish, sure to become a favorite, is especially delicious with Chicken and Sausage (page 142).

4 cups cold water
⅔ cup boiling water
1 teaspoon low-sodium beef bouillon
2 teaspoons low-sodium chicken bouillon
Black pepper to taste

2 teaspoons dried parsley
1 tablespoon unsalted margarine
2 cloves garlic, minced
2 leeks, chopped, including greens
6 cups broccoli flowerettes
3 tablespoons heavy cream

1. In saucepan, bring cold water to a boil over medium heat.
2. While cold water is boiling, in bowl, combine boiling water, beef and chicken bouillons, pepper, and parsley. Set aside.
3. In skillet, heat margarine over medium-low heat. Add garlic and leeks and sauté 2 minutes, stirring often. Set aside.
4. Add broccoli to boiling water and cook 2 minutes. Drain.
5. In saucepan, combine bouillon and leek mixtures. Turn heat to medium and bring to a slow boil.
6. Add broccoli and cream. Cook 2 minutes, stirring constantly.

Per serving: 74.9 calories; 18.8 mg. sodium; 10.5 gm. carbohydrates; 2.9 gm. fat.

Broccoli and Pine Nuts

SERVES 8

Simple and special, this southern-style dish is a flavorful accompaniment for Swordfish and Sweet Peppers (page 126) or Lemon-Basil Chicken (page 150).

2 tablespoons dry sherry
2 tablespoons lemon juice
2 tablespoons olive oil

4 cups broccoli flowerettes
¼ cup unsalted pine nuts
Black pepper to taste

1. In bowl, combine first 2 ingredients. Set aside.
2. In skillet, heat oil over low heat. Add broccoli and nuts and cook 2 minutes, stirring often.
3. Add sherry mixture and pepper. Stir to blend. Cover and cook 10 minutes, stirring occasionally.

Per serving: 78.3 calories; 8.8 mg. sodium; 4.3 gm. carbohydrates; 6.0 gm. fat.

Broccoli in Sherry Garlic

SERVES 4

An Italian favorite nationwide, this dish originated in the southern regions. The slightly browned garlic adds a nutty flavor to the broccoli, complementing it perfectly. It is a lovely accent for any main dish.

1 tablespoon olive oil
8 cloves garlic, minced
3 cups broccoli flowerettes

Black pepper to taste
2 tablespoons dry white wine

1. In skillet, heat oil over low heat. Add garlic and broccoli. Cover and cook 10 minutes, stirring often.
2. Stir in pepper and wine. Cook, uncovered, 2 minutes more, stirring occasionally.

Per serving: 87.7 calories; 16.2 mg. sodium; 9.9 gm. carbohydrates; 3.9 gm. fat.

Cabbage and Capers

SERVES 8

It is unusual to find the taste of mustard in southern-style dishes, but it is most welcome in this tangy blend which is delightful with Stuffed Burgers (page 166).

1 tablespoon olive oil
2 onions, sliced
6 cups cabbage, shredded
1 cup boiling water, divided
1 tablespoon low-sodium chicken
   bouillon

1½ tablespoons low-sodium
   Dijon mustard
2 tablespoons capers*

1. In large skillet, heat oil over low heat. Add onions and cook 5 minutes, stirring occasionally.
2. Add cabbage and ½ cup water. Cover and simmer 20 minutes.
3. While cabbage is cooking, in bowl, combine remaining water, bouillon, and mustard, stirring until mustard is dissolved.
4. Stir mustard mixture and capers into cabbage mixture. Cover and simmer 10 minutes more.

Per serving: 56.7 calories; 22.5 mg. sodium; 10.6 gm. carbohydrates;
   2.6 gm. fat.

* Preserved in vinegar only.

Carrots in Cheese Sauce SERVES 8

Four cups of cauliflowerettes would make a good substitute for the carrots in this terrific dish from Tuscany. Whichever vegetable you choose to feature, this recipe is especially wonderful with fish.

8 carrots, cut in 1-inch rounds	**⅛ teaspoon ground nutmeg**
2 cups Meat Stock (page 65)	**3 ounces low-sodium Gouda**
2 teaspoons dried mint	**cheese, minced**

1. In saucepan, combine all ingredients, except cheese. Turn heat to medium and bring to a slow boil.
2. Reduce heat to low. Cover and simmer ½ hour.
3. Add cheese. Cover and simmer 10 minutes more.

Per serving with carrots: 102.8 calories; 55.9 mg. sodium; 13.0 gm. carbohydrates; 4.1 gm. fat.
Per serving with cauliflower: 76.2 calories; 20.3 mg. sodium; 6.2 gm. carbohydrates; 4.1 gm. fat.

Carrots in Orange Wine SERVES 4

The Piedmont region gives us this elegant dish. Serve with Broiled Lamb Chops in Lemon-Parsley Sauce (page 168).

3 carrots, julienned	**1 orange, sliced**
2 cups water	**⅛ teaspoon ground nutmeg**
¾ cup dry red wine	**1 tablespoon dried parsley**
2 tablespoons raisins*	

1. In saucepan, combine first 2 ingredients. Turn heat to medium and bring to a slow boil. Continue boiling 20 minutes. Drain.
2. In saucepan, combine carrots and all remaining ingredients. Turn heat to low. Cover and simmer 20 minutes, stirring occasionally.

Per serving: 114.7 calories; 38.4 mg. sodium; 21.0 gm. carbohydrates; 0.3 gm. fat.

* Preserved in non-sodium ingredient.

Basil-Crumbed Cauliflower
SERVES 8

You may replace the cauliflower in this savory Sicilian dish with 6 cups broccoli flowerettes, or 1 pound green beans. It is wonderful with any main course.

1 tablespoon olive oil
1 onion, minced
2 cloves garlic, minced
6 cups cauliflowerettes, parboiled*
Black pepper to taste
1/16 teaspoon ground cinnamon

2 tablespoons unsalted margarine
1/4 cup low-sodium seasoned bread crumbs
2 teaspoons dried basil
2 teaspoons low-sodium chicken bouillon

1. In skillet, heat oil over low heat. Add onion and garlic and cook 5 minutes, stirring occasionally.
2. Add cauliflower, pepper, and cinnamon. Stir to blend. Cover and simmer 5 minutes.
3. While cauliflower is cooking, in second skillet, heat margarine over medium-low heat. Add bread crumbs, basil, and bouillon, stirring to blend thoroughly. Cook 2 minutes, stirring often.
4. Spoon bread crumb mixture over cauliflower mixture. Stir to blend.

Per serving with cauliflower: 96.3 calories; 17.3 mg. sodium; 11.6 gm. carbohydrates; 5.5 gm. fat.
Per serving with broccoli: 100.6 calories; 18.9 mg. sodium; 12.2 gm. carbohydrates; 5.5 gm. fat.
Per serving with green beans: 91.4 calories; 10.1 mg. sodium; 11.2 gm. carbohydrates; 5.4 gm. fat.

* Do not add salt to water.

Creamed Cauliflower and Peas SERVES 8

The touch of French cuisine is deliciously evident in this northern dish. It is fabulous with pasta and just as good with Tuna Sautéed in Wine (page 130).

1½ quarts cold water, divided
6 cups cauliflowerettes
½ pound fresh peas, shelled
1 cup boiling water
1 tablespoon low-sodium chicken
  bouillon

Dash of ground basil
1 tablespoon unsalted margarine
¼ cup heavy cream

1. In saucepan, bring 1 quart water to a boil over medium heat. Add cauliflower and cook 10 minutes, or until cauliflower is fork-tender. Drain.
2. While cauliflower is cooking, in second saucepan, bring remaining cold water to a boil over medium heat. Add peas and cook 10 minutes. Drain. Set aside.
3. While vegetables are cooking, in third saucepan, combine boiling water, bouillon, nutmeg, and basil. Turn heat to low. Cover and simmer 15 minutes. Set aside.
4. In skillet, heat margarine over low heat. Add peas and simmer 1 minute, stirring constantly.
5. Stir cream into bouillon mixture. Cover and simmer 1 minute.
6. In bowl, combine cauliflower, peas, and cream mixture, blending thoroughly.

Per serving: 91.9 calories; 16.2 mg. sodium; 9.5 gm. carbohydrates; 4.8 gm. fat.

Easy Eggplant Parmigiana SERVES 8

This is the almost instant version of the well-known dish. Of course, since Parmesan cheese is very high in sodium, we have replaced it with low-sodium Swiss cheese, which also has a distinctive, tangy bite. It is a great main dish served with Squid Salad Vinaigrette (page 111).

1 medium eggplant, cut in 1-inch rounds
¼ cup lemon juice
2 tablespoons low-sodium beef bouillon
4 cups Tomato Sauce II (page 243), divided

⅓ pound low-sodium mozzarella cheese, sliced
2 ounces low-sodium Swiss cheese, minced

1. Preheat oven to broil.
2. In 9 x 13-inch ovenproof casserole, place eggplant. Pour lemon juice over all. Then sprinkle bouillon over all.
3. Pour 2 cups tomato sauce around eggplant.
4. Lay mozzarella cheese on top of eggplant. Then sprinkle Swiss cheese over all.
5. Pour remaining sauce over all and broil 6 inches from heat 10 minutes, or until cheese starts to bubble on top.

Per serving: 120.3 calories; 18.9 mg. sodium; 17.6 gm. carbohydrates; 4.5 gm. fat.

Eggplant with Mushrooms   SERVES 8

The northern and central regions of Lombardy and Emilia-Romagna are the origins for the tasty recipe below, which is wonderful with any main dish.

1 tablespoon unsalted margarine
2 onions, minced
2 cloves garlic, minced
12 mushrooms, chopped
1 medium eggplant, peeled and diced
Black pepper to taste

2 teaspoons paprika
$\frac{1}{16}$ teaspoon ground cinnamon
1½ teaspoons dried oregano
1 tablespoon low-sodium chicken bouillon
1 tablespoon dry sherry

1. In skillet, heat margarine over low heat. Add onions and garlic and cook 10 minutes, or until onions are lightly browned, stirring often.
2. Add mushrooms and stir to blend.
3. Add all remaining ingredients, except sherry, stirring to blend. Cover and simmer 20 minutes, stirring occasionally.
4. Stir in sherry. Cover and simmer 5 minutes more.

Per serving: 61.9 calories; 10.4 mg. sodium; 12.1 gm. carbohydrates; 2.0 gm. fat.

Salmon-Stuffed Eggplant
SERVES 4

This is a superb southern presentation for this popular Italian vegetable. For an elegant variation, replace the salmon in Step 4 with ½ pound medium shrimp, shelled, deveined, and chopped, or 2 half chicken breasts, skinned, boned, and diced. Serve with Arugola Soup (page 66) for a lovely, light meal.

2 medium eggplant, halved,
   pulp removed and shells
   reserved
1 tablespoon olive oil
2 onions, minced
2 cloves garlic, minced
2 tomatoes, chopped
⅛ teaspoon celery seed*
½ teaspoon dried basil

1 teaspoon dried parsley
Black pepper to taste
½ pound salmon fillets, diced
1 tablespoon lemon juice
¼ cup low-sodium bread crumbs
2 ounces low-sodium Cheddar
   cheese, sliced thin
1 cup water

1. In bowl, chop eggplant pulp. Set aside.
2. In skillet, heat oil over low heat. Add onions and garlic and cook 5 minutes, or until onions turn golden, stirring occasionally.
3. Stir in tomatoes, celery seed, basil, parsley, and black pepper.
4. Push onion mixture to sides of skillet. To well created in center, add salmon and lemon juice. Raise heat to medium and cook 5 minutes, stirring often. Transfer mixture to bowl.
5. Preheat oven to 325°.
6. Stir eggplant pulp into salmon mixture, blending thoroughly.
7. Stuff salmon mixture into eggplant halves. Place stuffed eggplant in 9-inch square ovenproof casserole.
8. Sprinkle bread crumbs over eggplant halves. Top with cheese. Pour water around eggplant.
9. Bake, uncovered, ½ hour, or until cheese melts.

Per serving with salmon: 380.2 calories; 60.1 mg. sodium; 41.5 gm. carbohydrates; 17.4 gm. fat.
Per serving with shrimp: 308.2 calories; 103.5 mg. sodium; 42.4 gm. carbohydrates; 10.2 gm. fat.
Per serving with chicken: 311.2 calories; 48.5 mg. sodium; 41.5 gm. carbohydrates; 10.9 gm. fat.

* Do not use celery flakes, which contain salt.

Braised Fennel in Wine   SERVES 4

Cooking reduces the licorice taste of fennel to a tantalizing hint, enticing you to try just one more bite. This southern-style delicacy is just right with Carrot Soup with Capers (page 66) and Vermicelli with Oysters (page 195).

1 large fennel, sliced, tops removed	2 tablespoons lemon juice
¼ cup dry white wine	1 teaspoon low-sodium chicken bouillon
1 tablespoon olive oil	½ cup water
Dash of hot pepper flakes	

1. In skillet, combine first 2 ingredients. Turn heat to low. Cover and simmer 20 minutes, adding more wine, if necessary, to prevent sticking.
2. Stir in all remaining ingredients. Cover and simmer 20 minutes more.

Per serving: 69.8 calories; 3.3 mg. sodium; 5.3 gm. carbohydrates; 4.2 gm. fat.

Fennel in Cream Sauce   SERVES 8

The north also has its favorite fennel recipes. Try this flavorful dish from the Piedmont region with Parsley Flounder in Herb Sauce (page 120) or Marinated Rock Cornish Hens (page 156).

2 tablespoons unsalted margarine	1 cup boiling water
1 onion, chopped	1½ tablespoons low-sodium chicken bouillon
2 large fennel, sliced, tops removed	1 teaspoon dried basil
8 mushrooms, sliced	1/16 teaspoon ground nutmeg
Black pepper to taste	¼ cup heavy cream

1. In skillet, heat margarine over low heat. Add onion and cook 5 minutes, or until onion is wilted.
2. Add fennel, mushrooms, and pepper, stirring to blend. Cover and simmer 5 minutes.

3. While fennel is cooking, in bowl, combine all remaining ingredients, except cream. Stir into fennel mixture. Cover and cook ½ hour, stirring occasionally.
4. Stir in cream. Cover and cook 5 minutes more.

Per serving: 77.6 calories; 9.0 mg. sodium; 8.1 gm. carbohydrates; 5.0 gm. fat.

Buttery Green Beans with Mushrooms   SERVES 8

Shrimp in Spicy Tomato Sauce (page 135) or Veal Scallops and Leeks in Lemon-Basil Sauce (page 179) are two excellent follow-ups to this savory dish. For variety, add 2 ounces low-sodium minced Cheddar cheese to Step 6.

1½ quarts water
1 pound green beans, cut in
  2-inch pieces
3 tablespoons unsalted
  margarine, divided
2 cloves garlic, minced

12 mushrooms, sliced
Black pepper to taste
1 tablespoon low-sodium chicken
  bouillon
Dash of hot pepper flakes

1. In saucepan, bring water to a boil over high heat.
2. Reduce heat to medium. Add green beans and cook 7 minutes, or until beans are tender-crisp. Drain. Set aside.
3. While beans are cooking, in skillet, heat 1 tablespoon margarine over medium-low heat. Add garlic and sauté 5 minutes, or until garlic is lightly browned.
4. Add mushrooms and sauté 1 minute more, stirring constantly.
5. In bowl, combine mushroom mixture and green beans.
6. Add all remaining ingredients. Toss to blend thoroughly.

Per serving plain: 72.1 calories; 10.2 mg. sodium; 6.4 gm. carbohydrates;
  4.8 gm. fat.
Per serving with cheese: 100.5 calories; 11.5 mg. sodium; 6.6 gm. carbohydrates; 7.1 gm. fat.

Green Beans with Orange Slices

SERVES 4

Lobster Salad in Brandied Mayonnaise (page 108) is a perfect complement to this tasty dish from the Alto Adige region.

1 quart cold water
½ pound green beans
1 tablespoon unsalted margarine
1 orange, peeled and sectioned
2 teaspoons dry sherry

Black pepper to taste
¼ cup boiling water
1 teaspoon low-sodium chicken bouillon

1. In saucepan, bring cold water to a boil over high heat.
2. Reduce heat to medium. Add green beans and cook 7 minutes. Drain. Set aside.
3. While beans are cooking, in skillet, heat margarine over low heat. Add orange slices and cook 5 minutes, stirring often.
4. Add sherry and black pepper. Stir to blend.
5. Add green beans, boiling water, and bouillon, stirring to blend thoroughly. Cook 3 minutes more, stirring often.

Per serving: 77.1 calories; 6.3 mg. sodium; 10.9 gm. carbohydrates; 3.4 gm. fat.

Peas with Pork

SERVES 8

This southern-style dish balances the sweetness of peas with the pungent flavor of spiced pork. Fish Soup (page 68) or Basil and Tarragon Chicken Salad (page 114) is all you need for a wonderful meal.

1 quart water
1 tablespoon sugar
1 pound fresh peas, shelled
1 tablespoon olive oil, divided
2 onions, chopped

2 cloves garlic, minced
¼ pound pork shoulder, trimmed and diced
1/16 teaspoon hot pepper flakes

1. In saucepan, combine first 2 ingredients. Turn heat to medium

and bring to a slow boil. Add peas and boil 10 minutes. Drain. Set aside.

2. While peas are cooking, in skillet, heat 2 teaspoons oil over medium-low heat. Add onions and garlic and sauté 5 minutes, or until onions are golden, stirring occasionally.
3. Add remaining oil, pork, and hot pepper flakes. Raise heat to medium and sauté 5 minutes, or until pork is browned all over, stirring often.
4. In bowl, combine peas and pork mixture. Toss to blend thoroughly.

Per serving: 118.8 calories; 14.4 mg. sodium; 15.5 gm. carbohydrates;
    3.2 gm. fat.

Peas with Sweet Peppers   SERVES 4

An elegant and wonderfully tasty dish from the north. Serve with any meat, fish, or poultry recipe.

1 tablespoon unsalted margarine
1 onion, minced
1 clove garlic, minced
½ pound fresh peas, shelled
3 halves low-sodium sweet
  peppers, chopped

2 teaspoons low-sodium beef
  bouillon
¾ cup water

1. In skillet, heat margarine over low heat. Add onion and garlic and cook 5 minutes, or until onion is wilted.
2. Add peas and sweet peppers, blending thoroughly. Cover and simmer 5 minutes.
3. Add all remaining ingredients. Raise heat to medium and cook 10 minutes more, stirring occasionally. Drain.

Per serving: 119.3 calories; 28.6 mg. sodium; 20.1 gm. carbohydrates;
    3.9 gm. fat.

Meat-Stuffed Peppers

SERVES 4

This classic dish, created in the southern regions, is always sure to please. Choose either Spinach and Cheese Soup (page 76) or Green Bean and Carrot Salad (page 100) to complete your meal.

¾ pound chopped beef
2 tablespoons low-sodium beef bouillon
Black pepper to taste
2 teaspoons dried parsley
1 teaspoon dried oregano
2 tablespoons red wine vinegar

2 tablespoons low-sodium ketchup
¼ cup low-sodium seasoned bread crumbs
4 green peppers
2 cups water
2 cups Tomato Sauce I (page 242)

1. In bowl, combine first 8 ingredients, blending thoroughly. Set aside.
2. Cut 1 inch off tops of green peppers. Remove seeds and veins. Discard green pepper caps.
3. Preheat oven to 350°.
4. In deep 1-quart ovenproof casserole, place green peppers.
5. Pour water around green peppers. Then pour Tomato Sauce I over all.
6. Cover and bake 40 minutes. Uncover and bake 10 minutes more.

Per serving: 419.3 calories; 97.5 mg. sodium; 33.1 gm. carbohydrates; 21.2 gm. fat.

Rice-Stuffed Peppers   SERVES 8

A sophisticated dish worthy of the most special occasions. Try it with Salmon in Basil-Cream Sauce (page 121).

1 recipe Rice in Wine (page 201)	½ teaspoon lemon peel powder
2 leeks, chopped, including greens	¼ cup unsalted walnuts, chopped
⅛ teaspoon ground nutmeg	4 large green peppers

1. In bowl, combine first 5 ingredients, blending thoroughly. Set aside.
2. Preheat oven to 350°.
3. Cut 1 inch off tops of green peppers. Remove seeds and veins. Discard green pepper caps.
4. Stuff peppers with rice mixture.
5. Place each pepper in center of large piece of aluminum foil. Crimp foil around peppers.
6. On rack in oven, place peppers and bake for 40 minutes.
7. Halve peppers lengthwise before serving.

Per serving: 242.5 calories; 32.9 mg. sodium; 41.0 gm. carbohydrates; 7.1 gm. fat.

Shrimp-Stuffed Peppers

SERVES 8

A most unusual and delicious dish from Tuscany. You need only Baked Polenta with Tomatoes and Eggplant (page 205) to complete your meal. For a different taste experience, replace the green peppers with 4 large acorn squash, halved and seeded.

2 tablespoons unsalted
   margarine, divided
1 pound shrimp, shelled,
   deveined, and chopped
Black pepper to taste
2 tablespoons lemon juice
1 tablespoon dry red wine
2 tablespoons dried parsley

3 tomatoes, chopped
½ cup low-sodium ricotta cheese
1 tablespoon low-sodium chicken
   bouillon
8 green peppers
¼ cup low-sodium seasoned
   bread crumbs
1 teaspoon dried oregano

1. In skillet, heat margarine over low heat. Add shrimp and black pepper and cook 2 minutes, or until shrimp turn pink all over, stirring often.
2. Stir in lemon juice, wine, and parsley, stirring to blend. Transfer mixture to bowl.
3. Stir in tomatoes, cheese, and bouillon. Set aside.
4. Cut 1 inch off tops of green peppers. Remove seeds and veins. Discard green pepper caps.
5. Spoon shrimp mixture into green peppers. Set aside.
6. Preheat oven to 350°.
7. In bowl, combine last 2 ingredients. Sprinkle on top of peppers.
8. Place each pepper in center of large piece of aluminum foil. Crimp foil around peppers.
9. On rack in oven, place peppers. Bake ½ hour.
10. Halve peppers lengthwise before serving.

Per serving with peppers: 188.4 calories; 115.5 mg. sodium; 18.5 gm. carbohydrates; 6.5 gm. fat.
Per serving with squash: 219.9 calories; 89.6 mg. sodium; 28.1 gm. carbohydrates; 7.6 gm. fat.

Braised Spinach   SERVES 4

Variations of this wonderfully tasty dish are enjoyed from Florence to Palermo. It is a delightful accompaniment to any meal.

1 tablespoon olive oil
2 cloves garlic, minced
¾ pound spinach, chopped
Black pepper to taste
2 teaspoons low-sodium chicken
  bouillon

¼ cup dry white wine
⅛ teaspoon dried mint
2 tablespoons heavy cream

1. In skillet, heat oil over low heat. Add garlic and cook 10 minutes, or until garlic is lightly browned, stirring often.
2. Add all remaining ingredients, except cream, blending thoroughly. Cover and simmer 15 minutes.
3. Stir in cream. Cover and simmer 5 minutes more.

Per serving: 105.0 calories; 67.1 mg. sodium; 6.6 gm. carbohydrates;
    7.2 gm. fat.

Baked Stuffed Tomatoes

SERVES 4

This dish is as delicious as it is versatile. You can turn it into a main dish by replacing the carrots with 1 can (6½ ounces) low-sodium tuna; ½ pound shrimp, shelled, deveined, and chopped; 1 cup cooked chicken, cubed; or 1 cup cooked pork, cubed.

4 tomatoes, cored, pulp reserved
3 carrots, steamed* and diced
¼ teaspoon fennel seed

¼ cup unsalted, crushed walnuts
½ cup Piquant Mayonnaise
    (page 258)

1. Preheat oven to 350°.
2. In bowl, combine tomato pulp, carrots, fennel seed, walnuts, and mayonnaise, blending thoroughly.
3. Spoon carrot mixture into tomatoes. Set aside.
4. On rack in oven, place large piece of aluminum foil. Place tomatoes on foil and bake ½ hour.

Per serving plain: 186.5 calories; 47.7 mg. sodium; 15.8 gm. carbohydrates; 12.5 gm. fat.
Per serving with tuna: 205.2 calories; 39.1 mg. sodium; 15.8 gm. carbohydrates; 12.7 gm. fat.
Per serving with shrimp: 207.0 calories; 95.5 mg. sodium; 9.4 gm. carbohydrates; 12.8 gm. fat.
Per serving with chicken: 202.2 calories; 36.9 mg. sodium; 8.5 gm. carbohydrates; 13.4 gm. fat.
Per serving with pork: 259.6 calories; 45.5 mg. sodium; 8.5 gm. carbohydrates; 18.5 gm. fat.

* Do not add salt to water.

Spice-Broiled Tomatoes   SERVES 8

This dish is northern, but its appeal is universal. It is excellent with Snapper Stuffed with Seafood (page 124).

⅓ cup low-sodium seasoned
  bread crumbs
½ teaspoon dried oregano
½ teaspoon dried parsley
¼ teaspoon dried basil

¹⁄₁₆ teaspoon onion powder
Black pepper to taste
4 large tomatoes, halved
2 tablespoons unsalted margarine

1. Preheat oven to broil.
2. In bowl, combine first 6 ingredients, blending thoroughly. Set aside.
3. On shallow baking sheet, place tomatoes, cut side up. Sprinkle bread crumb mixture over all.
4. Dot with margarine and broil 6 inches from heat 7 minutes, or until bread crumbs are lightly browned.

Per serving: 76.6 calories; 7.4 mg. sodium; 10.2 gm. carbohydrates; 3.4 gm. fat.

Squash Melt

The flavorful goodness of squash is evident with every mouthful of this southern-style dish. Enjoy it with Parsley Beef in Brandy (page 163).

3 yellow squash, cut into spears
2 zucchini, cut into spears
¼ cup dry red wine
Black pepper to taste
1 tablespoon olive oil
4 cloves garlic, minced
2 leeks, chopped, including greens

2 ounces low-sodium Cheddar cheese, diced
2 ounces low-sodium ricotta cheese
1 cup water
2 teaspoons low-sodium beef bouillon
2 teaspoons dried oregano

1. Preheat oven to 350°.
2. In 9-inch square ovenproof casserole, combine first 4 ingredients. Set aside.
3. In skillet, heat oil over low heat. Add garlic and cook 10 minutes, or until garlic is lightly browned, stirring often.
4. In bowl, combine garlic and all remaining ingredients, blending thoroughly.
5. Spoon garlic mixture over squash and zucchini mixture. Cover and bake 35 minutes.

Per serving: 114.2 calories; 7.9 mg. sodium; 11.3 gm. carbohydrates; 6.3 gm. fat.

Squash with Orange-Nut Stuffing

SERVES 8

Save this northern dish for a special occasion. Two possible main course selections are Deviled Shrimp (page 134) and Roast Leg of Lamb (page 170).

4 acorn squash, halved and
  seeded
1 orange, peeled and chopped
2 tablespoons honey

¼ cup crushed, unsalted
  pine nuts
2 teaspoons dried mint

1. Preheat oven to 350°.
2. In 9 x 13-inch ovenproof casserole, place squash, cut side up, and bake ½ hour.
3. While squash is baking, in bowl, combine all remaining ingredients.
4. Spoon orange mixture into squash shells and bake 20 minutes more.

Per serving: 123.2 calories; 0.6 mg. sodium; 25.7 gm. carbohydrates; 3.7 gm. fat.

Sweet-and-Sour Zucchini   SERVES 8

This southern dish is so good you will eat it like candy. Try it with Swordfish in Pepper-Wine (page 127) or Roast Stuffed Chicken Italiano (page 152).

1 tablespoon olive oil	⅓ cup water
3 zucchini, cut into spears	2 tomatoes, chopped
2 cloves garlic, minced	2 teaspoons dried parsley
⅓ cup cider vinegar	⅛ teaspoon dried rosemary
3 tablespoons sugar	

1. In skillet, heat oil over low heat. Add zucchini and garlic and cook 2 minutes, stirring occasionally.
2. Stir in vinegar, sugar, and water. Raise heat to medium and cook until mixture starts to bubble around the edges.
3. Stir in all remaining ingredients. Reduce heat to medium-low. Cover and cook 15 minutes, stirring occasionally.

Per serving: 61.3 calories; 3.4 mg. sodium; 10.9 gm. carbohydrates; 2.0 gm. fat.

Sauces and Dressings

There are numerous and diverse sauces in the Italian culinary repertoire: meat sauces, herb sauces, and, of course, the classic tomato sauces. One or more is usually part of any given meal. Yet as important as they are, when compared to other cuisines, Italian sauces play only a supporting role.

In many other countries, sauces dominate the ingredients they adorn, or they are served separately as condiments. But in Italy, sauces play only a supporting role and, like other seasonings, are used only to enhance main ingredients.

We are most familiar with the spicy tomato-based sauces of southern Italy, pungent with garlic and olive oil. Two of our own examples are Tomato Sauce II (page 243) and Mustard-Tomato Sauce (page 246). But the subtle and light combinations of the north deserve our attention as well. In these regions, the more delicate flavor of butter replaces or combines with olive oil; garlic is seldom used; and herbs and spices are added with a lighter touch than in the south, or are, on occasion, the essence of a sauce. Pungent Basil Sauce (page 248) is one such example.

Italian sauces are surprisingly easy and quick to make, and most of them freeze very well. So whenever a touch of Italian strikes your fancy, remember a sauce is just minutes away.

Bechamel Sauce

MAKES 2½ CUPS

Salsa Besciamella or Balsamella was a mainstay in the cooking of ancient Romagna in northern Italy many years before the French discovered it and presented it to the world as bechamel. This classic white sauce will enhance any dish.

2 cups low-fat milk
4 tablespoons unsalted margarine
5 tablespoons all-purpose flour

1 tablespoon low-sodium chicken bouillon
¼ cup heavy cream

1. In saucepan, bring milk to a slow boil over medium-low heat.
2. While milk is cooking, in second saucepan, melt margarine over low heat.
3. Stir flour into margarine and continue stirring 2 minutes.
4. Gradually stir milk, 2 tablespoons at a time, into flour mixture.
5. Stir in bouillon and cream. Cook 2 minutes more, or until sauce thickens, stirring constantly.

Per recipe: 1,092.1 calories; 281.0 mg. sodium; 84.4 gm. carbohydrates; 71.5 gm. fat.
Per cup: 436.8 calories; 112.4 mg. sodium; 33.8 gm. carbohydrates; 28.6 gm. fat.
Per tablespoon: 27.3 calories; 7.0 mg. sodium; 2.1 gm. carbohydrates; 1.8 gm. fat.

Mushroom-Cheese Sauce MAKES 2½ CUPS

With pasta, with pork, with anything at all, this sauce is mouth-wateringly good.

1 tablespoon unsalted margarine
2 leeks, chopped, including
   greens
1 teaspoon all-purpose flour
2 cups boiling water
2 tablespoons low-sodium
   chicken bouillon

¼ cup low-sodium ricotta cheese
Black pepper to taste
8 mushrooms, chopped
2 tablespoons dry sherry
1 bunch watercress, chopped

1. In saucepan, melt margarine over low heat. Add leeks and cook 2 minutes, or until leeks start to brown, stirring often.
2. Stir in flour, blending thoroughly.
3. Stir in water, a little at a time. Then stir in bouillon, cheese, and pepper. Cook 10 minutes, or until mixture starts to thicken, stirring occasionally.
4. Stir in remaining ingredients. Cover and cook 10 minutes more.
5. Pour mixture into blender. Puree.
6. Refrigerate in tightly closed containers. Will keep up to 1 week.

Per recipe: 546.8 calories; 107.1 mg. sodium; 56.2 gm. carbohydrates;
   26.8 gm. fat.
Per cup: 218.7 calories; 42.8 mg. sodium; 22.5 gm. carbohydrates;
   10.7 gm. fat.
Per tablespoon: 13.7 calories; 2.7 mg. sodium; 1.4 gm. carbohydrates;
   0.7 gm. fat.

Tomato Sauce I

MAKES 6 CUPS

The recipes which follow are versions of classic Italian tomato sauce. In either recipe, for variety, add 2 green peppers, chopped, or ½ pound mushrooms, chopped, in the last half hour of cooking.

1 tablespoon olive oil
3 onions, chopped
6 cloves garlic, minced
1 can (29 ounces) unsalted
   tomato puree
1½ cups water
2 tablespoons red wine vinegar

3 tablespoons dry white (or red)
   wine
Black pepper to taste
½ tablespoon dried oregano
1 cup fresh basil, chopped, or
   1 tablespoon dried basil

1. In Dutch oven, heat oil over low heat. Add onions and garlic and cook 10 minutes, or until onions are lightly browned, stirring occasionally.
2. Add all remaining ingredients, except fresh basil. *Note:* If using dried basil, add at this time.
3. Cover and simmer 1½ hours, stirring occasionally. Add fresh basil. Cover and simmer 10 minutes more, stirring occasionally.
4. Let sauce cool 20 minutes. Then pour into containers. May be refrigerated up to 2 weeks, or frozen indefinitely.

Plain:
   Per recipe: 715.0 calories; 98.5 mg. sodium; 151.8 gm. carbohydrates;
      17.2 gm. fat.
   Per cup: 119.2 calories; 16.4 mg. sodium; 25.3 gm. carbohydrates;
      2.9 gm. fat.
   Per tablespoon: 7.4 calories; 1.0 mg. sodium; 1.6 gm. carbohydrates;
      0.2 gm. fat.

With green peppers:
   Per recipe: 803.0 calories; 150.5 mg. sodium; 171.0 gm. carbohydrates;
      18.0 gm. fat.
   Per cup: 133.8 calories; 25.1 mg. sodium; 28.5 gm. carbohydrates;
      3.0 gm. fat.
   Per tablespoon: 8.4 calories; 1.6 mg. sodium; 1.8 gm. carbohydrates;
      0.2 gm. fat.

With mushrooms:
   Per recipe: 779.0 calories; 132.7 mg. sodium; 162.2 gm. carbohydrates;
      17.2 gm. fat.
   Per cup: 129.8 calories; 22.1 mg. sodium; 27.0 gm. carbohydrates;
      2.9 gm. fat.
   Per tablespoon: 8.1 calories; 1.4 mg. sodium; 1.7 gm. carbohydrates;
      0.2 gm. fat.

Tomato Sauce II

MAKES 8 CUPS

1 tablespoon olive oil
3 onions, chopped
6 cloves garlic, minced
3 pounds tomatoes, chopped
½ tablespoon dried oregano
1 can (6 ounces) low-sodium
   tomato paste

2 cups water
Black pepper to taste
2 bay leaves
2 cups fresh basil, chopped, or
   2 tablespoons dried basil

1. In Dutch oven, heat oil over low heat. Add onions and garlic and cook 10 minutes, or until onions are lightly browned, stirring occasionally.
2. Add tomatoes, oregano, and tomato paste. Cook 5 minutes, stirring once.
3. Add all remaining ingredients, except fresh basil. *Note:* If using dried basil, add at this time.
4. Cover and simmer 1 hour, stirring occasionally. Add fresh basil. Cover and simmer 10 minutes more, stirring occasionally.
5. Discard bay leaves.
6. Let sauce cool 20 minutes. Then pour into containers. May be refrigerated up to 2 weeks, or frozen indefinitely.

Plain:
   Per recipe: 772.4 calories; 101.0 mg. sodium; 169.1 gm. carbohydrates; 19.1 gm. fat.
   Per cup: 96.6 calories; 12.6 mg. sodium; 21.1 gm. carbohydrates; 2.4 gm. fat.
   Per tablespoon: 6.0 calories; 0.8 mg. sodium; 1.3 gm. carbohydrates; 0.1 gm. fat.

With green peppers:
   Per recipe: 860.4 calories; 153.0 mg. sodium; 188.3 gm. carbohydrates; 19.9 gm. fat.
   Per cup: 107.6 calories; 19.1 mg. sodium; 23.5 gm. carbohydrates; 2.5 gm. fat.
   Per tablespoon: 6.7 calories; 1.2 mg. sodium; 1.5 gm. carbohydrates; 0.2 gm. fat.

With mushrooms:
   Per recipe: 836.4 calories; 135.2 mg. sodium; 179.5 gm. carbohydrates; 19.1 gm. fat.
   Per cup: 104.6 calories; 16.9 mg. sodium; 22.4 gm. carbohydrates; 2.4 gm. fat.
   Per tablespoon: 6.5 calories; 1.1 mg. sodium; 1.4 gm. carbohydrates; 0.1 gm. fat.

Mock Red Clam Sauce — MAKES 3 CUPS

Two of the most popular sauces in Italian cuisine are red clam sauce and white clam sauce, most often served over spaghetti or fettuccine. No Italian cookbook would be complete without them. But at a minimum of 181 milligrams sodium per 3½ ounces, clams are too high in sodium for most salt-restricted diets. That is why we have substituted the succulent oyster for the two sauces which follow. We think you will find the results delicious. However, if your diet permits, by all means try the classic version by replacing the oysters with 1 dozen small littleneck clams, steamed open and chopped.

1 tablespoon olive oil
3 cloves garlic, minced
1 can (3⅜ ounces) low-sodium
 sardines, chopped
1 tablespoon dried parsley
½ teaspoon dried oregano
6 tomatoes, chopped

½ cup boiling water
1 tablespoon low-sodium chicken
 bouillon
Black pepper to taste
1 pint oysters, shucked and
 chopped, including liquid

1. In skillet, heat oil over medium heat. Add garlic and cook 5 minutes, or until garlic is lightly browned, stirring occasionally.
2. Add sardines, parsley, oregano, and tomatoes, stirring to blend.
3. Stir in water, bouillon, and pepper. Reduce heat to low. Cover and simmer 20 minutes.
4. Stir in oysters, plus liquid. Cover and simmer 5 minutes more.
5. Refrigerate in tightly closed containers. Will keep up to 1 week.

With oysters:
 Per recipe: 855.2 calories; 440.8 mg. sodium; 113.7 gm. carbohydrates;
  38.2 gm. fat.
 Per cup: 285.1 calories; 146.9 mg. sodium; 37.9 gm. carbohydrates;
  12.7 gm. fat.
 Per tablespoon: 17.8 calories; 9.2 mg. sodium; 2.4 gm. carbohydrates;
  0.8 gm. fat.

With clams:
 Per recipe: 720.3 calories; 397.4 mg. sodium; 60.7 gm. carbohydrates;
  33.0 gm. fat.
 Per cup: 240.1 calories; 132.5 mg. sodium; 20.2 gm. carbohydrates;
  11.0 gm. fat.
 Per tablespoon: 15.0 calories; 8.3 mg. sodium; 1.3 gm. carbohydrates;
  0.7 gm. fat.

Mock White Clam Sauce   MAKES 3½ CUPS

Our version of the white sauce classic is less robust than Mock Red Clam Sauce (page 244), but is just as flavorful.

1 tablespoon olive oil
4 cloves garlic, minced
⅛ teaspoon hot pepper flakes
2 cups boiling water
2½ tablespoons low-sodium chicken bouillon
¼ cup dry white wine

3 tablespoons dried parsley
½ teaspoon dried basil
1 pint oysters, shucked and chopped, including liquid
1 tablespoon unsalted margarine
2 ounces low-sodium Cheddar cheese, minced

1. In skillet, heat oil over low heat. Add garlic and hot pepper flakes and cook 5 minutes, or until garlic is golden, stirring occasionally.
2. Add water, bouillon, wine, parsley, and basil, stirring to blend.
3. Raise heat to medium and bring to a slow boil, stirring occasionally.
4. Reduce heat to low. Cover and simmer 10 minutes.
5. Add oysters, plus liquid, margarine, and cheese. Cover and simmer 5 minutes more.
6. Refrigerate in tightly closed jars. Will keep up to 1 week.

With oysters:
   Per recipe: 924.3 calories; 324.4 mg. sodium; 42.8 gm. carbohydrates;
      52.5 gm. fat.
   Per cup: 264.1 calories; 92.7 mg. sodium; 12.2 gm. carbohydrates;
      15.0 gm. fat.
   Per tablespoon: 16.5 calories; 5.8 mg. sodium; 0.8 gm. carbohydrates;
      0.9 gm. fat.

With clams:
   Per recipe: 789.4 calories; 281.0 mg. sodium; 36.1 gm. carbohydrates;
      47.3 gm. fat.
   Per cup: 225.5 calories; 80.3 mg. sodium; 10.3 gm. carbohydrates;
      13.5 gm. fat.
   Per tablespoon: 14.1 calories; 5.0 mg. sodium; 0.6 gm. carbohydrates;
      0.8 gm. fat.

Mustard-Tomato Sauce　　MAKES 6 CUPS

The unexpected tang of mustard gives a delicious twist to a classic tomato sauce. Good on just about everything.

1 can (29 ounces) unsalted
　tomato puree
3 tomatoes, chopped
2 cups water
¼ cup sugar

⅓ cup red wine vinegar
2 bay leaves
2 tablespoons dried oregano
3 tablespoons low-sodium Dijon
　mustard

1. In Dutch oven, combine first 4 ingredients. Turn heat to medium and bring to a slow boil, stirring often.
2. Reduce heat to low. Add all remaining ingredients, except mustard. Cover and simmer 1 hour, stirring occasionally.
3. Stir in mustard. Cover and simmer ½ hour more, stirring occasionally.
4. Discard bay leaves.
5. Store in tightly closed containers. May be refrigerated up to 3 weeks, or frozen indefinitely.

Per recipe: 906.2 calories; 72.1 mg. sodium; 213.3 gm. carbohydrates;
　5.3 gm. fat.
Per cup: 151.0 calories; 12.0 mg. sodium; 35.6 gm. carbohydrates;
　0.9 gm. fat.
Per tablespoon: 9.4 calories; 0.8 mg. sodium; 2.2 gm. carbohydrates;
　0.1 gm. fat.

Wine-Cream Sauce　　MAKES 3¾ CUPS

Elegant and delicious, this sauce will turn any chicken or fish dish into a stellar event. Also excellent on fettuccine.

¼ cup unsalted margarine
3 tablespoons all-purpose flour
2½ cups low-fat milk
1 tablespoon low-sodium chicken
　bouillon

½ cup dry sherry
¼ cup heavy cream

1. In saucepan, melt margarine over low heat. Stir in flour, blending thoroughly.

2. Gradually add milk, blending thoroughly.
3. Stir in bouillon and sherry. Cover and simmer 10 minutes, stirring occasionally.
4. Stir in cream. Cook, uncovered, 5 minutes more, stirring occasionally.
5. Refrigerate in tightly closed containers. Will keep up to 3 days.

Per recipe: 1,126.2 calories; 345.6 mg. sodium; 73.8 gm. carbohydrates; 71.5 gm. fat.
Per cup: 300.3 calories; 92.2 mg. sodium; 19.7 gm. carbohydrates; 19.1 gm. fat.
Per tablespoon: 18.8 calories; 5.8 mg. sodium; 1.2 gm. carbohydrates; 1.2 gm. fat.

Spicy Green Sauce MAKES 5½ CUPS

This sauce is a versatile staple throughout Italy because it is an equally excellent accompaniment for meat, fish, and poultry.

1 can (3⅜ ounces) low-sodium sardines
2 cloves garlic, chopped
1 tablespoon green peppercorns*
1 tablespoon capers*
½ cup olive oil
1¼ cups boiling water

1 tablespoon low-sodium Dijon mustard
¼ cup red wine vinegar
3 tablespoons dried parsley
1 teaspoon dried thyme
Black pepper to taste

1. In blender, combine first 4 ingredients. Grind briefly. Transfer to bowl.
2. In second bowl, combine oil, water, and mustard, stirring until mustard is completely dissolved.
3. To oil mixture, stir in vinegar, parsley, thyme, and pepper, blending thoroughly.
4. Stir in sardine mixture, blending well.
5. Pour mixture into jars, leaving ½-inch headspace. Will keep in tightly closed jars up to 2 weeks if refrigerated.

Per recipe: 1,293.7 calories; 161.5 mg. sodium; 12.3 gm. carbohydrates; 131.9 gm. fat.
Per cup: 235.2 calories; 29.4 mg. sodium; 2.2 gm. carbohydrates; 24.0 gm. fat.
Per tablespoon: 14.7 calories; 1.8 mg. sodium; 0.1 gm. carbohydrates; 1.5 gm. fat.

* Preserved in vinegar only.

Pungent Basil Sauce　　　MAKES 3¾ CUPS

The refreshing bite of this zesty sauce is exceptional with cold fish.
You might also try it as a basting sauce for broiled chicken or veal.

2 cups low-sodium ketchup
1 can (8 ounces) low-sodium
　tomato sauce
2 tablespoons dry sherry
2 teaspoons low-sodium
　Worcestershire sauce

1 small onion, minced
1 cup chopped, fresh basil, or
　2 tablespoons dried basil

1. In jar, combine first 5 ingredients. Shake to blend thoroughly.
2. If using fresh basil, stir into mixture 1 hour before serving to
   allow flavors to blend. Without the fresh basil, mixture can be
   frozen indefinitely or refrigerated up to 1 month.
3. If using dried basil, stir into mixture, which can be frozen
   indefinitely or refrigerated up to 1 month.

Per recipe: 366.9 calories; 117.0 mg. sodium; 108.6 gm. carbohydrates;
　　6.6 gm. fat.
Per cup: 97.8 calories; 31.2 mg. sodium; 29.0 gm. carbohydrates;
　　1.8 gm. fat.
Per tablespoon: 6.1 calories; 2.0 mg. sodium; 1.8 gm. carbohydrates;
　　0.1 gm. fat.

Herb Sauce

MAKES 3½ CUPS

One of the most delectable sauces to ever grace your table, this is perfect for basting poultry and meat.

1 tablespoon olive oil
1 onion, minced
2 cups Chicken Stock (page 64)
1 cup sour cream (or plain yogurt)
¼ cup lemon juice
1 cup fresh basil, chopped, or
   3 tablespoons dried basil

1 tablespoon dried tarragon
½ tablespoon dried dill
1 teaspoon dried rosemary
2 tablespoons brandy

1. In saucepan, heat oil over low heat. Add onion and cook until lightly browned, stirring occasionally.
2. Add stock. Raise heat to medium and cook until mixture bubbles around the edges.
3. Reduce heat to low. Stir in all remaining ingredients, except brandy, blending thoroughly. Cover and cook 20 minutes, stirring occasionally.
4. Stir in brandy. Cook, uncovered, 5 minutes more.
5. Refrigerate in tightly closed jars, leaving ½-inch headspace. Will keep up to 1 week.

With sour cream:
   Per recipe: 1,219.7 calories; 146.9 mg. sodium; 47.3 gm. carbohydrates;
      112.4 gm. fat.
   Per cup: 348.5 calories; 42.0 mg. sodium; 13.5 gm. carbohydrates;
      32.1 gm. fat.
   Per tablespoon: 21.8 calories; 2.6 mg. sodium; 0.8 gm. carbohydrates;
      2.0 gm. fat.

With yogurt:
   Per recipe: 528.3 calories; 190.1 mg. sodium; 52.9 gm. carbohydrates;
      30.0 gm. fat.
   Per cup: 150.9 calories; 54.3 mg. sodium; 15.1 gm. carbohydrates;
      8.5 gm. fat.
   Per tablespoon: 9.4 calories; 3.4 mg. sodium; 0.2 gm. carbohydrates;
      0.1 gm. fat.

Hot Sauce

MAKES 4½ CUPS

This is, without doubt, one of the great barbecue sauces.

6 low-sodium cucumber pickles, chopped
2 onions, chopped
6 cloves garlic, minced
1 can (29 ounces) unsalted tomato puree

3 tablespoons low-sodium Dijon mustard
½ teaspoon hot pepper flakes
¼ cup low-sodium ketchup
1 cup water

1. In blender, combine first 3 ingredients. Grind briefly. Transfer to Dutch oven.
2. To Dutch oven, add all remaining ingredients. Turn heat to medium-low and cook 20 minutes, stirring occasionally.
3. Reduce heat to low. Cover and simmer ½ hour more, stirring occasionally.
4. Store in tightly closed containers. May be refrigerated up to 2 weeks, or frozen indefinitely.

Per recipe: 499.6 calories; 97.2 mg. sodium; 130.1 gm. carbohydrates; 5.0 gm. fat.
Per cup: 111.0 calories; 21.6 mg. sodium; 28.9 gm. carbohydrates; 1.1 gm. fat.
Per tablespoon: 6.9 calories; 1.4 mg. sodium; 4.8 gm. carbohydrates; 0.07 gm. fat.

Wine-Caper Sauce   MAKES 1½ CUPS

This sophisticated sauce is especially appropriate for fish and poultry. It is also surprisingly delicious on rice and pasta.

1 cup boiling water
2 tablespoons low-sodium
  chicken bouillon
2 tablespoons dried parsley
Black pepper to taste

¼ cup dry white wine
4 tablespoons capers*
2 tablespoons lemon juice
2 tomatoes, chopped

1. In saucepan, combine first 4 ingredients. Turn heat to low. Cover and simmer 10 minutes, stirring occasionally.
2. Raise heat to medium. Add wine, capers, and lemon juice. Cook, uncovered, 5 minutes more, or until mixture starts to boil.
3. Stir in tomatoes. Reduce heat to low. Cover and simmer 20 minutes more, stirring occasionally.
4. Store in tightly closed containers. May be refrigerated up to 2 weeks, or frozen indefinitely.

Per recipe: 244.3 calories; 60.1 mg. sodium; 33.5 gm. carbohydrates;
    6.9 gm. fat.
Per cup: 162.9 calories; 40.1 mg. sodium; 22.3 gm. carbohydrates;
    4.6 gm. fat.
Per tablespoon: 10.2 calories; 2.5 mg. sodium; 1.4 gm. carbohydrates;
    0.3 gm. fat.

* Preserved in vinegar only.

Rosemary-Wine Sauce MAKES 2¼ CUPS

Perfectly wonderful on meat, poultry, and fish, this sauce has an exquisite taste to match its heady aroma. It also imparts an exotic flavor to rice.

1 tablespoon unsalted margarine	2 teaspoons dried rosemary
2 onions, diced	⅛ teaspoon black pepper
1 cup Chicken Stock (page 64)	1/16 teaspoon ground cinnamon
2 cups dry sherry (or dry vermouth)	

1. In saucepan, melt margarine over low heat. Add onions and cook until golden, stirring occasionally.
2. Add stock. Raise heat to medium and cook until mixture bubbles around the edges.
3. Add remaining ingredients, stirring to blend. Cook until mixture bubbles around the edges, stirring occasionally.
4. Reduce heat to low and simmer 15 minutes more, stirring occasionally.
5. Store in tightly closed jars, leaving ½-inch headspace. Will keep up to 2 weeks if refrigerated, or indefinitely if frozen.

Per recipe: 652.5 calories; 77.9 mg. sodium; 67.6 gm. carbohydrates; 17.5 gm. fat.
Per cup: 290.0 calories; 34.6 mg. sodium; 30.0 gm. carbohydrates; 7.8 gm. fat.
Per tablespoon: 18.1 calories; 22.4 mg. sodium; 19.2 gm. carbohydrates; 0.5 gm. fat.

Raspberry Sauce

MAKES 3 CUPS

An exquisite sauce, marvelous on chicken and veal, and tasty on beef and pork as well. For variety, replace the raspberries with 1 dozen dried apricots, chopped, and soaked in 1 cup boiling water ½ hour.

1 pint raspberries	4 cloves garlic, minced
½ cup cider vinegar	½ cup fresh basil, chopped, or
¼ cup dry white wine	2 teaspoons dried basil
1 tablespoon unsalted margarine	Black pepper to taste

1. In bowl, combine first 2 ingredients. Cover and refrigerate 1 hour to allow flavors to blend.
2. In blender, combine raspberry mixture and wine. Puree. Set aside.
3. In saucepan, heat margarine over low heat. Add garlic and cook 5 minutes, or until garlic is golden.
4. Add puree. Cover and simmer 5 minutes.
5. Add basil and pepper, stirring to blend. Cover and simmer 10 minutes more.
6. Store in tightly closed containers. May be refrigerated up to 1 week, or frozen up to 1 month.

With raspberries:
  Per recipe: 385.6 calories; 23.6 mg. sodium; 51.2 gm. carbohydrates; 13.0 gm. fat.
  Per cup: 128.5 calories; 7.9 mg. sodium; 17.1 gm. carbohydrates; 4.3 gm. fat.
  Per tablespoon: 8.0 calories; 0.5 mg. sodium; 1.1 gm. carbohydrates; 0.3 gm. fat.

With apricots:
  Per recipe: 433.6 calories; 39.1 mg. sodium; 65.7 gm. carbohydrates; 11.6 gm. fat.
  Per cup: 144.5 calories; 13.0 mg. sodium; 21.9 gm. carbohydrates; 3.9 gm. fat.
  Per tablespoon: 9.0 calories; 0.8 mg. sodium; 1.4 gm. carbohydrates; 0.2 gm. fat.

Oil and Vinegar Dressing   MAKES 2½ CUPS

This recipe and the one which follows are two variations of the classic oil and vinegar dressing. Each is distinct and delicious: one with the pungent flavor of garlic; the other with the bite of hot pepper flakes. Both utilize the trick of boiling water to "stretch" the oil and so minimize the calories but not the flavor.

½ cup olive oil
1½ cups boiling water
2 teaspoons low-sodium Dijon
  mustard
2 teaspoons garlic powder

2 teaspoons dried oregano
1 teaspoon dried basil
Black pepper to taste
½ cup red wine vinegar

1. In jar, combine all ingredients. Shake to blend thoroughly.
2. Refrigerate in tightly closed containers. Will keep indefinitely.

Per recipe: 1,032.7 calories; 8.7 mg. sodium; 6.9 gm. carbohydrates;
    119.0 gm. fat.
Per cup: 413.1 calories; 3.5 mg. sodium; 2.8 gm. carbohydrates;
    47.6 gm. fat.
Per tablespoon: 25.8 calories; 0.2 mg. sodium; 0.2 gm. carbohydrates;
    3.0 gm. fat.

Italian Vinaigrette   MAKES 2½ CUPS

½ cup olive oil
1¼ cups boiling water
½ teaspoon sugar
1 tablespoon dried parsley
1 teaspoon dried basil

1 teaspoon dried oregano
1⁄16 teaspoon hot pepper flakes
1 small onion, minced
⅔ cup red wine (or cider) vinegar

1. In jar, combine all ingredients. Shake to blend thoroughly.
2. Refrigerate in tightly closed container. Will keep indefinitely.

Per recipe: 1.077.4 calories; 25.7 mg. sodium; 27.0 gm. carbohydrates;
    118.7 gm. fat.
Per cup: 431.0 calories; 10.3 mg. sodium; 10.8 gm. carbohydrates;
    47.5 gm. fat.
Per tablespoon: 26.9 calories; 0.6 mg. sodium; 0.7 gm. carbohydrates;
    3.0 gm. fat.

Honey-Vinegar Dressing   MAKES 2 CUPS

A highly unusual, pungent sweet-and-sour blend. Will dress up any vegetable or salad, and makes a wonderful glaze for pork, poultry, and fish.

¼ cup lemon juice
1 cup cider vinegar
¼ cup honey
½ cup boiling water
2 teaspoons garlic powder

2 teaspoons dried basil
2 teaspoons paprika
1 teaspoon dried rosemary
Black pepper to taste

1. In bowl, combine first 2 ingredients.
2. In second bowl, combine honey and boiling water, stirring until honey is thoroughly blended.
3. Stir lemon juice mixture into honey mixture, blending thoroughly.
4. Stir in remaining ingredients.
5. Refrigerate in tightly closed jars. Will keep indefinitely.

Per recipe: 218.8 calories; 19.2 mg. sodium; 64.4 gm. carbohydrates;
    0 gm. fat.
Per cup: 109.4 calories; 9.6 mg. sodium; 32.2 gm. carbohydrates; 0 gm. fat.
Per tablespoon: 6.8 calories; 0.6 mg. sodium; 2.0 gm. carbohydrates;
    0 gm. fat.

Mustard-Garlic Sauce   MAKES 2¾ CUPS

Wonderful on chilled salads or vegetables. For a special treat, use this sauce to glaze any meat or poultry.

½ cup olive oil
1¼ cups boiling water
⅓ cup low-sodium Dijon mustard

⅔ cup red wine vinegar
10 cloves garlic, minced
Black pepper to taste

1. In bowl, combine first 3 ingredients, stirring until mustard is completely dissolved.
2. Stir in remaining ingredients.
3. Refrigerate in tightly closed containers. Will keep indefinitely.

Per recipe: 1,196.2 calories; 22.0 mg. sodium; 30.6 gm. carbohydrates;
    124.2 gm. fat.
Per cup: 435.1 calories; 8.0 mg. sodium; 11.1 gm. carbohydrates;
    45.2 gm. fat.
Per tablespoon: 27.2 calories; 0.5 mg. sodium; 0.7 gm. carbohydrates;
    2.8 gm. fat.

Creamy Garlic Dressing   MAKES 2½ CUPS

So delicious you will want to use this dressing on everything.

6 cloves garlic, ground
½ cup low-sodium mayonnaise
½ cup sour cream
⅛ teaspoon ground nutmeg
1 tablespoon dried parsley
2 teaspoons dried basil

Black pepper to taste
1 cup boiling water
4 teaspoons low-sodium chicken
    bouillon
¼ cup cider vinegar

1. In bowl, combine first 7 ingredients, stirring to blend thoroughly.
2. In second bowl, combine water and bouillon, stirring until bouillon is completely dissolved.
3. Stir bouillon mixture into mayonnaise mixture.
4. Stir in vinegar.

5. Refrigerate in tightly closed containers. Will keep up to 1 month.

Per recipe: 1,327.5 calories; 127.6 mg. sodium; 28.8 gm. carbohydrates;
  135.4 gm. fat.
Per cup: 531.0 calories; 51.0 mg. sodium; 11.5 gm. carbohydrates;
  54.2 gm. fat.
Per tablespoon: 33.2 calories; 3.2 mg. sodium; 0.7 gm. carbohydrates;
  3.4 gm. fat.

Herbed Mayonnaise Dressing   MAKES 1⅓ CUPS

The wine gives this dressing its delicate taste, and guarantees pleasing results on cold meat, fish, and poultry. Of course, it is an excellent topping for salads and vegetables as well.

⅓ cup low-sodium mayonnaise
½ cup cider vinegar
1 tablespoon lemon juice
2 tablespoons sugar

2 tablespoons dried parsley
½ tablespoon dried oregano
Black pepper to taste
3 tablespoons dry white wine

1. In bowl, combine all ingredients, stirring to blend thoroughly.
2. Refrigerate in tightly closed containers. Will keep indefinitely.

Per recipe: 711.6 calories; 44.6 mg. sodium; 40.0 gm. carbohydrates;
  58.9 gm. fat.
Per cup: 535.0 calories; 33.5 mg. sodium; 30.1 gm. carbohydrates;
  44.3 gm. fat.
Per tablespoon: 33.4 calories; 2.1 mg. sodium; 1.9 gm. carbohydrates;
  2.8 gm. fat.

Piquant Mayonnaise MAKES 2 CUPS

Here is a mayonnaise with a captivating flavor that is wonderful on fish, poultry, vegetables, and as a dip. You will love it.

½ cup low-sodium mayonnaise
1 jar (3½ ounces) capers,*
  including liquid
¼ teaspoon onion powder
¹⁄₁₆ teaspoon garlic powder

1 teaspoon dried basil
2 teaspoons dried dill
1 can (3⅜ ounces) low-sodium
  sardines, chopped (optional)
¼ cup lemon juice

1. In bowl, combine first 6 ingredients, stirring to blend thoroughly.
2. Stir in sardines, if desired, and lemon juice.
3. Refrigerate in tightly closed containers. Will keep up to 2 weeks with sardines; indefinitely without sardines.

With sardines:
  Per recipe: 1,048.0 calories; 175.5 mg. sodium; 6.4 gm. carbohydrates;
    100.5 gm. fat.
  Per cup: 524.0 calories; 87.8 mg. sodium; 3.2 gm. carbohydrates;
    50.3 gm. fat.
  Per tablespoon: 32.8 calories; 5.5 mg. sodium; 0.2 gm. carbohydrates;
    3.1 gm. fat.

Without sardines:
  Per recipe: 823.2 calories; 42.4 mg. sodium; 4.4 gm. carbohydrates;
    88.2 gm. fat.
  Per cup: 411.6 calories; 21.2 mg. sodium; 2.2 gm. carbohydrates;
    44.1 gm. fat.
  Per tablespoon: 25.7 calories; 1.3 mg. sodium; 0.1 gm. carbohydrates;
    2.8 gm. fat.

* Preserved in vinegar only.

Cucumber Dressing

MAKES 2 CUPS

Cool, refreshing, a flavorful treat, this dressing will perk up a salad and turn a simply prepared vegetable into a prize. It is also great with cold fish and poultry.

¼ cup low-sodium mayonnaise
½ cup plain yogurt
½ cup orange juice
1 teaspoon dried oregano
1 tablespoon dried parsley

4 scallions, chopped, including
  greens
Black pepper to taste
1 cucumber, diced

1. In bowl, combine first 3 ingredients, blending thoroughly.
2. Stir in remaining ingredients.
3. Refrigerate in tightly closed containers. Will keep up to 3 days.
   Note: If you are not planning to use within 3 days, do not add cucumber until ready to serve. Mixture will then keep up to 1 week.

Per recipe: 609.3 calories; 133.7 mg. sodium; 24.4 gm. carbohydrates;
    44.8 gm. fat.
Per cup: 304.6 calories; 66.9 mg. sodium; 12.2 gm. carbohydrates;
    22.4 gm. fat.
Per tablespoon: 19.0 calories; 4.2 mg. sodium; 0.8 gm. carbohydrates;
    1.4 gm. fat.

Desserts

The art of cake- and pastry-making originated with the Italians, mainly in the prosperous homes of twelfth-century Venice. Indeed, Venetian chefs took such pride in their skill that many became specialists in sweet confections, and are still so today. Now, however, the rich treats they make are generally served only on holidays and other special occasions, and sometimes as between-meal substitutes for the popular pizza snack.

Everyday desserts are fruit and cheese and, when the weather is hot, ice cream. But here, too, the Italian flair is in evidence. Ice cream is usually flavored with one or more fruits; cheese and fruits are whipped with cream, liqueurs, or eggs. And whatever the dessert, it often contains one or more kinds of nuts, for which Italians have great fondness.

When you try such delectable offerings as Italian Cheese Pie (page 263), Nut Cake (page 267), and Glazed Oranges with Raspberry Cream (page 272), we are sure you will agree that the Italian reputation for dessert-making is well-deserved.

Italian Pie Dough   MAKES 2 6-INCH CRUSTS

This recipe produces a crust that is as light and flaky as the most delicate French pastry; the lemon peel and sherry give it a uniquely Italian air. Wonderful with any filling you choose.

2 cups all-purpose flour	¼ cup sugar
½ cup unsalted margarine	2 tablespoons dry sherry
1 tablespoon lemon peel powder	2 tablespoons ice water
3 egg yolks	

1. In bowl, combine flour and margarine, blending thoroughly.
2. Stir in lemon peel powder and egg yolks.
3. Beat in sugar and sherry.
4. Beat in ice water.
5. Form dough into balls. Wrap balls in waxed paper and refrigerate at least 1 hour.

Per recipe: 2,814.9 calories; 192.7 mg. sodium; 370.5 gm. carbohydrates;
    105.5 gm. fat.
Per crust: 1,407.5 calories; 96.4 mg. sodium; 185.3 gm. carbohydrates;
    52.8 gm. fat.

Italian Cheese Pie

SERVES 20

Neither as creamy nor as rich as American cheese pie, but scrumptious all the same, this pie probably originated in Lazio, the region Rome calls its own. This is a pie fit for the gods.

1 pound low-sodium ricotta
 cheese
3 eggs, separated, divided
⅓ cup sugar
1 teaspoon lemon peel powder

1 teaspoon vanilla extract
2 tablespoons banana liqueur
1 recipe Italian Pie Dough
 (page 262)

1. In skillet, heat cheese over medium-low heat 5 minutes, stirring constantly. Drain off excess fluid.
2. Transfer cheese to cheesecloth. Wring out any excess moisture.
3. Transfer cheese to bowl.
4. Beat in 2 egg yolks. Set aside.
5. In second bowl, beat together 3 egg whites, sugar, and lemon peel powder.
6. Beat egg white mixture into cheese mixture.
7. Beat in vanilla and banana liqueur. Set aside.
8. Place dough between 2 sheets of waxed paper and roll out to ¼-inch thickness.
9. Carefully peel off top layer of waxed paper and turn dough into 8-inch pie plate.
10. Trim off overlapping dough. Shape it into a ball. Place it between 2 pieces of waxed paper and roll out to ¼-inch thickness.
11. Carefully peel off top layer of waxed paper. Cut dough into 1-inch wide strips. Set aside.
12. Preheat oven to 350°.
13. Spoon cheese mixture into pie crust. Top with dough strips arranged in lattice-like fashion, and pressed against the sides of the pie plate.
14. Brush remaining egg yolk over dough strips.
15. Bake pie ½ hour, or until crust is golden brown.

Per serving: 209.0 calories; 20.0 mg. sodium; 23.3 gm. carbohydrates;
 9.1 gm. fat.

Mixed Fruit Cobbler
SERVES 24

The Austro-German love of creamy fruit desserts is in evidence in this exquisite dish from the region of Alto Adige.

2 cups all-purpose flour
⅓ cup brown sugar
2 teaspoons orange peel powder
3 teaspoons low-sodium baking powder
½ cup water
¼ cup low-fat milk
2 eggs
3 peaches, peeled, pitted, and sliced thin

2 pears, peeled, cored, and sliced thin
2 apples, peeled, cored, and sliced thin
1 cup blueberries
1½ teaspoons ground cinnamon
¼ teaspoon clove powder
2 tablespoons unsalted margarine

1. In bowl, combine first 4 ingredients, blending thoroughly.
2. Gradually beat in water, milk, and eggs, blending thoroughly.
3. Pour batter into 9 x 13-inch ovenproof casserole.
4. Preheat oven to 350°.
5. Scatter peach, pear, and apple slices and blueberries into batter.
6. Stir in cinnamon and clove powder.
7. Dot mixture with margarine and bake ½ hour, or until mixture is set and knife inserted in center comes out clean.

Per serving: 129.5 calories; 7.4 mg. sodium; 25.3 gm. carbohydrates; 1.7 gm. fat.

Fruit-Filled Log

SERVES 48

The balmy southern Mediterranean climate of Campania yields luscious tropical fruits like those featured in the wonderful dessert below.

1 cup golden raisins*
12 dates, pitted and chopped
8 dried figs, chopped
8 dried peaches, chopped
½ cup strawberry jam†
3 eggs
¾ cup sugar

½ cup vegetable oil
¾ cup apple juice
1 teaspoon almond extract
3½ cups all-purpose flour
4 teaspoons low-sodium baking
   powder

1. In bowl, combine first 5 ingredients, blending thoroughly. Set aside.
2. In second bowl, beat together eggs, sugar, oil, apple juice, and almond extract.
3. In third bowl, combine flour and baking powder, blending thoroughly.
4. At medium speed, gradually beat flour mixture into egg mixture, until a smooth dough is formed.
5. Turn dough onto lightly floured board and divide into 3 equal sections.
6. Roll out each section to ⅛-inch thickness.
7. Spread fruit mixture over each dough section. Then roll up dough.
8. Preheat oven to 325°.
9. Place logs, seam side down, on greased and floured baking sheets. Bake ½ hour, or until dough is golden brown.

Per serving: 112.3 calories; 6.1 mg. sodium; 27.9 gm. carbohydrates;
   0.5 gm. fat.

* Preserved in non-sodium ingredient.
† Without sodium or pectin.

Lemony Coconut Cake   SERVES 32

Sweet and tart, light and refreshing as a southern breeze.

2 cups sugar
½ cup unsalted margarine
3 eggs
2 cups all-purpose flour
2 teaspoons low-sodium baking
  powder

½ cup lemon juice
½ cup low-fat milk
1 teaspoon vanilla extract
¼ cup shredded coconut

1. Preheat oven to 350°.
2. In bowl, cream together first 2 ingredients.
3. Stir in eggs, blending thoroughly. Set aside.
4. In second bowl, combine flour and baking powder, blending thoroughly.
5. Stir in lemon juice, milk, and vanilla, blending thoroughly.
6. Stir in coconut, blending thoroughly.
7. Gradually stir flour mixture into sugar mixture, blending thoroughly.
8. Spoon batter into greased and floured 8-inch square baking pan and bake 40 minutes, or until toothpick inserted in center comes out clean.

Per serving: 152.2 calories; 9.7 mg. sodium; 26.5 gm. carbohydrates;
    4.1 gm. fat.

Nut Cake

SERVES 20

Nuts are a favorite food throughout Italy. So it is no wonder these favorites should be combined into this rich, thoroughly enjoyable cake.

½ cup sugar
½ cup unsalted margarine
2 eggs
1 teaspoon ground cinnamon
2 tablespoons brandy
½ cup unsalted walnuts, crushed

¼ cup unsalted pecans, chopped
¼ cup unsalted pine nuts
1¼ cups all-purpose flour
2½ teaspoons low-sodium
   baking powder

1. In bowl, cream together sugar and margarine.
2. Stir in eggs, cinnamon, and brandy, blending thoroughly.
3. Stir in walnuts, pecans, and pine nuts.
4. In second bowl, combine flour and baking powder, blending thoroughly.
5. Fold flour mixture into sugar mixture, blending thoroughly.
6. Preheat oven to 350°.
7. Pour batter into greased and floured 9-inch square baking pan.
8. Bake 45 minutes, or until toothpick inserted in center comes out clean.

Per serving: 70.9 calories; 6.4 mg. sodium; 5.7 gm. carbohydrates; 5.1 gm. fat.

Nut Balls   MAKES 48 NUT BALLS

Sicily inspired this nut-filled delight.

4 cups all-purpose flour
3 teaspoons low-sodium baking
    powder
1½ cups sugar
1 teaspoon orange peel powder
½ teaspoon ground cinnamon
⅔ cup unsalted margarine
⅓ cup low-fat milk
2 tablespoons dry red wine

2 eggs
1 teaspoon vanilla extract
½ cup unsalted walnuts,
    chopped
½ cup unsalted almonds,
    chopped
½ cup unsalted cashews,
    chopped

1. In bowl, combine first 5 ingredients, blending thoroughly.
2. Cream in margarine. Set aside.
3. In second bowl, beat together milk. wine, eggs, vanilla, and
   nuts.
4. Fold nut mixture into flour mixture, blending thoroughly.
5. Preheat oven to 375°.
6. Break off walnut-size pieces of dough. Roll into balls and place
   on greased and floured baking sheet.
7. Bake 10 minutes, or until nut balls are golden brown.

Per serving: 143.9 calories; 4.5 mg. sodium; 22.4 gm. carbohydrates;
   5.2 gm. fat.

Spice Sponge Cake   SERVES 24

Of no particular region, this delicately spiced variation on a perennial favorite is sure to please.

1½ cups all-purpose flour
⅛ teaspoon aniseed, ground
⅛ teaspoon allspice powder
⅛ teaspoon clove powder

2 teaspoons orange peel powder
8 eggs, separated
3 tablespoons ice water
1⅓ cups sugar, divided

1. In bowl, combine first 5 ingredients, blending thoroughly. Set
   aside.

2. In second bowl, beat together egg yolks, water, and ⅔ cup sugar.
3. Stir flour mixture into egg yolk mixture, blending thoroughly.
4. In third bowl, beat together egg whites and remaining sugar.
5. Beat egg white mixture into flour mixture.
6. Preheat oven to 350°.
7. Pour batter into 2 8-inch square baking pans.
8. Bake 20 minutes, or until toothpick inserted in center comes out clean.

Per serving: 126.9 calories; 18.8 mg. sodium; 23.3 gm. carbohydrates;
 1.4 gm. fat.

Easter Cookies MAKES 72 COOKIES

These crunchy, tangy, crumbly treats are usually served at Easter, but once you try them you will want to enjoy them all year long.

4 cups all-purpose flour	5 eggs
1 tablespoon low-sodium baking powder	⅓ cup vegetable oil
	2 tablespoons rum
½ teaspoon ground nutmeg	1 teaspoon almond extract
1 cup sugar	3 tablespoons lemon juice

1. In bowl, combine first 4 ingredients, blending thoroughly.
2. Beat in eggs, one at a time.
3. Beat in all remaining ingredients, blending to form stiff dough.
4. Preheat oven to 375°.
5. Break off walnut-size pieces of dough. Shape into balls and place on greased and floured baking sheets about 1½ inches apart.
6. Bake 10 minutes, or until cookies are golden brown.

Per cookie: 74.6 calories; 4.2 mg. sodium; 12.7 gm. carbohydrates; 1.4 gm. fat.

Pecan Cookies   MAKES 40 COOKIES

A variation of the buttery, delectable cookie traditionally served as a Christmas treat. For a wonderful licorice-flavored variation, add ½ teaspoon aniseed, ground, to Step 2.

⅓ cup sugar
¾ cup unsalted margarine
1 teaspoon vanilla extract
2 tablespoons Kahlua

1¾ cups all-purpose flour
1 teaspoon orange peel powder
¼ teaspoon ground nutmeg
¾ cup unsalted pecans, chopped

1. In bowl, cream together sugar and margarine.
2. Stir in vanilla and Kahlua, blending thoroughly.
3. In second bowl, combine flour, orange peel powder, and nutmeg, blending thoroughly.
4. Stir flour mixture into sugar mixture, blending thoroughly.
5. Stir in pecans, blending thoroughly.
6. Preheat oven to 325°.
7. Break off walnut-size pieces of dough. Shape into balls and place on greased and floured baking sheet 1½ inches apart.
8. Bake 15 minutes, or until cookies are golden brown.

Per cookie: 95.3 calories; 0.8 mg. sodium; 9.8 gm. carbohydrates; 5.4 gm. fat.

Apples Baked in Cranberry-Coconut Sauce   SERVES 8

An unusual and totally wonderful baked apple dish. Four pears, halved and cored, make a lovely alternate to the apples.

½ package (6 ounces) fresh
   cranberries
3 cups water
1 tablespoon dried mint
½ teaspoon clove powder

½ teaspoon ground nutmeg
4 apples, halved and cored
½ cup dry sherry
8 teaspoons shredded coconut

1. In saucepan, combine first 5 ingredients. Turn heat to medium and bring to a slow boil.

2. Reduce heat to low and simmer ½ hour. Set aside.
3. Preheat oven to 350°.
4. In 9-inch square ovenproof casserole, place apples, cut side down.
5. Spoon cranberry mixture around apples.
6. Pour sherry over all.
7. Sprinkle coconut over all.
8. Cover and bake 40 minutes, or until apples are fork tender.

Per serving with apples: 106.1 calories; 2.1 mg. sodium; 20.0 gm. carbohydrates; 2.6 gm. fat.
Per serving with pears: 110.1 calories; 3.1 mg. sodium; 20.8 gm. carbohydrates; 2.4 gm. fat.

Bananas in Strawberry Cream SERVES 8

This is one of the tastiest desserts you will ever enjoy.

1 pint strawberries, hulled and chopped
¾ cup pineapple juice

½ cup heavy cream
6 bananas, peeled and diced

1. In blender, combine first 3 ingredients. Puree. Transfer to bowl. Cover and refrigerate until ready to serve.
2. Divide bannanas equally among 8 dessert cups. Spoon strawberry cream over all.

Per serving: 163.7 calories; 6.7 mg. sodium; 29.4 gm. carbohydrates; 6.0 gm. fat.

Glazed Oranges
with Raspberry Cream
SERVES 8

You may replace the oranges with 8 peach halves, and replace the raspberries with 1 pint hulled strawberries. The result will be equally tasty.

¼ cup water
1 pint raspberries, divided
⅓ cup heavy cream
4 oranges, sliced in ½-inch
  rounds

8 tablespoons honey
¼ cup Grand Marnier

1. Preheat oven to broil.
2. In blender, combine water, ⅓ cup raspberries, and cream. Puree. Set aside.
3. On baking sheet, place orange rounds. Drizzle with honey and broil 6 inches from heat 5 minutes.
4. Pour on Grand Marnier. Flame.
5. Transfer orange rounds to platter.
6. Spoon raspberry puree over all.
7. Garnish with remaining raspberries.

Per serving with oranges and raspberries:
    163.3 calories; 5.1 mg. sodium; 28.2 gm. carbohydrates; 4.0 gm. fat.
Per serving with peaches and strawberries:
    134.2 calories; 4.6 mg. sodium; 20.9 gm. carbohydrates; 3.9 gm. fat.

Peach Ice

The succulent peach flavor of this chilled dish will be more satisfying than any sherbet or ice cream. For a tangy alternative, substitute ½ pint raspberries and 2 apples, peeled, cored, and diced, for the peaches.

½ cup sugar	8 peaches, peeled, pitted, and
⅓ cup water	chopped
2 egg whites	½ teaspoon vanilla extract
2 tablespoons lemon juice	1 cup heavy cream

1. In saucepan, combine first 2 ingredients. Bring to a boil over medium heat. Continue boiling 5 minutes, or until mixture is the consistency of heavy syrup.
2. While sugar mixture is heating, in bowl, beat egg whites and lemon juice until stiff peaks are formed.
3. To egg mixture, gradually add sugar mixture, beating at high speed until stiff. Cover and refrigerate ½ hour.
4. In blender, combine peaches and vanilla. Puree. Cover and refrigerate 20 minutes.
5. In second bowl, beat cream until stiff. Fold into cooled sugar mixture. Then fold in peach mixture.
6. Spoon mixture into 12 parfait glasses or dessert cups. Freeze at least 6 hours before serving.

Per serving with peaches:
    102.1 calories; 3.9 mg. sodium; 17.3 gm. carbohydrates; 3.7 gm. fat.
Per serving with apples and raspberries:
    98.0 calories; 3.6 mg. sodium; 16.1 gm carbohydrates; 3.9 gm. fat.

Brandied Pears
SERVES 12

This delicious dish is an elegant yet easy way to add a special finishing touch to any meal.

1 cup water
1 cup pear brandy, divided

2 teaspoons dried mint
6 pears, peeled, cored, and sliced

1. Preheat oven to 350°.
2. In 9 x 13-inch casserole, pour water and ½ cup brandy.
3. Stir in mint.
4. Add pears, cut side down.
5. Pour remaining brandy over all and bake 20 minutes, or until pears are fork tender.

Per serving: 118.2 calories; 2.2 mg. sodium; 15.3 gm. carbohydrates;
    0.4 gm. fat.

Creamy Rum Fruit
SERVES 16

Sour cream adds the zest and mild bite to this frozen confection which was probably inspired by Italy's Swiss or German neighbors.

1 cup low-fat milk, divided
1 package unflavored gelatin
3 tablespoons sugar
4 tablespoons rum
1 pint sour cream

1 pint strawberries, hulled and
    chopped
2 cups seedless green grapes
4 peaches, pitted and chopped
1 orange, peeled and sectioned

1. In saucepan, combine ½ cup milk and gelatin. Turn heat to low and simmer 2 minutes, stirring to dissolve gelatin.
2. Transfer mixture to bowl. Stir in sugar, blending thoroughly.
3. Stir in remaining milk, rum, sour cream, and strawberries. Place bowl in freezer. Let set 20 minutes.
4. Stir in grapes and peaches. Divide mixture among 16 dessert cups.
5. Garnish with orange sections.

Per serving: 174.8 calories; 18.1 mg. sodium; 14.7 gm. carbohydrates;
    11.4 gm. fat.

Dried Fruit in Brandy Wine

SERVES 8

Below is our version of a traditional Italian dessert—a combination of fruit and wine. It is marvelous.

½ cup raisins*
12 dried figs, chopped
16 dried peaches, chopped
16 dried pears, chopped

½ cup dry red wine
2 tablespoons brandy
2 cloves
½ teaspoon ground cinnamon

In bowl, combine all ingredients. Toss to blend. Cover and refrigerate at least 4 hours before serving, stirring occasionally.

Per serving: 199.6 calories; 13.5 mg. sodium; 43.7 gm. carbohydrates; 0.5 gm. fat.

* Preserved in non-sodium ingredient.

An Italian Menu for Entertaining

Except for antipasti which add flavor and flair to cocktail parties, Italian food is probably not top of mind when you are planning a party. That is because we are all too happily familiar with its delights in our everyday meals and, therefore, think it not exotic enough or impressive enough for special occasions.

We urge you to think again. Of all the Italian meals you have eaten, more than likely most have been tomato-based. Spaghetti and meatballs, eggplant or veal parmigiana, pizza, and so on, are easy, fast, fun, and sure to please the fussiest eaters, which is why, by the way, they make perfect party foods.

But Italian food offers so much more than these universally popular dishes that if the unusual is your preference, you will find a wealth of selections in the Italian kitchen. What could turn a breakfast of eggs into a fancy feast? Why Italian Sausage and Eggs (page 175), of course. Or provide a more elegant lunch or dinner than Lobster in Creamy Wine Sauce (page 132) or Veal with Braised Watercress (page 181).

As we stated earlier, Italian antipasti is wonderful cocktail food, but there are also many hearty and zesty recipes which are perfect for large buffets, as well. Try Mixed Vegetable Appetizer (page 44) and Fried Cheese Puffs (page 60), to name but two.

Because Italian food is as easy to make as it is good to eat, your job as hostess will be worry-free if you take note of a few simple rules of organization:

- *Make a checklist* of all the ingredients you will need at least one week in advance so you can have everything at hand and avoid last-minute panic runs to the store.
- *Rely on tried-and-true successes* which have become favorites with your own family and guests over time. Sticking to proven and popular dishes will give you confidence and will guarantee your company's pleasure and appreciation.

• *Balance your menu* for color and texture, as well as for taste. Food is a sensual experience. Your meal will be on its way to success if it pleases the eye and will be even more appreciated if the tastes and textures complement rather than echo each other.

For example, the sweet and delicate Chicken in Parsley Wine (page 144) is a perfect counterpoint to the puckery Sweet-and-Sour Zucchini (page 238).

• *Consider preparation time* and structure your menu not only to make it one your guests will enjoy, but also one that minimizes work and aggravation for you. To wit, choose some dishes that can be made ahead of time and served cold; others that can simmer for hours, freeing you to do other things.

Italian cuisine lends itself beautifully to these planning guides. Cold antipasti are as delicious as hot; many dishes can be leisurely braised; sauces can be made well in advance; and still other recipes, like pasta or veal scallops, can be prepared in a matter of minutes. Moreover, the mingling of northern and southern specialties will produce memorable eating and fun for you as well as your friends.

Last but not least, when you cook Italian, you are bound to receive kudos. Everyone, the world over, appreciates the tantalizing flavors of this cuisine. So enjoy this chapter. It contains 20 menus, all designed to prove that a little something Italian can give your party that special touch.

Brunch for 4

Broiled Oysters (page 133)
Basil and Tarragon Chicken Salad (page 114)
Green Beans with Orange Slices (page 228)
Nut Cake (page 267)

Preparation Tips:
1. Prepare Nut Cake up to 2 days before ready to serve. *Note:* Leftover cake will keep up to 3 weeks if refrigerated; up to 2 months if frozen.
2. Prepare Basil and Tarragon Chicken Salad 1 hour before serving. Cover and refrigerate until ready to serve.

3. Prepare Broiled Oysters* through Step 3, 20 minutes before ready to serve.
4. Prepare Green Beans with Orange Slices through Step 4, 15 minutes before ready to serve.
5. Finish preparation of Broiled Oysters 5 minutes before ready to serve.
6. Finish preparation of Green Beans with Orange Slices 3 minutes before ready to serve.

* If you are not allowed shellfish, substitute 1 pound cod, minced, in Step 4, and increase broiling time to 6 minutes.

◆━━◆◀◆▶◆━━◆

Brunch for 4

Sausage, Peppers, and Eggs (page 175)
Baked Stuffed Tomatoes (page 234)
Italian Flat Bread (page 85)
Pears Baked in Cranberry-Coconut Sauce (page 270)

Preparation Tips:
1. Prepare Italian Flat Bread at least 3½ hours before ready to serve. *Note:* Bread may be prepared up to 2 days before serving and will keep 1 week if refrigerated.
2. Prepare Baked Stuffed Tomatoes through Step 3, 1 hour before ready to serve.
3. Prepare Pears Baked in Cranberry-Coconut Sauce through Step 7, 40 minutes before ready to serve.
4. Finish preparation of Baked Stuffed Tomatoes ½ hour before ready to serve.
5. Finish preparation of Pears Baked in Cranberry-Coconut Sauce 20 minutes before ready to serve.
6. Prepare Sausage, Peppers, and Eggs* 15 minutes before ready to serve.

* The Sausage Napoli (page 172) used in this recipe may be prepared up to 6 months before ready to use.

◆━▶◉◀━◆

Brunch for 8

Chicken and Caper Salad (page 115)
Rice-Stuffed Peppers (page 231)
Spicy Apple Relish (page 61)
Lemony Coconut Cake (page 266)

Preparation Tips:
1. Prepare Spiced Apple Relish the day before ready to use. Keep refrigerated until ready to serve. *Note:* This relish may be prepared and refrigerated up to 3 months before ready to use.
2. Prepare Chicken and Caper Salad through Step 4, 3 hours before serving. Cover and refrigerate until ready to serve.
3. Prepare Rice-Stuffed Peppers through Step 5, 2 hours before ready to serve.
4. Prepare Lemony Coconut Cake through Step 7, 1 hour before ready to serve.
5. Continue preparation of Rice-Stuffed Peppers through Step 6, 40 minutes before ready to serve.
6. Finish preparation of Lemony Coconut Cake 40 minutes before ready to serve.
7. Finish preparation of Chicken and Caper Salad 5 minutes before ready to serve.
8. Finish preparation of Rice-Stuffed Peppers immediately before serving.

◆━▶◉◀━◆

Brunch for 8

Swordfish and Sweet Peppers (page 126)
Baked Polenta with Tomatoes and Eggplant (page 205)
Dried Fruit in Brandy Wine (page 275)

Preparation Tips:
1. Prepare Dried Fruit in Brandy Wine 6 hours before ready to serve.

2. Prepare Swordfish and Sweet Peppers through Step 1, 4 hours before ready to serve.
3. Prepare Baked Polenta with Tomatoes and Eggplant through Step 8, 1½ hours before ready to serve.
4. Finish preparation of Swordfish and Sweet Peppers ½ hour before ready to serve.
5. Finish preparation of Baked Polenta with Tomatoes and Eggplant 15 minutes before ready to serve.

Brunch for 16

Zucchini, Tomato, and Sardine Salad (page 107)
Meat-Stuffed Flat Bread (page 86)
Glazed Oranges with Raspberry Cream (page 272)

Preparation Tips:
1. Prepare Meat-Stuffed Flat Bread through Step 3, 3 hours before ready to serve.
2. Prepare Zucchini, Tomato, and Sardine Salad* through Step 2, 45 minutes before ready to serve.
3. Finish preparation of Meat-Stuffed Flat Bread ½ hour before ready to serve.
4. Prepare Glazed Oranges with Raspberry Cream† 12 minutes before ready to serve.
5. Finish preparation of Zucchini, Tomato, and Sardine Salad immediately before ready to serve.

* Four times the recipe. The Honey-Vinegar Dressing (page 255) used in this recipe may be prepared any time before ready to use.
† Double the recipe.

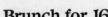

Brunch for 16

Chicken Picante (page 155)
Roast Peppers and Beet Salad (page 105)
Potato Bread (page 84)
Creamy Rum Fruit (page 274)

Preparation Tips:
1. Prepare Potato Bread at least 5 hours before ready to serve. *Note:* Bread may be prepared the day before serving and will keep up to 2 weeks if refrigerated.
2. Prepare Chicken Picante* 50 minutes before ready to serve.
3. Prepare Creamy Rum Fruit through Step 3, 45 minutes before ready to serve.
4. Prepare Roast Peppers and Beet Salad† 15 minutes before ready to serve.
5. Finish preparation of Creamy Rum Fruit 10 minutes before ready to serve.
6. Finish preparation of Roast Peppers and Beet Salad 5 minutes before ready to serve.

* Double the recipe.
† The Oil and Vinegar Dressing (page 254) used in this recipe may be prepared any time before ready to use.

Lunch for 4

Mushroom-Rice Soup (page 70)
Squid and Shrimp Salad (page 110)
Raspberry and Apple Ice (page 273)

Preparation Tips:
1. Prepare Raspberry and Apple Ice the day before ready to use.
2. Prepare Mushroom-Rice Soup through Step 3, 50 minutes before ready to serve.

3. Prepare Squid and Shrimp Salad* through Step 2, 20 minutes before ready to serve.
4. Finish preparation of Mushroom-Rice Soup 10 minutes before ready to serve.
5. Finish preparation of Squid and Shrimp Salad immediately before ready to serve.

* The Italian Vinaigrette (page 254) used in this recipe may be prepared any time before ready to use. If you are not allowed shellfish, substitute ½ can (3⅜ ounces) low-sodium salmon in Step 3.

Lunch for 4

Braised Endive Salad (page 99)
Chicken with Lemon Sauce (page 143)
Rice in Spicy Green Sauce (page 200)
Easter Cookies (page 269)

Preparation Tips:
1. Prepare Easter Cookies at least 1½ hours before ready to serve. *Note:* Cookies may be prepared up to 1 week before serving and will keep indefinitely.
2. Prepare Chicken with Lemon Sauce through Step 4, 1 hour and 5 minutes before ready to serve.
3. Prepare Rice in Spicy Green Sauce* 20 minutes before ready to serve.
4. Prepare Braised Endive Salad 15 minutes before ready to serve.
5. Finish preparation of Chicken with Lemon Sauce immediately before ready to serve.

* The Spicy Green Sauce (page 247) used in this recipe may be prepared up to 2 weeks before ready to use.

Lunch for 8

Mixed Salad Surprise (page 103)
Chicken and Oyster Lasagna Rolls (page 188)
Glazed Peaches with Raspberry Cream (page 272)

Preparation Tips:
1. Prepare Chicken and Oyster Lasagna Rolls* 50 minutes before ready to serve.
2. Prepare Mixed Salad Surprise† 20 minutes before ready to serve.
3. Prepare Glazed Peaches with Raspberry Cream 12 minutes before ready to serve.

* If you are not allowed shellfish, substitute 1 half chicken breast, skinned, boned, and cubed in Step 3 of this recipe.
† The Oil and Vinegar Dressing (page 254) used in this recipe may be prepared any time before ready to use.

Lunch for 8

Baked Snapper (page 123)
Potato and Green Salad (page 102)
Apples Baked in Cranberry-Coconut Sauce (page 270)

Preparation Tips:
1. Prepare Baked Snapper through Step 1, 2 hours and 15 minutes before ready to serve.
2. Prepare Apples Baked in Cranberry-Coconut Sauce through Step 7, 80 minutes before ready to serve.
3. Prepare Potato and Green Bean Salad* 1 hour before ready to serve.
4. Finish preparation of Apples Baked in Cranberry-Coconut Sauce 40 minutes before ready to serve.
5. Finish preparation of Baked Snapper 20 minutes before ready to serve.

* The Italian Vinaigrette (page 254) used in this recipe may be prepared any time before ready to use.

Dinner for 4

Beet Salad (page 97)
Chicken Milano (page 147)
Basil Rice and Leeks (page 198)
Carrots in Orange Wine (page 220)
Lemony Coconut Cake (page 266)

Preparation Tips:
1. Prepare Lemony Coconut Cake at least 2 hours before ready to serve. *Note:* Cake may be prepared up to 1 week before serving and will keep 2 weeks.
2. Prepare Chicken Milano 1 hour before ready to serve.
3. Prepare Carrots in Orange Wine 45 minutes before ready to serve.
4. Prepare Basil Rice and Leeks 25 minutes before ready to serve.
5. Prepare Beet Salad 5 minutes before ready to serve.

Dinner for 4

Lemon-Mint Artichokes (page 214)
Veal Como (page 176)
Shells with Mushroom-Cheese Sauce (page 191)
Braised Fennel in Wine (page 226)
Fruit-Filled Log (page 265)

Preparation Tips:
1. Prepare Fruit-Filled Log at least 2 hours before ready to serve. *Note:* Log may be prepared up to 2 days before serving and will keep up to 3 weeks if refrigerated.
2. Prepare Lemon-Mint Artichokes 1 hour and 15 minutes before ready to serve.
3. Prepare Braised Fennel in Wine through Step 1, 45 minutes before ready to serve.

4. Prepare Mushroom-Cheese Sauce* through Step 3, ½ hour before ready to serve.
5. Prepare Veal Como through Step 3, ½ hour before ready to serve.
6. Finish preparation of Braised Fennel in Wine 20 minutes before ready to serve.
7. Continue preparation of Veal Como through Step 4, 20 minutes before ready to serve.
8. Continue preparation of Shells with Mushroom-Cheese Sauce 15 minutes before ready to serve.
9. Finish preparation of Veal Como 10 minutes before ready to serve.
10. Finish preparation of Shells with Mushroom-Cheese Sauce immediately before serving.

* Make ½ the recipe.

Dinner for 8

Cauliflower Salad (page 98)
Rosemary Chicken with Green Peppercorns (page 153)
Rice Primavera (page 202)
Apples Baked in Cranberry-Coconut Sauce (page 270)

Preparation Tips:
1. Prepare Apples Baked in Cranberry-Coconut Sauce through Step 7, 1½ hours before ready to serve.
2. Prepare Rosemary Chicken with Green Peppercorns through Step 1, 55 minutes before ready to serve.
3. Prepare Rice Primavera* through Step 3, 45 minutes before ready to serve.
4. Continue preparation of Rosemary Chicken with Green Peppercorns through Step 2, 45 minutes before ready to serve.
5. Finish preparation of Apples Baked in Cranberry-Coconut Sauce 40 minutes before ready to serve.
6. Finish preparation of Rosemary Chicken with Green Peppercorns 40 minutes before ready to serve.

* The Chicken Stock (page 64) used in this recipe may be prepared up to 1 week before ready to use.

7. Finish preparation of Rice Primavera 35 minutes before ready to serve.
8. Prepare Cauliflower Salad† 25 minutes before ready to serve.

† The Hot Sausage (page 171) used in this recipe may be prepared up to 6 months before ready to use. The Oil and Vinegar Dressing (page 254) used in this recipe may be prepared any time before ready to use.

Dinner for 8

Braised Arugola Salad (page 96)
Fish Soup (page 68)
Spaghetti with Mustard-Garlic Sauce (page 256)
Buttery Green Beans with Mushrooms (page 227)
Nut Cake (page 267)

Preparation Tips:
1. Prepare Nut Cake up to 2 days before ready to serve. *Note:* Leftover cake will keep up to 3 weeks if refrigerated; up to 2 months, if frozen.
2. Prepare Fish Soup* through Step 4, 2 hours and 10 minutes before ready to serve.
3. In Dutch oven, boil ¾ pound spaghetti in 2 quarts water† 15 minutes before ready to serve. Drain. Set aside.
4. Prepare Buttery Green Beans with Mushrooms through Step 4, 15 minutes before ready to serve.
5. Finish preparation of Fish Soup 10 minutes before ready to serve.
6. Prepare Braised Arugola Salad 7 minutes before ready to serve.
7. Finish preparation of Buttery Green Beans with Mushrooms immediately before serving.
8. Toss spaghetti with Mustard-Garlic Sauce‡ immediately before serving.

* The Chicken Stock (page 64) used in this recipe may be prepared up to 1 week before ready to use. If you are not allowed shellfish, substitute ½ pound cod, cut in 1-inch chunks, in Step 5.
† Do not add salt to water.
‡ The Mustard-Garlic Sauce (page 256) used in this recipe may be prepared any time before ready to use.

Buffet for 12

Mushrooms in Mustard Marinade (page 48)
Italian Coleslaw (page 102)
Braised Pork (page 173)
Baked Cod Venezia (page 118)
Rice in Wine-Caper Sauce (page 201)
Nut Balls (page 268)

Preparation Tips:
1. Prepare Mushrooms in Mustard Marinade* up to 2 weeks before ready to serve.
2. Prepare Italian Coleslaw† at least 4 hours before ready to serve. Keep refrigerated until ready to serve.
3. Prepare Nut Balls at least 3 hours before ready to serve. *Note:* Nut Balls may be prepared the day before serving and will keep up to 1 month.
4. Prepare Braised Pork through Step 3, 2 hours before ready to serve.
5. Prepare Baked Cod Venezia‡ through Step 5, 40 minutes before ready to serve.
6. Prepare Rice in Wine-Caper Sauce§ 35 minutes before ready to serve.
7. Finish preparation of Braised Pork ½ hour before ready to serve.
8. Finish preparation of Baked Cod Venezia 20 minutes before ready to serve.

* The Mustard-Garlic Sauce (page 256) used in this recipe may be prepared any time before ready to use.
† The Sausage Sicilian (page 172) used in this recipe may be prepared up to 6 months before ready to use. The Herbed Mayonnaise Dressing (page 257) used in this recipe may be prepared any time before ready to use.
‡ Triple the recipe.
§ The Wine-Caper Sauce (page 251) used in this recipe may be prepared up to 2 weeks before ready to use.

Buffet for 16

Potato and Green Bean Salad (page 187)
Chicken and Artichokes (page 140)
Tender Meat Balls (page 167)
with Tomato Sauce I (page 242)
Tomato-Plum Relish (page 62)
Glazed Oranges with Raspberry Cream (page 272)

Preparation Tips:
1. Prepare Tomato Sauce I* 2 days before ready to use. Keep refrigerated until ready to use.
2. Prepare Tomato-Plum Relish the day before ready to use. Keep refrigerated until ready to serve. *Note:* This relish may be prepared and refrigerated up to 3 months before ready to use.
3. Prepare Potato and Green Bean Salad† 2 hours before serving. Cover and refrigerate until ready to serve.
4. Prepare Tender Meat Balls‡ with Tomato Sauce I 1½ hours before ready to serve.
5. Prepare Chicken and Artichokes‡ 1 hour before ready to serve.
6. Prepare Glazed Oranges with Raspberry Cream† 15 minutes before ready to serve.

* The Tomato Sauce I (page 242) used in this recipe may be prepared up to 2 weeks before ready to use.
† Double the recipe. The Italian Vinaigrette (page 254) used in this recipe may be prepared any time before ready to use.
‡ Double the recipe.

‹———›✦‹———›

Buffet for 24

Baked Stuffed Mushrooms (page 47)
Chicken and Caper Salad (page 115)
Shrimp in Spicy Tomato Sauce (page 135)
Rice and Sausage (page 198)
Mixed Fruit Cobbler (page 264)

Preparation Tips:
1. Prepare Chicken and Caper Salad* through Step 4, 2 hours and 20 minutes before ready to serve.
2. Prepare Baked Stuffed Mushrooms through Step 5, 1 hour before ready to serve.
3. Prepare Mixed Fruit Cobbler 45 minutes before ready to serve.
4. Prepare Rice and Sausage† through Step 4, ½ hour before ready to serve.
5. Prepare Shrimp in Spicy Tomato Sauce‡ through Step 4, ½ hour before ready to serve.
6. Finish preparation of Baked Stuffed Mushrooms 20 minutes before ready to serve.
7. Finish preparation of Rice and Sausage 10 minutes before ready to serve.
8. Finish preparation of Shrimp in Spicy Tomato Sauce 3 minutes before ready to serve.
9. Finish preparation of Chicken and Caper Salad immediately before ready to serve.

* Triple the recipe.
† Triple the recipe. The Meat Stock (page 65) used in this recipe may be prepared up to 1 week before ready to use. The Sausage Napoli (page 172) used in this recipe may be prepared up to 6 months before ready to use.
‡ Double the recipe. If you are not allowed shellfish, substitute 3 pounds snapper fillets in Step 1 and increase cooking time to 15 minutes in Step 5 of this recipe.

* ➤◆◀ *

Cocktails for 16

Zucchini Strips (page 48)
Broiled Chicken Wings in Tomato Sauce (page 54)
Rosemary Lamb Kebobs (page 58)
Salmon Spread (page 53)
Garlic Bread (page 80)

Preparation Tips:
1. Prepare Salmon Spread the day before serving. Cover and refrigerate until ready to use.
2. Prepare Rosemary Lamb Kebobs* through Step 1, 1½ hours before ready to serve.
3. Prepare Garlic Bread† 25 minutes before ready to serve.
4. Prepare Boiled Chicken Wings in Tomato Sauce‡ 20 minutes before ready to serve.
5. Finish preparation of Rosemary Lamb Kebobs 15 minutes before ready to serve.
6. Prepare Zucchini Strips 5 minutes before ready to serve.

* Triple the recipe.
† The Basic Italian White Bread (page 82) used in the recipe may be prepared the day before ready to use and will keep up to 2 weeks if refrigerated.
‡ Triple the recipe. The Tomato Sauce I (page 242) used in this recipe may be prepared up to 2 weeks before ready to use.

Cocktails for 24

Antipasto Mixed Fry (page 46)
with Hot Sauce (page 250)
Sweet Pepper-Stuffed Eggs (page 50)
Marinated Chopped Beef (page 56)
Spiced Apple Relish (page 61)
Herbed Vegetable Bread (page 83)

Preparation Tips:
1. Prepare Spiced Apple Relish the day before ready to use. Keep refrigerated until ready to serve. *Note:* This relish may be prepared and refrigerated up to 3 months before ready to use.
2. Prepare Hot Sauce up to 2 weeks before ready to use.
3. Prepare Herbed Vegetable Bread the day before ready to serve. *Note:* Leftover bread will keep up to 2 weeks if refrigerated.
4. Prepare Marinated Chopped Beef through Step 2 up to 24 hours before ready to serve.
5. Prepare Sweet Pepper-Stuffed Eggs* at least 4 hours before serving. Cover and refrigerate until ready to use.
6. Slice each loaf of Herbed Vegetable Bread into 18 slices. Then quarter each slice and set out 1 hour before ready to serve.
7. Finish preparation of Marinated Chopped Beef ½ hour before ready to serve.
8. Prepare Antipasto Mixed Fry 25 minutes before ready to serve.

* Double the recipe.

➤➤◆◀— ◆

Cocktails for 32

Sweet Pickled Vegetables (page 45)
Fried Cheese Puffs (page 60)
Garlic Shrimp (page 52)
Melon and Pork (page 58)
Chicken-Stuffed Eggplant (page 225)

Preparation Tips:
1. Prepare Sweet Pickled Vegetables up to 1 week before ready to use. *Note:* Leftover vegetables will keep indefinitely if refrigerated.
2. Prepare Fried Cheese Puffs through Step 3 at least 3 hours before ready to serve.
3. Prepare Chicken-Stuffed Eggplant through Step 8, 1½ hours before ready to serve.
4. Continue preparation of Fried Cheese Puffs through Step 9, 1 hour before ready to serve.
5. Continue preparation of Chicken-Stuffed Eggplant through Step 9, 45 minutes before ready to serve.
6. Prepare Melon and Pork* through Step 1, 40 minutes before ready to serve.
7. Prepare Garlic Shrimp† 25 minutes before ready to serve.
8. Finish preparation of Chicken-Stuffed Eggplant 15 minutes before ready to serve as follows: Cut each eggplant half in half and quarter each half.
9. Finish preparation of Fried Cheese Puffs 10 minutes before ready to serve.
10. Finish preparation of Melon and Pork immediately before serving.

* The Braised Pork (page 173) used in this recipe should be prepared, covered, and refrigerated the day before ready to use.
† Triple the recipe. If you are not allowed shellfish, substitute 3 pounds swordfish steak, cut into 1-inch chunks, in Step 2 of this recipe and increase cooking time to 10 minutes, turning chunks occasionally.

An Italian Diet

A healthy diet has many objectives:

- to reduce (or gain) weight.
- to maintain a desired weight.
- to address specific medical problems.

To help the dieter it should:

- be easy to follow.
- be adaptable on an on-going basis.
- offer a variety of interesting, good-tasting dishes.

Quite a list—but one which, believe it or not, a diet of Italian food meets on every count.

That Italian food is delicious was never in dispute. But whether it was nutritious was in question, and to think of it as diet food was, well, unthinkable. The reason for this prejudice was clear. Any cuisine based on pasta, pizza, olive oil, and sauces had to be fattening.

Nothing could be more wrong. The pasta and, for that matter, the rice which provide bulk in the Italian diet are excellent sources of fiber which we now know is so good for us. Moreover, the abundance of fresh vegetables, served daily at every Italian table, provide additional natural fiber, vitamins, and minerals.

These complex carbohydrates give the body energy. They fuel the brain; they help metabolize fat. No wonder, then, that athletes, like tennis star, Martina Navratilova, attribute much of their winning styles to a combination of proper exercise and high-fiber diets. In fact, complex carbohydrates should make up one half to two thirds of our daily fare.

So, contrary to popular belief, carbohydrates are not fattening at all. In fact, an average portion of pasta or rice, or a potato, all contain fewer calories than ½ cup of cottage cheese. Yet carbohydrates are the one group most fad diets eliminate. While it is true that many of these diets produce weight loss, they do so at great potential risk to the body because they concentrate on an excessive amount of protein.

Too much protein strains the body's vital organs, especially the kidneys, and forces excessive loss of water, and with it, key nutrients, including potassium and calcium. Dehydration can result, along with a form of toxicity known as ketosis. In the most severe cases, such as those brought on by liquid protein diets, death can result.

Of course, some protein is important. It helps build bones and tone muscle, and should account for 20 to 25 percent of the food you eat each day. Meat, poultry, and fish are high in protein, but as good as they are, about 6 ounces are all you need to meet your daily requirement.

Here, too, Italian food fits the bill because traditionally protein is usually served in small amounts, to leave ample room for the pasta or rice and vegetables. Moreover, the emphasis is always on lean meats, poultry, and seafood.

Like Mexico, the subject of our last book, Italy is surrounded by waters abounding in seafood. Not surprisingly, *la frutta da mare* is served at one or more meals daily, perfect for dieters because fish is not only high in protein but also low in calories, fat, and sodium. In addition, it is an important source of calcium.

Shellfish is another matter. Their sodium content is generally too high for low-sodium dieters, and their high iodine levels produce allergic reactions in many people.

In Italy, the ways in which poultry and meat are prepared eliminate excess fat, an excellent practice because animal fats are saturated and can raise the blood cholesterol. Although fats are a dietary necessity and should make up 25 to 30 percent of our daily food intake, they should be primarily polyunsaturated or monounsaturated fats, which are usually vegetable derivatives.

Fats supply concentrated energy to the body and, quite literally, grease the way for the ingestion of other nutrients. What is more, the right fats (those noted above) may have positive health benefits.

Scientists have long observed that people of Greek and Italian origin have lower blood cholesterol levels than many other nationalities, and a corresponding lower rate of heart disease. Studies now suggest that the use of olive oil, a monounsaturated fat, is the probable cause. This is a valuable finding because at one time monounsaturated fats were not thought to have any effect on blood cholesterol.

Research studies at the University of Texas Health Science Center in Dallas indicate otherwise. Scott Grundy, a physician with a doctorate in biochemistry, conducted the research which indicates that not only may monounsaturated fats be better for you than polyunsaturated fats but also that they may be so in slightly higher quantities.

With regard to Italian food, let us review whether it satisfies the objectives of a healthy diet, stated earlier. Can Italian food help you lose, gain, or maintain weight? The answer is yes. Can it be appropriate for those with special dietary needs? Both intrinsically and with the help of this book, the answer again is yes. Is an Italian diet easy to follow and is it adaptable? Yes, because Italian cuisine uses the simplest foods and cooking methods along with uncomplicated, basic seasonings. Does it offer variety and good taste? Without doubt.

There is one thing more. The best eating pattern is one based on small meals and nutritious between-meal snacks. Most Italians practice *la nuova cucina*, the Italian version of *nouvelle cuisine*. What is more, the Italian propensity for snacks throughout the day provides healthy bursts of carbohydrate energy.

A diet of Italian food succeeds on every level, being at once varied enough to inspire continuation and easy to assimilate into your life-style. However, beyond any dietary basics, there are some additional considerations which everyone with special requirements must remember. So we would like to restate some of the guidelines offered in *The Mexican Salt-Free Diet Cookbook*:

Those of us with hypertension, cardiovascular disease, arteriosclerosis, kidney dysfunction, or edema must limit not only our salt intake but fat and calories as well. Those who have hypoglycemia or diabetes must monitor and control their sugar and/or complex carbohydrate consumption, and must also be prudent about fat, salt, and calories.

The easiest and wisest way to address our individual and, in some instances, mutual requirements is to follow a balanced and healthy eating program—the common denominator being the avoidance of weight gain.

You are probably thinking, Easier said than done. Indeed, which one of us has not experienced the physical and emotional rigors of dieting. Bland, tasteless food, predictable, inflexible routines, and chronic hunger pains eventually lead to cheating or total abandonment of the diet. In short, most diets are a perfect Catch-22, wickedly designed to trap us into failure.

However, history does not have to repeat itself because, with minor adjustments, Italian food is excellent for dieters, whatever their concerns may be. As we explained, the nutritional basics are there, and, happily, the variety of taste experiences in Italian cuisine will take the onus off dieting—so much so, it will not seem like dieting at all. With a minor change here and there, an Italian diet will help you to easily make the transition to a healthier, happier, and thinner way of life.

As for the particulars, using the recipes in this book, we have prepared a diet based on the following:

1. *Two weeks' duration* because it takes at least this long for your palate to adjust to the absence of salt and to appreciate new flavors. After the initial two-week period, you can repeat the basic plan with different dishes.

2. *Under 1,200 calories* to show you how much food and satisfaction you can have and still lose weight.

   To determine the proper calorie level for yourself, keep the following points in mind:

   • If you want to maintain your weight, multiply your ideal weight by 13.5 to determine your daily calorie level.

   • If you want to lose weight—or gain it for that matter— just remember that slowly and steadily is the safest, healthiest way to reach and hold onto your goal. That translates to a one-and-a-half-pound gain or loss over a two-week period.

   Add to that the knowledge that 3,500 calories equal one pound. So if you cut out 250 calories per day, you will lose that pound in 14 days; add the same 250 calories, you will gain that pound in the prescribed time.

3. *Under 500 milligrams sodium* to prove how easy it is to live and dine happily and deliciously on a so-called restricted diet.

   If your sodium limits—self-imposed or otherwise—are more liberal, consult a sodium guide (some of which are listed in this book's bibliography) to see what additional options are available to you.

   For example, if you love calf's liver or shrimp, enjoy them. Just remember to stay within your limits and not to exceed 1,500 milligrams per day, more than enough sodium for anyone.

   If, like me, you must get by with less than 500 milligrams

sodium per day, just replace all shellfish on the menu with meat, poultry, or another fish. Or delete some dairy products. It is just that simple.

At the end of these two weeks, we hope you will realize that a diet is neither a curse nor a punishment. It is not one of life's aberrations but rather the way of life which is healthiest and best for you. And, as we hope you now realize, Italian food is one of the healthiest, as well as tastiest, life-styles you can follow.

Note: The menus on the following pages were specifically designed for the salt-free dieter. Thus, if you do use sugar substitutes, please be sure they are not only sugar-free but low-sodium (calcium saccharin or Nutra-Sweet) as well.

In addition, much consideration was given to the needs of those with diabetes, which accounts for the carbohydrate snacks throughout the day. (By the way, deliciously healthy, energy-releasing snacking is good for all of us and helps cut down the urge to splurge.) But if you are a diabetic, pass on sugary desserts and, in fact, check this program with your own doctor or nutritionist to see if adjustments are necessary.

One final word. Read the entire diet before you begin. It contains a lot of tips, such as using leftovers and switching meals, designed to save you time and work, and make it both easy and pleasant for you to stick to your goal.

TIPS FOR DAY ONE

You are about to start an unforgettable, unbelievable experience—a diet of fettuccine and tomato sauce, cheese dressings and creamy desserts. That is, in the next two weeks, you are going to discover that even so-called fattening Italian food can be slimming, as well as nutritious and delicious.

Sound good? Well, there is more. You will see that with a little common sense, a little discipline, and an appreciation as well as an enjoyment of food, you can drop the word "diet" from your vocabulary forever.

The fact is once you reach your desired weight and learn the few guidelines we have outlined on nutrition, healthy eating in all its tasty variations will be an automatic and pleasurable way of life for you.

We are almost ready to begin. Just a few final hints:

1. Do not skip meals or snacks. Diet does not mean deprivation, and the body needs regular doses of nourishment and energy.
2. Relax. The best way to lose weight and keep it off is slow but steady. So, let it happen, and like the fictitious tortoise, you will win the race looking and feeling good.
3. Have fun. Good-tasting food is not synonymous with fattening. At the end of these two weeks, you *will* see a slimmer you in the mirror.

	Calories	Sodium (mg.)	Carbo-hydrates (gm.)	Fat (gm.)
BREAKFAST				
3½ ounces orange juice	46.0	1.0	10.3	0.3
1 soft-boiled egg	78.0	55.0	0.4	4.3
1 slice Herbed Vegetable Bread*	168.7	5.1	30.7	2.7
Coffee or tea	—	—	—	—
1 teaspoon sugar substitute	2.0	0	1.4	0
1 tablespoon low-fat milk	6.3	7.1	0.75	0.1
Total	301.0	68.2	43.55	7.4
LUNCH				
Chicken in Wine*	200.1	58.4	5.3	7.6
1 cup steamed green beans	32.0	7.0	0.2	7.1
½ tomato, chopped	15.7	2.1	3.4	0.1
Coffee or tea	—	—	—	—
1 teaspoon sugar substitute	2.0	0	1.4	0
1 tablespoon low-fat milk	6.3	7.1	0.75	0.1
Total	256.1	74.6	11.15	14.9
SNACK				
½ ounce low-sodium Cheddar cheese	56.9	6.0	0.3	4.6
2 low-sodium crackers	22.0	1.7	2.9	1.0
Iced tea with lemon	—	—	—	—
Total	78.9	7.7	3.2	5.6

* See index for recipe page number.

	Calories	Sodium (mg.)	Carbo-hydrates (gm.)	Fat (gm.)
DINNER				
1 cup shredded lettuce	18.0	9.0	3.5	0.3
½ tomato, chopped	15.7	2.1	3.4	0.1
¼ cucumber, chopped	41.0	17.7	2.9	0.1
2 tablespoons Honey-Vinegar Dressing*	13.6	1.2	4.0	0
Salmon, Eggplant, and Capers*	151.3	46.9	13.4	5.5
Potatoes Baked in Pungent Basil Sauce*	130.4	18.8	32.8	1.7
Nut Cake*	70.9	6.4	5.7	5.1
Coffee or tea	—	—	—	—
1 teaspoon sugar substitute	2.0	0	1.4	0
1 tablespoon low-fat milk	6.3	7.1	0.75	0.1
Total	449.2	109.2	67.85	12.9
SNACK				
½ cup strawberries	20.8	0.7	5.5	0.3
Grand Total	1,106.0	260.4	131.3	41.1

* See index for recipe page number.

TIPS FOR DAY TWO

After one day of feasting on bread and chicken and salmon and cake, you are probably thinking, "This is my kind of diet." Well, that is the idea, and more good things lie in store for you today and in the days to come.

In the meantime, a few tips: Leftover Herbed Vegetable Bread will keep up to two weeks if refrigerated, and leftover Nut Cake will keep up to three weeks if refrigerated and up to two months if frozen.

Now, for the second day of your trip to a new you.

	Calories	Sodium (mg.)	Carbo-hydrates (gm.)	Fat (gm.)
BREAKFAST				
½ banana	43.0	0.5	11.0	0.1
¼ cup low-sodium cottage cheese	45.0	31.0	4.0	1.0
2 low-sodium crackers	22.0	1.7	2.9	1.0
Coffee or tea	—	—	—	—
1 teaspoon sugar substitute	2.0	0	1.4	0
1 tablespoon low-fat milk	6.3	7.1	0.75	0.1
Total	118.3	40.3	20.05	2.2

	Calories	Sodium (mg.)	Carbo-hydrates (gm.)	Fat (gm.)
LUNCH				
Green Bean and Carrot Salad*	77.6	24.4	6.9	4.3
Salmon, Eggplant, and Capers*	151.3	46.9	13.4	5.5
Coffee or tea	—	—	—	—
1 teaspoon sugar substitute	2.0	0	1.4	0
1 tablespoon low-fat milk	6.3	7.1	0.75	0.1
Total	237.2	78.4	22.45	9.9
SNACK				
1 apple	116.0	12.0	0.6	9.2
DINNER				
Braised Endive Salad*	60.7	19.2	5.9	3.5
Veal and Mushroom Stew*	246.7	82.4	4.9	17.5
Basil Rice and Leeks*	149.3	10.7	30.0	1.7
Pears Baked in Cranberry-Coconut Sauce*	110.1	3.1	20.8	2.4
Coffee or tea	—	—	—	—
1 teaspoon sugar substitute	2.0	0	1.4	0
1 tablespoon low-fat milk	6.3	7.1	0.75	0.1
Total	575.1	122.5	63.75	25.2

* See index for recipe page number.

	Calories	Sodium (mg.)	Carbo-hydrates (gm.)	Fat (gm.)
SNACK				
½ ounce low-sodium Swiss cheese	50.7	4.0	0.3	3.9
2 low-sodium crackers	22.0	1.7	2.9	1.0
Iced tea with lemon	—	—	—	—
Total	77.7	5.7	3.2	4.9
Grand Total	1,124.3	258.9	110.1	51.4

* See index for recipe page number.

TIPS FOR DAY THREE

By now, you should be right in the swing of things. Dieting can be fun. It really is not dieting at all. That is the right attitude. Keep it up. By the way, a little exercise will help you keep your positive energy.

First, exercise will start your adrenalin flowing, giving you a sweet rush of well-being. Second, it will firm your body as you slim down, so you will lose inches as well as weight. Third, exercise decreases your appetite, leaving you easily satisfied by the goodies on your plate.

So take a brisk walk twice a day. Do 15 minutes of stretching in the morning or evening. You will feel as good as today's menu will taste.

As for leftovers: Pears Baked in Cranberry-Coconut Sauce will keep up to one week if refrigerated. Or you can enjoy them tonight in place of Glazed Oranges with Raspberry Cream.

	Calories	Sodium (mg.)	Carbo-hydrates (gm.)	Fat (gm.)
BREAKFAST				
½ cup pineapple	26.0	0.5	6.9	0.1
½ cup oatmeal	62.9	2.0	11.1	1.1
Coffee or tea	—	—	—	—
1 teaspoon sugar substitute	2.0	0	1.4	0
1 tablespoon low-fat milk	6.3	7.1	0.75	0.1
Total	97.2	9.6	20.15	1.2

	Calories	Sodium (mg.)	Carbo-hydrates (gm.)	Fat (gm.)
LUNCH				
1 cup chopped lettuce	18.0	9.0	3.5	0.3
Veal and Mushroom Stew*	246.7	82.4	4.9	17.5
1 cup steamed broccoli	36.6	0.3	6.7	17.1
Coffee or tea	—	—	—	—
1 teaspoon sugar substitute	2.0	0	1.4	0
1 tablespoon low-fat milk	6.3	7.1	0.75	0.1
Total	309.6	98.8	17.25	35.0
SNACK				
½ ounce low-sodium Gouda cheese	56.9	6.0	0.3	4.6
2 low-sodium crackers	22.0	1.7	2.9	1.0
Iced tea with lemon	—	—	—	—
Total	78.9	7.7	3.2	5.6

* See index for recipe page number.

	Calories	Sodium (mg.)	Carbo-hydrates (gm.)	Fat (gm.)
DINNER				
1 cup shredded lettuce	18.0	9.0	3.5	0.3
¼ green pepper, chopped	11.0	6.5	2.4	0.1
2 tablespoons Cucumber Dressing*	38.0	8.4	1.6	2.8
Lemon-Basil Chicken*	221.2	58.2	11.7	7.4
Fettuccine in Parsley-Cream Sauce*	253.1	29.1	35.0	10.6
1 serving low-sodium lime gelatin	9.0	11.0	0	0
Coffee or tea	—	—	—	—
1 teaspoon sugar substitute	2.0	0	1.4	0
1 tablespoon low-fat milk	6.3	7.1	0.75	0.1
Total	558.6	129.3	56.35	21.3
SNACK				
Glazed Oranges with Raspberry Cream*	163.3	5.1	28.2	4.0
Grand Total	1,207.6	250.5	125.2	67.1

* See index for recipe page number.

TIPS FOR DAY FOUR

Today you are halfway through the first week. You are feeling terrific, alert, in control. You feel lighter, tighter, although you might not see a weight loss yet.

Not to worry. It takes time for your body to adjust to its new food signals. But it will. Any day now you'll see that first drop on the scale, and it will be all wonderfully downhill from there.

Note: Leftover Veal and Mushroom Stew may replace the London Broil Vinaigrette for dinner on Day Five, or, if frozen, it may be reheated and replace the Seafood Fettuccine dinner on Day Seven. Otherwise, it will keep up to one month if frozen. Leftover Glazed Oranges with Raspberry Cream will keep up to one week if refrigerated, or can replace the Creamy Rum Fruit dessert on Day Eight.

Now, take a break from your busy day and see that movie you have had on your list for so long. You deserve it.

	Calories	Sodium (mg.)	Carbohydrates (gm.)	Fat (gm.)
BREAKFAST				
3½ ounces apple juice	47.0	1.0	11.9	0.1
1 poached egg	78.0	55.0	0.4	4.3
1 Cheese and Sausage Biscuit*	64.0	7.8	6.5	3.2
Coffee or tea	—	—	—	—
1 teaspoon sugar substitute	2.0	0	1.4	0
1 tablespoon low-fat milk	6.3	7.1	0.75	0.1
Total	197.3	70.9	20.95	7.7

* See index for recipe page number.

	Calories	Sodium (mg.)	Carbo-hydrates (gm.)	Fat (gm.)
LUNCH				
1 cup shredded lettuce	18.0	9.0	3.5	0.3
½ tomato, chopped	15.7	2.1	3.4	0.1
2 tablespoons Creamy Garlic Dressing*	66.4	6.4	1.4	6.8
Lemon-Basil Chicken*	221.2	58.2	11.7	7.4
Coffee or tea	—	—	—	—
1 teaspoon sugar substitute	2.0	0	1.4	0
1 tablespoon low-fat milk	6.3	7.1	0.75	0.1
Total	329.6	82.8	22.15	14.7
SNACK				
1 peach	43.4	1.1	11.1	0.1
DINNER				
Tomato and Mozzarella Salad*	97.9	6.2	6.0	7.1
Swordfish in Pepper-Wine Sauce*	141.2	6.9	2.5	5.7
Stuffed Baked Potatoes*	137.1	20.0	20.9	5.7
Eggplant with Mushrooms*	61.9	10.4	12.1	2.0
1 pear	62.0	2.0	15.3	0.4
Coffee or tea	—	—	—	—
1 teaspoon sugar substitute	2.0	0	1.4	0
1 tablespoon low-fat milk	6.3	7.1	0.75	0.1
Total	508.4	52.6	58.95	21.0

* See index for recipe page number.

	Calories	Sodium (mg.)	Carbo-hydrates (gm.)	Fat (gm.)
SNACK				
½ ounce low-sodium Cheddar cheese	56.9	6.0	0.3	4.6
2 low-sodium crackers	22.0	1.7	2.9	1.0
Iced tea with lemon	—	—	—	—
Total	78.9	7.7	3.2	5.6
Grand Total	1,157.6	215.1	116.4	49.1

TIPS FOR DAY FIVE

By now, you should be bursting with confidence and energy, getting more out of every day. For it is widely known that good eating can improve your emotional as well as your physical state.

No doubt, your food tastes better, too. Not only because you have a healthy appetite, not only because you are eating without guilt, but because your taste buds are adjusting to the lack of salt and you can really taste food for the first time.

Isn't it wonderful?

Leftover Cheese and Sausage Biscuits will keep up to one week, if refrigerated, or can be substituted for the breakfast bread recommendations on Days Seven, Eight, and Ten.

Leftover Stuffed Baked Potatoes can replace the Potato and Green Bean Salad at lunch, or will keep up to three days if refrigerated. Leftover Eggplant with Mushrooms can replace tonight's dinner salad, or the Carrot Soup with Capers on Day Eight.

In other words, with the right foundation, you can also eat what you like when you want to. What could be better?

	Calories	Sodium (mg.)	Carbo-hydrates (gm.)	Fat (gm.)
BREAKFAST				
½ grapefruit	62.9	1.4	16.4	0.14
¼ cup plain yogurt	70.9	53.7	5.6	3.9
1 Cinnamon Fruit Biscuit*	80.2	4.3	15.4	1.4
Coffee or tea	—	—	—	—
1 teaspoon sugar substitute	2.0	0	1.4	0
1 tablespoon low-fat milk	6.3	7.1	0.75	0.1
Total	222.3	66.5	39.55	5.54

* See index for recipe page number.

	Calories	Sodium (mg.)	Carbo-hydrates (gm.)	Fat (gm.)
LUNCH				
1 cup shredded lettuce	18.0	9.0	3.5	0.3
Potato and Green Bean Salad*	138.2	9.4	17.5	7.8
Swordfish in Pepper-Wine Sauce*	141.2	6.9	2.5	5.7
Coffee or tea	—	—	—	—
1 teaspoon sugar substitute	2.0	0	1.4	0
1 tablespoon low-fat milk	6.3	7.1	0.75	0.1
Total	305.7	32.4	25.65	13.9
SNACK				
½ apple	58.0	6.0	0.3	4.6
Iced tea with lemon	—	—	—	—
Total	58.0	6.0	0.3	4.6

	Calories	Sodium (mg.)	Carbo-hydrates (gm.)	Fat (gm.)
DINNER				
1 cup shredded lettuce	18.0	9.0	3.5	0.3
½ tomato, sliced	15.7	2.1	3.4	0.1
¼ green pepper, chopped	11.0	6.5	2.4	0.1
3 tablespoons lemon juice	9.9	0.3	3.3	0
London Broil Vinaigrette*	285.4	76.2	1.4	16.9
½ cup boiled white rice	124.6	0.1	27.7	0.1
Squash Melt*	114.2	7.9	11.3	6.3
Coffee or tea	—	—	—	—
1 teaspoon sugar substitute	2.0	0	1.4	0
1 tablespoon low-fat milk	6.3	7.1	0.75	0.1
Total	587.1	109.2	55.15	23.9
SNACK				
½ cup grapes	39.4	1.7	9.0	0.6
1 serving low-sodium lime gelatin	9.0	11.0	0	0
Total	48.4	12.7	9.0	0.6
Grand Total	1,222.4	226.8	129.7	48.5

* See index for recipe page number.

TIPS FOR DAY SIX

One week is almost over. You know you can do it, and you should, by now, have the added incentive of your first weight loss.

So celebrate. Invite some people in to share your "diet" dinner. You may even indulge in a glass of wine in place of the Nut Cake, and drink a toast. A toast to you.

By the way, if you have to keep your daily sodium intake to 250 milligrams, replace the milk at breakfast with ½ ounce of your favorite low-sodium cheese, and replace the Macaroni and Spinach at dinner with leftover Potato and Green Bean Salad; otherwise, the salad will keep up to one week if refrigerated.

Leftover Cinnamon Fruit Biscuits are a wonderful breakfast bread option on Days Seven, Eight, and Ten, or will keep up to two weeks if refrigerated.

	Calories	Sodium (mg.)	Carbo- hydrates (gm.)	Fat (gm.)
BREAKFAST				
½ cup blueberries	62.0	1.0	15.3	0.5
½ cup oatmeal	62.9	2.0	11.1	1.1
¼ cup low-fat milk	25.0	28.6	3.0	0.5
Coffee or tea	—	—	—	—
1 teaspoon sugar substitute	2.0	0	1.4	0
1 tablespoon low-fat milk	6.3	7.1	0.75	0.1
Total	158.2	38.7	31.55	2.2

* See index for recipe page number.

	Calories	Sodium (mg.)	Carbo-hydrates (gm.)	Fat (gm.)
LUNCH				
Salad Roma* with Wine-Caper Sauce*	92.9	36.9	15.2	1.4
London Broil Vinaigrette*	285.4	76.2	1.4	16.9
Coffee or tea	—	—	—	—
1 teaspoon sugar substitute	2.0	0	1.4	0
1 tablespoon low-fat milk	6.3	7.1	0.75	0.1
Total	386.6	120.2	18.75	18.4
SNACK				
¼ cantaloupe	42.9	17.1	10.7	0.1
DINNER				
1 tomato, sliced	31.4	4.2	6.8	0.2
Chicken and Mushrooms*	190.6	60.4	6.9	7.2
Macaroni and Spinach*	175.0	28.6	32.9	2.0
1 orange	98.0	2.0	24.4	0.4
Coffee or tea	—	—	—	—
1 teaspoon sugar substitute	2.0	0	1.4	0
1 tablespoon low-fat milk	6.3	7.1	0.75	0.1
Total	503.3	102.3	73.15	9.9
SNACK				
Nut Cake*	70.9	6.4	5.7	5.1
Iced tea with lemon	—	—	—	—
Total	70.9	6.4	5.7	5.1
Grand Total	1,184.5	285.1	145.5	35.5

* See index for recipe page number.

TIPS FOR DAY SEVEN

You should be very proud of yourself. You are halfway there. All you have to do today is enjoy yourself, plan something fun, and look forward to the week ahead.

You are in control, and doesn't it feel great.

Speaking of control, if you are not allowed shellfish, replace the shrimp in Seafood Fettuccine with ½ pound red snapper fillets, cut into 1-inch chunks, and add it during Step 3. Your daily sodium count will be reduced by almost 18 milligrams. If that is not enough, replace the breakfast cottage cheese with ½ ounce of your preferred low-sodium cheese or substitute Braised Endive Salad for the Minestrone.

That is all there is to it.

	Calories	Sodium (mg.)	Carbo-hydrates (gm.)	Fat (gm.)
BREAKFAST				
1 peach, pitted and chopped	43.4	1.1	11.1	0.1
¼ cup low-sodium cottage cheese	45.0	31.0	4.0	1.0
1 slice Almond Bread with Aniseed*	124.1	5.1	24.6	2.0
Coffee or tea	—	—	—	—
1 teaspoon sugar substitute	2.0	0	1.4	0
1 tablespoon low-fat milk	6.3	7.1	0.75	0.1
Total	220.8	44.3	41.85	3.2

* See index for recipe page number.

	Calories	Sodium (mg.)	Carbo-hydrates (gm.)	Fat (gm.)
LUNCH				
Italian Coleslaw*	122.1	42.7	12.8	6.8
Chicken and Mushrooms*	190.6	60.4	6.9	7.2
Coffee or tea	—	—	—	—
1 teaspoon sugar substitute	2.0	0	1.4	0
1 tablespoon low-fat milk	6.3	7.1	0.75	0.1
Total	321.0	110.2	21.85	14.1
SNACK				
½ grapefruit	62.9	1.4	16.4	0.14
2 low-sodium crackers	22.0	1.7	2.9	1.0
Total	84.9	3.1	19.3	1.14
DINNER				
Minestrone*	165.2	44.1	19.9	10.1
Seafood Fettuccine*	274.8	73.7	39.1	3.7
Brandied Pears*	118.2	2.7	15.3	0.4
Coffee or tea	—	—	—	—
1 teaspoon sugar substitute	2.0	0	1.4	0
1 tablespoon low-fat milk	6.3	7.1	0.75	0.1
Total	566.5	127.6	76.45	14.3
SNACK				
1 cup low-sodium chicken bouillon	18.0	5.0	2.0	1.0
Grand Total	1,211.2	290.2	161.5	33.7

* See index for recipe page number.

TIPS FOR DAY EIGHT

After the success of your first week, you should be feeling almost smug over your ability to handle Week Two. In fact, since every day has undoubtedly been easier than the day before, this week should be effortless.

How do you like that feeling of power?

If you have leftover Almond Bread with Aniseed, you can sample it again in place of the suggested breakfast breads on Days Eight, Ten, or Fourteen. Or you may keep it up to two weeks if refrigerated.

Leftover Italian Coleslaw can be substituted for the Zucchini, Tomato, and Oyster Salad and steamed broccoli at dinner on Day Nine, or for the Braised Endive Salad at lunch on Day Fourteen. Otherwise, it will keep up to one week if refrigerated.

Leftover Minestrone can also replace the Zucchini, Tomato, and Oyster Salad plus steamed broccoli noted above, or the Squash with Orange-Nut Stuffing at dinner on Day Ten. This soup will also keep up to one week if refrigerated, and up to one month if frozen.

Last, but delectably not least, leftover Brandied Pears will make wonderful substitutes for the late snacks on Days Nine, Eleven, and Twelve. Or they will keep up to one week if refrigerated.

As for your daily sodium requirement, if you need to keep it to 250 milligrams per day, forego your breakfast egg. That plus the previously suggested variation for the Seafood Fettuccine, explained on page 309, will do the job.

	Calories	Sodium (mg.)	Carbo-hydrates (gm.)	Fat (gm.)
BREAKFAST				
½ cup strawberries	20.8	0.7	5.5	0.3
1 soft-boiled egg	78.0	55.0	0.4	4.3
1 slice Dilled Cheese Bread*	99.7	6.7	14.4	2.7
Coffee or tea	—	—	—	—
1 teaspoon sugar substitute	2.0	0	1.4	0
1 tablespoon low-fat milk	6.3	7.1	0.75	0.1
Total	206.8	69.5	22.45	7.4
LUNCH				
1 cup shredded lettuce	18.0	9.0	3.5	0.3
½ tomato, chopped	15.7	2.1	3.4	0.1
¼ green pepper, chopped	11.0	6.5	2.4	0.1
2 tablespoons lemon juice	6.6	0.2	2.2	0
Seafood Fettuccine*	274.8	73.7	39.1	3.7
Coffee or tea	—	—	—	—
1 teaspoon sugar substitute	2.0	0	1.4	0
1 tablespoon low-fat milk	6.3	7.1	0.75	0.1
Total	334.4	98.6	52.75	4.3
SNACK				
½ ounce low-sodium Gouda cheese	56.9	6.0	0.3	4.6
2 low-sodium crackers	22.0	1.7	2.9	1.0
Iced tea with lemon	—	—	—	—
Total	78.9	7.7	3.2	5.6

* See index for recipe page number.

	Calories	Sodium (mg.)	Carbo-hydrates (gm.)	Fat (gm.)
DINNER				
Carrot Soup with Capers*	99.9	56.6	14.3	4.3
Basil and Tarragon Pork Salad*	230.7	58.4	6.7	16.7
Creamy Rum Fruit*	174.8	18.1	14.7	11.4
Coffee or tea	—	—	—	—
1 teaspoon sugar substitute	2.0	0	1.4	0
1 tablespoon low-fat milk	6.3	7.1	0.75	0.1
Total	513.7	140.2	37.85	32.5
SNACK				
1 tomato, sliced	31.4	4.2	6.8	0.2
Iced tea with lemon	—	—	—	—
Total	31.4	4.2	6.8	0.2
Grand Total	1,165.2	320.2	123.1	50.0

* See index for recipe page number.

TIPS FOR DAY NINE

By now, you should be a believer. The good life is everything it is supposed to be and more. Good eating. Good living. Good feeling. Good looking.

And since things are going so well, why not start planning now for the celebration you are going to have in just a few more days.

Leftover Dilled Cheese Bread can replace the breakfast bread selections on Days Ten and Fourteen, or will keep up to two weeks if refrigerated. In addition, any remaining Creamy Rum Fruit can replace either tonight's late-night snack, or that on Day Eleven. Otherwise, it will keep up to one week if refrigerated.

	Calories	Sodium (mg.)	Carbo- hydrates (gm.)	Fat (gm.)
BREAKFAST				
½ cup pineapple	26.0	0.5	6.9	0.1
½ cup oatmeal	62.9	2.0	11.1	1.1
Coffee or tea	—	—	—	—
1 teaspoon sugar substitute	2.0	0	1.4	0
1 tablespoon low-fat milk	6.3	7.1	0.75	0.1
Total	97.2	9.6	20.15	1.3

* See index for recipe page number.

	Calories	Sodium (mg.)	Carbo-hydrates (gm.)	Fat (gm.)
LUNCH				
Basil and Tarragon Pork Salad*	230.7	58.4	6.7	16.7
¼ cup Spiced Apple Relish*	61.6	5.9	16.4	0.3
Coffee or tea	—	—	—	—
1 teaspoon sugar substitute	2.0	0	1.4	0
1 tablespoon low-fat milk	6.3	7.1	0.75	0.1
Total	300.6	71.4	25.25	20.1
SNACK				
½ ounce low-sodium mozzarella cheese	42.5	4.3	0.3	3.5
½ tomato, sliced	15.7	2.1	3.4	0.1
2 low-sodium crackers	22.0	1.7	2.9	1.0
Iced tea with lemon	—	—	—	—
Total	80.2	8.1	6.6	4.6

	Calories	Sodium (mg.)	Carbo-hydrates (gm.)	Fat (gm.)
DINNER				
Zucchini, Tomato, and Oyster Salad*	104.4	42.3	11.2	3.5
Honey-Vinegar Baked Chicken*	186.4	60.5	26.5	2.5
Creamy Garlic Potatoes*	121.1	11.1	20.4	4.0
1 cup steamed broccoli	36.6	0.3	6.7	17.1
Coffee or tea	—	—	—	—
1 teaspoon sugar substitute	2.0	0	1.4	0
1 tablespoon low-fat milk	6.3	7.1	0.75	0.1
Total	456.8	121.3	66.95	27.2
SNACK				
Italian Cheese Pie*	209.0	20.0	23.3	9.1
1 peach	43.4	1.1	11.1	0.1
Iced tea with lemon	—	—	—	—
Total	252.4	21.1	34.3	9.2
Grand Total	1,187.2	231.5	153.3	62.4

* See index for recipe page number.

TIPS FOR DAY TEN

You are on the home stretch, and you probably do feel you could race a mile. Perhaps you already have. Do I detect a smile? Well, good for you.

Leftover Spiced Apple Relish will keep up to three months if refrigerated. Any extra Creamy Garlic Potatoes would be a tasty alternate to the Hot Sauce Shells planned for dinner on Day Eleven, or will keep up to three days if refrigerated. And if there is any Italian Cheese Pie left, it will keep up to one week if refrigerated.

You see? All these tasty foods are offering you a head start on next week's menu planning.

One thing more: If you are not allowed shellfish, eliminate the oysters from the evening's Zucchini, Tomato, and Oyster Salad, or replace the entire salad with the Minestrone left over from Day Seven.

	Calories	Sodium (mg.)	Carbo-hydrates (gm.)	Fat (gm.)
BREAKFAST				
½ cup blueberries	62.0	1.0	15.3	0.5
¼ cup low-sodium cottage cheese	45.0	31.0	4.0	1.0
1 slice Italian Flat Bread* with walnuts	141.4	1.6	22.3	3.7
Coffee or tea	—	—	—	—
1 teaspoon sugar substitute	2.0	0	1.4	0
1 tablespoon low-fat milk	6.3	7.1	0.75	0.1
Total	256.7	40.7	43.75	5.3

* See index for recipe page number.

	Calories	Sodium (mg.)	Carbo-hydrates (gm.)	Fat (gm.)
LUNCH				
Chicken and Caper Salad*	206.1	74.1	10.6	9.8
1 plum	66.0	2.0	0.2	11.9
Coffee or tea	—	—	—	—
1 teaspoon sugar substitute	2.0	0	1.4	0
1 tablespoon low-fat milk	6.3	7.1	0.75	0.1
Total	280.4	83.2	12.95	21.8
SNACK				
¼ cup Spiced Eggplant Relish*	48.5	6.0	13.0	0.7
2 low-sodium crackers	22.0	1.7	2.9	1.0
Iced tea with lemon	—	—	—	—
Total	70.5	7.7	15.9	1.7
DINNER				
Flounder in Cheesy Dill Sauce*	164.2	74.4	3.6	8.7
Rice, Cabbage, and Sweet Peppers*	198.2	30.4	40.2	1.8
Squash with Orange-Nut Stuffing*	123.2	0.6	25.7	3.7
Coffee or tea	—	—	—	—
1 teaspoon sugar substitute	2.0	0	1.4	0

* See index for recipe page number.

	Calories	Sodium (mg.)	Carbo-hydrates (gm.)	Fat (gm.)
1 tablespoon low-fat milk	6.3	7.1	0.75	0.1
Total	493.9	112.5	71.65	14.3

SNACK

	Calories	Sodium (mg.)	Carbo-hydrates (gm.)	Fat (gm.)
1 serving low-sodium lime gelatin	9.0	11.0	0	0
Grand Total	1,110.5	255.1	144.3	43.1

* See index for recipe page number.

TIPS FOR DAY ELEVEN

So, what is it going to be? A trip to the Caribbean to show off that svelte body of yours? A new outfit you have had your eye on? Whatever you choose, just remember two things: Your reward is only a few days away, and you have definitely earned it.

Lots of leftovers to consider. First, leftover Italian Flat Bread can replace the Potato Bread for brunch on Day Fourteen. Or it will keep up to one week if refrigerated.

Extra Chicken and Capers Salad will make a lovely, light substitute for the Stuffed Burgers at lunch on Day Twelve, or it will keep up to four days if refrigerated.

Any remaining Spiced Eggplant Relish will keep up to three months if refrigerated. Lastly, leftover Squash with Orange-Nut Stuffing may replace today's luncheon salad and dressing, or will keep up to two days if refrigerated.

If today's sodium total is too high for you, replace your morning egg with ¼ cup low-sodium cottage cheese or ½ cup oatmeal.

Keep it up. Only three more days.

	Calories	Sodium (mg.)	Carbo-hydrates (gm.)	Fat (gm.)
BREAKFAST				
3½ ounces tomato juice	19.0	3.0	4.3	0.1
1 poached egg	78.0	55.0	0.4	4.3
1 Cheese and Sausage Biscuit*	64.0	7.8	6.5	3.2
Coffee or tea	—	—	—	—
1 teaspoon sugar substitute	2.0	0	1.4	0
1 tablespoon low-fat milk	6.3	7.1	0.75	0.1
Total	169.3	72.9	13.35	7.7

* See index for recipe page number.

	Calories	Sodium (mg.)	Carbo-hydrates (gm.)	Fat (gm.)
LUNCH				
1 cup shredded lettuce	18.0	9.0	3.5	0.3
¼ green pepper, chopped	11.0	6.5	2.4	0.1
2 tablespoons Cucumber Dressing*	38.0	8.4	1.6	2.8
Flounder in Cheesy Dill Sauce*	164.2	74.4	3.6	8.7
Coffee or tea	—	—	—	—
1 teaspoon sugar substitute	2.0	0	1.4	0
1 tablespoon low-fat milk	6.3	7.1	0.75	0.1
Total	239.5	105.4	13.25	12.0
SNACK				
1 banana	86.0	1.0	22.0	0.2
Iced tea with lemon	—	—	—	—
Total	86.0	1.0	22.0	0.2

	Calories	Sodium (mg.)	Carbo-hydrates (gm.)	Fat (gm.)
DINNER				
1 cup shredded lettuce	18.0	9.0	3.5	0.3
½ tomato, chopped	15.7	2.1	3.4	0.1
2 tablespoons Honey-Vinegar Dressing*	13.6	1.2	4.0	0
Stuffed Burgers*	307.3	48.4	5.9	19.2
Hot Sauce Shells*	136.7	9.2	30.0	0.7
1 cup steamed green beans	32.0	7.0	0.2	7.1
Coffee or tea	—	—	—	—
1 teaspoon sugar substitute	2.0	0	1.4	0
1 tablespoon low-fat milk	6.3	7.1	0.75	0.1
Total	531.6	84.0	49.15	27.5
SNACK				
Glazed Oranges with Raspberry Cream*	163.3	5.1	28.2	4.0
Iced tea with lemon	—	—	—	—
Total	163.3	5.1	28.2	4.0
Grand Total	1,189.7	268.4	126.0	51.4

* See index for recipe page number.

TIPS FOR DAY TWELVE

Excited? The finish line is in sight, and you are just hitting your stride. You are in complete control. And free to be happy, healthy, and thin on your own terms.

So get ready for the next two weeks and the weeks after. Put your own menus together to fit your lifestyle and your tastes. You can do it. What is more, you know you can.

Maybe some of today's leftovers will give you a few ideas. For example, leftover Cheese and Sausage Biscuits can replace the oatmeal at breakfast on Day Thirteen, or the morning Potato Bread on Day Fourteen. Leftover Hot Sauce Shells can substitute for Spaghetti in Spicy Green Sauce at dinner on Day Thirteen, or will keep up to three days if refrigerated.

If it is necessary to lower today's sodium count, we are sure you know by now how easily that can be done. Simply replace the morning yogurt with ½ ounce of the low-sodium cheese you prefer.

	Calories	Sodium (mg.)	Carbo-hydrates (gm.)	Fat (gm.)
BREAKFAST				
½ grapefruit	62.9	1.4	16.4	0.14
¼ cup plain yogurt	70.9	53.7	5.6	3.9
2 low-sodium crackers	22.0	1.7	2.9	1.0
Coffee or tea	—	—	—	—
1 teaspoon sugar substitute	2.0	0	1.4	0
1 tablespoon low-fat milk	6.3	7.1	0.75	0.1
Total	164.1	63.9	27.05	5.14

* See index for recipe page number.

	Calories	Sodium (mg.)	Carbo-hydrates (gm.)	Fat (gm.)
LUNCH				
1 cup shredded lettuce	18.0	9.0	3.5	0.3
¼ green pepper, chopped	11.0	6.5	2.4	0.1
2 tablespoons lemon juice	6.6	0.2	2.2	0
Stuffed Burgers*	307.3	48.4	5.9	19.2
¼ cup Tomato-Plum Relish*	55.8	4.0	15.0	0.8
Coffee or tea	—	—	—	—
1 teaspoon sugar substitute	2.0	0	1.4	0
1 tablespoon low-fat milk	6.3	7.1	0.75	0.1
Total	407.0	75.2	31.15	20.5
SNACK				
1 pear	62.0	2.0	15.3	0.4
DINNER				
1 cup shredded lettuce	18.0	9.0	3.5	0.3
Chicken Stew Roma*	194.7	77.0	15.6	5.7
Mashed Potatoes with Pork Bits*	206.4	30.6	19.9	7.3
Coffee or tea	—	—	—	—
1 teaspoon sugar substitute	2.0	0	1.4	0
1 tablespoon low-fat milk	6.3	7.1	0.75	0.1
Total	427.4	123.7	41.15	13.4

* See index for recipe page number.

	Calories	Sodium (mg.)	Carbo-hydrates (gm.)	Fat (gm.)
SNACK				
Spice Sponge Cake*	126.9	18.8	23.3	1.4
Iced tea with lemon	—	—	—	—
Total	126.9	18.8	23.3	1.4
Grand Total	1,187.4	283.6	138.0	40.8

* See index for recipe page number.

TIPS FOR DAY THIRTEEN

Thirteen can be lucky because by now you not only feel and look better, you probably look younger, too, because a confident, joyous attitude does erase the years—just one more plus from your new way of life.

As for leftovers, Tomato-Plum Relish will keep up to three months if refrigerated, as will the Spice Sponge Cake.

Think of today as New Year's Eve. Tomorrow starts a brand-new year, and your resolutions are already well in hand.

	Calories	Sodium (mg.)	Carbo-hydrates (gm.)	Fat (gm.)
BREAKFAST				
½ apple, chopped	58.0	6.0	0.3	4.6
½ cup oatmeal	62.9	2.0	11.1	1.1
Coffee or tea	—	—	—	—
1 teaspoon sugar substitute	2.0	0	1.4	0
1 tablespoon low-fat milk	6.3	7.1	0.75	0.1
Total	129.2	15.1	13.55	5.8
LUNCH				
1 cup shredded lettuce	18.0	9.0	3.5	0.3
Chicken Stew Roma*	194.7	77.0	15.6	5.7
Coffee or tea	—	—	—	—
1 teaspoon sugar substitute	2.0	0	1.4	0
1 tablespoon low-fat milk	6.3	7.1	0.75	0.1
Total	221.0	93.1	21.25	6.1

* See index for recipe page number.

	Calories	Sodium (mg.)	Carbo-hydrates (gm.)	Fat (gm.)
SNACK				
¼ cup low-sodium cottage cheese	45.0	31.0	4.0	1.0
½ cup grapes	39.4	1.7	9.0	0.6
Iced tea with lemon	—	—	—	—
Total	84.4	32.7	13.0	1.6
DINNER				
1 cup shredded lettuce	18.0	9.0	3.5	0.3
1 tablespoon Creamy Garlic Dressing*	33.2	3.2	0.7	3.4
Tuna Sautéed in Wine*	255.1	50.0	14.5	11.5
Spaghetti in Spicy Green Sauce*	229.9	12.3	30.4	9.5
Sweet-and-Sour Zucchini*	61.3	3.4	10.9	2.0
Coffee or tea	—	—	—	—
1 teaspoon sugar substitute	2.0	0	1.4	0
1 tablespoon low-fat milk	6.3	7.1	0.75	0.1
Total	605.8	85.0	62.15	26.4
SNACK				
½ ounce low-sodium Gouda cheese	56.9	6.0	0.3	4.6
1 orange	98.0	2.0	24.4	0.4
Iced tea with lemon	—	—	—	—
Total	154.9	8.0	24.7	5.0
Grand Total	1,195.3	233.9	134.7	44.9

TIPS FOR DAY FOURTEEN

Happy New Year! Look how far you have come, how much you have accomplished.

You are no doubt thinner and feeling better about your body and yourself, as well. Remember, these two weeks have established the rule, rather than the exception. "Take charge" are your passwords now, and they will always serve you well.

Back to the day's details for just a moment. Leftover Sweet-and-Sour Zucchini would be a tangy alternative to the Braised Endive Salad planned for lunch today. Or it will keep up to two days if refrigerated.

From today's menu, leftover Leg of Lamb would be a delicious start for your new year, or it will keep up to three days if refrigerated. In addition, any remaining Rice with Tomatoes and Cheese will keep up to two days if refrigerated.

What you do with leftovers is up to your imagination. What you do for your body and the rest of your life is up to your innate good sense and your desire to make every day as rewarding as the last two weeks have been.

You can do it because you have already proven you are a winner.

	Calories	Sodium (mg.)	Carbo-hydrates (gm.)	Fat (gm.)
BREAKFAST				
3½ ounces low-sodium tomato juice	19.0	3.0	4.3	0.1
1 soft-boiled egg	78.0	55.0	0.4	4.3
1 slice Potato Bread*	154.6	2.3	31.4	0.3
Coffee or tea	—	—	—	—
1 teaspoon sugar substitute	2.0	0	1.4	0
1 tablespoon low-fat milk	6.3	7.1	0.75	0.1
Total	259.9	67.4	38.25	4.8
LUNCH				
Braised Endive Salad*	60.7	19.2	5.9	3.5
Tuna Sautéed in Wine*	255.1	50.0	14.5	11.1
Coffee or tea	—	—	—	—
1 teaspoon sugar substitute	2.0	0	1.4	0
1 tablespoon low-fat milk	6.3	7.1	0.75	0.1
Total	324.1	76.3	22.55	14.7
SNACK				
½ ounce low-sodium Gouda cheese	56.9	6.0	0.3	4.6
2 low-sodium crackers	22.0	1.7	2.9	1.0
Iced tea with lemon	—	—	—	—
Total	78.9	7.7	3.2	5.6

	Calories	Sodium (mg.)	Carbo-hydrates (gm.)	Fat (gm.)
DINNER				
1 cup shredded	18.0	9.0	3.5	0.3
1 tablespoon Oil and Vinegar Dressing*	25.8	0.2	0.2	3.0
Roast Leg of Lamb*	241.8	88.2	3.6	8.8
Rice with Tomatoes and Cheese*	181.9	8.3	30.1	5.6
Coffee or tea	—	—	—	—
1 teaspoon sugar substitute	2.0	0	1.4	0
1 tablespoon low-fat milk	6.3	7.1	0.75	0.1
Total	475.8	112.8	39.55	17.8
SNACK				
½ cup strawberries	20.8	0.7	5.5	0.3
Iced tea with lemon	—	—	—	—
Total	20.8	0.7	5.5	0.3
Grand Total	1,159.5	264.9	109.1	43.2

* See index for recipe page number.

Tables of Nutritional Values

The following tables provide an easy reference for nutritional values of all foods used (or suggested) in this book. Specifically included are the calorie, sodium, carbohydrate, and fat content per 100 grams (approximately 3½ ounces).

We ask that you note the following:

1. Nutritional values are based on raw ingredients unless otherwise noted.
2. Zero connotes no presence.
3. A dash connotes trace amounts.

	Calories	Sodium (mg.)	Carbo-hydrates (gm.)	Fat (gm.)
ALCOHOLIC BEVERAGES				
Brandy	295.0	1.0	—	0
Champagne	85.0	5.0	4.2	0
Kahlua	295.0	1.0	—	0
Liqueur	295.0	1.0	—	0
Rum	249.0	1.0	—	0
Vermouth	85.0	5.0	4.2	0
Wine (dry sherry, red and white)	85.0	5.0	4.2	0

	Calories	Sodium (mg.)	Carbo-hydrates (gm.)	Fat (gm.)
CONDIMENTS				
Applesauce	41.0	2.0	10.8	0.2
Capers[1]	10.0	10.0	2.0	0.2
Honey	304.0	5.0	82.3	0

[1] Preserved in vinegar only.

	Calories	Sodium (mg.)	Carbo-hydrates (gm.)	Fat (gm.)
CONDIMENTS (*continued*)				
Hot cherry peppers, low-sodium	19.6	24.5	4.9	0
Jams and preserves	272.0	12.0	70.0	0.1
Ketchup				
Chili, low-sodium	56.0	30.0	1.0	0
Regular, low-sodium	42.0	20.0	1.0	0
Mayonnaise, low-sodium	100.0	3.0	0	11.0
Mustard, low-sodium	91.0	7.0	5.3	6.3
Pickles, butter, low-sodium	73.0	5.0	2.2	0.2
Sugar				
Brown	373.0	30.0	96.4	0
Regular	385.0	1.0	99.5	0
Substitute[2]	42.0	0	9.8	0
Sweet pepper slices, low-sodium	35.0	24.5	8.8	0
Tomato paste, low-sodium	91.0	10.0	18.6	0.4
Tomato puree, unsalted	39.0	6.0	8.9	0.2
Tomato sauce, low-sodium	39.0	6.0	8.9	0.2
Vinegar				
Cider and red	14.0	1.0	5.9	0
White	12.0	1.0	5.0	0
Worcestershire sauce, low-sodium	304.0	5.0	82.3	0

[2] Low-sodium, as well as sugar-free.

	Calories	Sodium (mg.)	Carbo-hydrates (gm.)	Fat (gm.)
DAIRY				
Cheese				
Cheddar, low-sodium	398.0	18.0	2.1	32.2
Cottage, low-sodium	106.0	18.0	2.9	4.2
Cream, low-sodium	374.0	12.0	2.1	37.7
Gouda, low-sodium	345.0	35.0	1.7	28.0
Mozzarella, low-sodium	106.0	12.0	2.9	4.2
Ricotta, low-sodium	175.0	8.8	3.5	14.0
Swiss, low-sodium	355.0	30.0	1.7	28.0
Cream	352.0	32.0	3.1	37.6
Egg[3]	163.0	122.0	0.9	11.5
Margarine, unsalted	720.0	15.0	0.4	81.0
Milk, low-fat	48.0	145.0	5.5	1.0
Sour cream	352.0	32.0	3.1	37.6
Yogurt, plain, low-fat	50.0	51.0	5.2	1.7

	Calories	Sodium (mg.)	Carbo-hydrates (gm.)	Fat (gm.)
FISH AND SEAFOOD				
Cod	78.0	70.0	0	0.3
Flounder	79.0	78.0	0	0.8
Haddock	79.0	61.0	0	0.1
Lobster[4]	91.0	210.0	0.3	1.9
Oysters, shucked	66.0	73.0	3.4	1.8
Red snapper	93.0	67.0	0	0.9

[3] One medium egg is approximately 2 ounces.
[4] A 1-pound lobster has approximately 4 ounces of meat.

	Calories	Sodium (mg.)	Carbo-hydrates (gm.)	Fat (gm.)
FISH AND SEAFOOD (*continued*)				
Salmon				
Raw	217.0	64.0	0	13.4
canned,				
low-sodium	145.0	70.0	0	5.9
Sardines, canned,				
low-sodium	203.0	120.2	—	11.1
Shrimp	91.0	140.0	1.5	0.8
Squid	84.0	—	1.5	0.9
Swordfish	118.0	—	0	4.0
Trout	188.0	—	0	9.8
Tuna				
Raw	145.0	37.0	0	4.1
Canned,				
low-sodium	108.0	51.0	0	0.8

	Calories	Sodium (mg.)	Carbo-hydrates (gm.)	Fat (gm.)
FRUIT				
Apple	58.0	1.0	14.5	0.6
Apricots, dried[5]	260.0	26.0	66.5	0.5
Banana	85.0	1.0	22.0	0.2
Blueberries[6]	62.0	1.0	15.3	0.5
Cantaloupe	30.0	12.0	7.5	0.1
Coconut, dried	548.0	—	53.2	39.1
Cranberries	46.2	2.1	10.9	0.7
Dates[7]	275.0	1.0	72.9	0.5
Figs[8]				
Raw	80.0	2.0	20.3	0.3
Dried	274.0	34.0	69.1	1.3
Grapefruit	44.0	1.0	11.5	0.1

[5] 1 cup equals 3 ounces; 5 dried equals 1 ounce.
[6] 1 cup equals 3 ounces.
[7] 4 dates equal 1 ounce.
[8] 1 raw equals 3½ ounces; 3 dried equal 1 ounce.

	Calories	Sodium (mg.)	Carbo-hydrates (gm.)	Fat (gm.)
FRUIT (*continued*)				
Grapes	69.0	3.0	15.7	1.0
Honeydew melon	33.0	12.0	7.7	0.3
Lemon	27.0	5.0	8.2	0.3
Orange	49.0	1.0	12.2	0.2
Peach				
Raw	38.0	1.0	9.7	0.1
Dried[9]	262.0	16.0	0.7	3.1

	Calories	Sodium (mg.)	Carbo-hydrates (gm.)	Fat (gm.)
Pear				
Raw	62.0	2.0	15.3	0.4
Dried[9]	268.0	7.0	1.8	3.1
Pineapple	52.0	1.0	13.7	0.2
Plum	66.0	2.0	17.8	—
Prunes[10]	255.0	8.0	67.4	0.6
Raisins[11]	289.0	27.0	77.4	0.2
Raspberries[6]	251.0	4.0	59.8	2.2
Strawberries[12]	37.0	1.0	8.4	0.5

	Calories	Sodium (mg.)	Carbo-hydrates (gm.)	Fat (gm.)
JUICE				
Apple	47.0	1.0	11.9	—
Lemon	23.0	1.0	7.6	0.1
Orange	48.0	1.0	11.2	0.2
Pineapple	55.0	1.0	13.5	0.1
Tomato, low-sodium	19.0	3.0	4.3	0.1

9 2 dried equal 1 ounce.
10 3 prunes equal 1 ounce.
11 1 cup equals 6 ounces.
12 1 cup equals 5½ ounces.

	Calories	Sodium (mg.)	Carbo-hydrates (gm.)	Fat (gm.)
MEAT				
Beef				
Bottom round	197.0	65.0	0	12.3
Chopped	286.0	47.0	0	20.3
Chuck (ground beef)	286.0	47.0	0	20.3
Flank (London broil)	191.0	65.0	0	6.6
Stewing	158.0	60.0	0	7.4
Lamb				
Leg	192.0	75.0	0	7.7
Loin	197.0	75.0	0	8.6
Rib	224.0	75.0	0	12.1
Shank	65.7	25.0	0	2.9
Liver, chicken	129.0	70.0	2.9	3.7
Pork				
Loin	254.0	70.0	0	14.2
Roast	254.0	70.0	0	14.2
Shoulder	244.0	70.0	0	14.3
Veal				
Loin (scallops)	156.0	90.0	0	8.0
Rib	207.0	90.0	0	14.0
Shoulder (ground veal)	240.0	90.0	0	18.0
Stewing	231.0	90.0	0	17.0

	Calories	Sodium (mg.)	Carbo-hydrates (gm.)	Fat (gm.)
NUTS[13]				
Almonds	98.0	4.0[14]	19.5	54.2
Cashews	561.0	15.0[14]	29.3	45.7
Pecans	687.0	—[14]	14.6	71.2
Pine nuts	552.0	0 [14]	11.6	47.4
Sesame seeds	582.0	—[14]	17.6	53.4
Walnuts				
Black	628.0	3.0[14]	14.8	59.3
English	651.0	2.0[14]	15.8	64.0

[13] ¼ cup equals approximately 2 ounces.
[14] Unsalted only.

	Calories	Sodium (mg.)	Carbohydrates (gm.)	Fat (gm.)
POULTRY				
Chicken[15]				
Fryers				
Flesh and skin (whole)	126.0	58.0	0	5.1
Flesh only (whole)	107.0	78.0	0	2.7
Breast	110.0	50.0	0	2.4
Drumstick	115.0	67.0	0	3.9
Wing	146.0	50.0	0	7.4
Roasters				
Flesh and skin (whole)	197.0	58.0	0	12.6
Flesh only (whole)	131.0	58.0	0	4.5
Dark meat, without skin	132.0	67.0	0	4.7
Light meat, without skin	128.0	50.0	0	3.2
Rock Cornish hen	110.0	50.0	0	2.4

	Calories	Sodium (mg.)	Carbohydrates (gm.)	Fat (gm.)
VEGETABLES				
Artichoke[16]				
Raw	47.0	43.0	10.6	0.2
Hearts, frozen	23.5	46.6	6.0	0
Arugola[17]	18.0	9.0	3.5	0.3
Asparagus	26.0	2.0	5.0	0.2
Avocados	167.0	4.0	6.3	16.4
Beans[18]				

[15] Approximately 60 percent of a whole chicken is actually meat.
[16] An average-size raw artichoke is approximately 10 ounces; 2 hearts equal 1 ounce.
[17] 1 bunch equals 2 ounces; 1 cup equals 3 ounces.
[18] 1 cup equals 6 ounces.

	Calories	Sodium (mg.)	Carbo-hydrates (gm.)	Fat (gm.)
VEGETABLES (*continued*)				
Kidney	343.0	10.0	61.9	1.5
Navy	340.0	19.0	61.3	1.6
Pinto	349.0	10.0	63.7	1.2
Beets, canned, low-sodium	32.0	46.0	7.8	—
Broccoli[19]	32.0	15.0	5.9	0.3
Cabbage[20]	24.0	20.0	5.4	0.2
Carrots	42.0	43.0	9.7	0.2
Cauliflower[21]	27.0	13.0	5.2	0.2
Chiles, green	37.0	25.0	9.1	0.2
Cucumbers	48.0	20.6	3.4	0.1
Eggplant	25.0	2.0	5.6	0.2
Endive	20.0	14.0	4.1	0.1
Escarole	20.0	14.0	4.1	0.1
Fennel	28.0	—	5.1	0.4
Garlic	137.0	19.0	30.8	0.2
Green beans	32.0	7.0	7.1	0.2
Leeks	52.0	5.0	11.2	0.3
Lettuce[22]	18.0	9.0	3.5	0.3
Mushrooms[23]	28.0	15.0	4.4	0.3
Onions	38.0	10.0	17.4	0.2
Parsley	44.0	45.0	8.5	0.6
Pasta				
Raw	362.0	2.0	75.2	1.2
Cooked	148.0	2.0	30.1	0.5
Peas				
Raw	84.0	2.0	14.4	0.4
Canned, low-sodium	78.0	3.0	14.3	0.4
Peppers				
Bell, green	22.0	13.0	4.8	0.2
Bell, red	31.0	25.0	7.1	0.3

[19] 1 spear equals 5 ounces; 1 head equals 20 ounces.
[20] 1 cup equals 4 ounces.
[21] 1 cup equals 4 ounces; 1 head equals 24 ounces.
[22] 1 cup equals 3½ ounces; 1 head equals 1 pound.
[23] 2 mushrooms equal 1 ounce.

	Calories	Sodium (mg.)	Carbo-hydrates (gm.)	Fat (gm.)
VEGETABLES (*continued*)				
Potatoes				
Baked	93.0	4.0	21.7	1.0
Boiled	76.0	3.0	17.1	1.0
Radishes[24]	17.0	18.0	3.6	0.1
Rice				
Raw[18]	363.0	5.0	80.4	0.4
Cooked[25]	109.0	5.0	24.2	0.1
Scallions	36.0	5.0	8.2	0.2
Spinach	26.0	71.0	4.3	0.3
Squash				
Acorn	44.0	0.1	11.2	1.0
Yellow	20.0	1.0	4.3	0.2
Zucchini	17.0	1.0	3.6	0.1
Tomatoes				
Raw	22.0	3.0	4.7	0.2
Plum, canned, low-sodium	20.0	3.0	4.2	0.2
Watercress[26]	19.0	51.9	0.3	0.6

	Calories	Sodium (mg.)	Carbo-hydrates (gm.)	Fat (gm.)
WHEAT AND GRAIN				
Bread, low-sodium[27]	241.0	3.5	49.3	2.6
Bread crumbs, low-sodium[28]	364.0	35.0	77.0	7.0
Crackers, low-sodium[29]	195.0	4.3	25.5	9.0
Oatmeal, cooked	55.0	4.0	9.7	1.0

[24] 2 radishes equal 1 ounce.
[25] 1 cup equals 8 ounces.
[26] 1 bunch equals 2½ ounces; 1 cup equals 3½ ounces.
[27] 1 slice equals 1 ounce.
[28] 1 cup equals 4 ounces.
[29] Eleven equal 1 ounce.

	Calories	Sodium (mg.)	Carbo-hydrates (gm.)	Fat (gm.)
MISCELLANY				
Baking powder, low-sodium	83.0	40.0	20.1	—
Barley	348.0	—	77.2	1.1
Bouillon				
Beef, low-sodium[30]	378.0	210.0	42.0	21.0
Chicken, low-sodium[31]	378.0	105.0	42.0	21.0
Cornmeal (not self-rising)	355.0	1.0	73.7	8.3
Flour				
All-purpose	365.0	2.0	74.5	1.2
Wheat	333.0	3.0	71.0	2.0
Gelatin, unflavored[32]	335.0	2.0	0	0.1
Oil	884.0	0	0	100.0
Shortening	902.0	—	0	100.0
Yeast	282.0	52.0	38.9	1.6

[30] Content per tablespoon equals 54 calories, 30 milligrams sodium, 3 grams carbohydrates, 3 grams fat.
[31] Content per tablespoon equals 54 calories, 15 milligrams sodium, 3 grams carbohydrates, 3 grams fat.
[32] One package equals 2 tablespoons equals 1 ounce.

Bibliography

American Diabetes Association, Inc., and The American Dietetic Association. *A Guide for Professionals: The Effective Application of "Exchange Lists for Meal Planning,"* 1977.

American Diabetes Association, Inc., and The American Dietetic Association. *Exchange Lists for Meal Planning,* 1976.

American Heart Association Booklets: *Your 500 Milligrams Sodium Diet. Your 1000 Milligrams Sodium Diet, Your Mild Sodium-Restricted Diet.* Dallas, Texas: American Heart Association, 1957.

American Spice Trade Association Booklets: *A Glossary of Spices. A Guide to Spices. A History of Spices. Low-Calorie Spice Tips. Low-Cholesterol Spice Tips. Low-Fat Spice Tips. Low-Sodium Spice Tips. Spice Attitude and Usage Study. The Spice and Diet Cookbooklet. What You Should Know About Spices.*

Bond, Clara-Beth Young, R.D.; Dobbin, E. Virginia, R.D.; Gofman, Helen F., M.D.; Jones, Helen C.; and Lyon, Lenore. *The Low Fat, Low Cholesterol Diet.* Revised and Enlarged Edition. New York: Doubleday & Company, Inc., 1971.

Brody, Jane. *Jone Brody's Nutrition Book.* New York: W. W. Norton & Company, Inc., 1981.

Carper, Jean, and Krause, Patricia A. *The All-In-One Calorie Counter.* New York: Bantam Books, Inc., 1979.

Carper, Jean, and Krause, Patricia A. *The All-In-One Carbohydrate Gram Counter.* New York: Bantam Books, Inc., 1977.

Chaback, Elaine. *The Complete Calorie Counter.* New York: Dell Publishing Co., Inc., 1979.

Dong, Collin H., M.D., and Banks, Jane. *The Arthritic's Cookbook.* New York: Bantam Books, Inc., 1978.

350 · Bibliography

Gersoff, Stanley N., Ph.D., Editor. *Tufts University Diet and Nutrition Letter*. Vol. 4, No. 3, May, 1986. 475 Park Avenue South, New York, New York 10016.

Hausman, Patricia. *The Calcium Bible*. New York: Rawson Associates Publishers, Inc., 1986.

Joslin Clinic. *Diabetic Diet Guide*. Boston, Mass.

Margie, Joyce Daly, M.S., and Hunt, James C., M.D. *Living With High Blood Pressure*. Bloomfield, New Jersey: HLS Press, Inc., 1978.

Moore, Richard, Editor. *Fodor's Italy 1985*. New York: Fodor's Travel Guides, 1985.

Morrison, Lester, M.D. *The Low-Fat Way to Health & Longer Life*. New York: Arc Books, Inc., 1971.

Pezzini, Wilma. *Fisher Annotated Travel Guides. Italy 1985*. New York: New American Library, 1985.

Revell, Dorothy. *Cholesterol Control*. Denver, Colorado: Royal Publications, Inc., 1961.

Rosenthal, Sylvia. *Live High on Low Fat*. New Enlarged Edition. New York: J.B. Lippincott Company, 1975.

Simon, Kate. *Italy: The Places in Between*. Revised and Expanded Edition. New York: Harper & Row Publishers, Inc., 1970.

Schell, Merle. *The Chinese Salt-Free Diet Cookbook*. New York: New American Library, 1985.

Schell, Merle. *The Mexican Salt-Free Diet Cookbook*. New York: New American Library, 1986.

Schell, Merle. *Tasting Good. The International Salt-Free Diet Cookbook*. New York: New American Library, 1981.

United States Department of Agriculture. *Handbook No. 8*. U.S. Government Printing Office. Washington, D.C. 20402, 1963.

U.S. Department of Health, Education, and Welfare. *Healthy People. The Surgeon General's Report on Health Promotion and Disease Prevention*. Washington, D.C. 20402, 1979.

U.S. Department of Health and Human Services. *Diet and Nutrition for People with Diabetes*. Selected Annotations. NIH Publication No. 80-1872. Washington, D.C.: National Diabetes Information Clearinghouse, 1979.

Index

Abruzzi, cuisine of, 7
Acorn squash:
  with orange-nut stuffing, 237
  shrimp-stuffed, 232
Adapting your favorite Italian
    recipes, 30–31
Alcohol, 12
  see also Brandy; Champagne;
    Rum; Wine
Allspice, 12–13
Almond(s):
  bread with aniseed, 87
  nut balls, 268
Aniseed, 13
  bread with, almond, 87
  pecan cookies, 270
Antipasti, 43–62
  beef:
    marinated chopped, 56
    meatballs in creamy mustard-
      garlic sauce, 57
  cheese:
    dip, combination, 59
    puffs, fried, 60
  chicken:
    liver spread, 55
    wings, broiled in tomato
      sauce, 54
    wings, wine-baked, 54
  eggs:
    Genovese, stuffed, 49
    sweet pepper-stuffed, 50
  melon and pork, 58
  mushrooms:
    baked stuffed, 47
    in mustard marinade, 48

    oysters, baked stuffed, 51
  relish:
    spiced apple, 61
    tomato-plum, 62
  salmon spread, 53
  sardine spread, 53
  shrimp, garlic, 52
  tuna spread, 53
  vegetable(s):
    mixed, appetizer, 44
    mixed fry, 46
    sweet pickled, 45
  zucchini strips, 48
Apple(s):
  baked in cranberry-coconut
    sauce, 270–71
  fruit cobbler, mixed, 264
  ice, 273
  pork and, 58
  relish, spiced, 61
  stuffing with sausage, Italian,
    92
Applesauce, braised chicken with,
    138
Apricot sauce, 253
Artichokes:
  chicken and, 140
  lemon-mint, 214
  stuffed, 215
  veal with, and mushrooms,
    180
Artificial sweeteners, *see* Sugar
    substitutes
Arugola, 13
  salad, braised, 96
  soup, 66

Asparagus:
   other suggested sauces for, 216
   in spicy cheese sauce, 216
   vinaigrette, 216

Baking powder, low-sodium, 21
Bananas in strawberry cream, 271
Barley soup:
   green bean and, 69
   zucchini and, 69
Basil, 13
   chicken salad, tarragon and, 114
   -crumbed cauliflower, 221
   lemon-,
      chicken, 150–51
      veal scallops and leeks in,
         sauce, 179
   pizza with topping I, 90
   pungent, sauce, 248
      potatoes baked in, 208
   rice and leeks, 198
   salmon in, -cream sauce, 121
   sauce, pungent, 248
   tomato and mozzarella salad,
      106
Bay leaf, 14
Bean(s):
   navy:
      hens and, Rock Cornish, 157
      pork and, 174
      tomatoes and, 212
   pinto:
      soup, pork, pasta, and, 73
      soup, tomato-, 77
Bechamel sauce, 240
Beef, 159
   burgers, stuffed, 166
   London broil vinaigrette, 161
   marinated chopped, 56
   meatballs, tender, 167
   meatballs in creamy mustard-
      garlic sauce, 57
   meat loaf with cream, 162
   meat-stuffed flat bread, 86
   meat-stuffed peppers, 230
   parsley, in brandy, 163
   pot roast Bologna, 164

   as protein source, 296
   sausage Napoli, 172
      peppers, and eggs, 175
   steak and cheese, 165
   stew, Italian, 160
   stock, 65
Beet(s):
   salad, 97
      mixed vegetable, 104
      roast peppers and, 105
Biscuits:
   cheese and sausage, 80
   cinnamon fruit, 88
Blueberries for mixed fruit
      cobbler, 264
Bouillon, low-sodium, 21–22, 30
Brandy, 14
   beef in, parsley, 163
   brandied mayonnaise, lobster
      salad in, 108
   dried fruit in, wine, 275
Bread crumbs:
   basil-crumbed cauliflower, 221
   burgers, stuffed, 166
   low-sodium, 22
   spice-broiled tomatoes, 235
   topping, squid with, 125
Breads, 79–93
   almond, with aniseed, 87
   basic Italian white, 82
   biscuits:
      cheese and sausage, 80
      cinnamon fruit, 88
   cheese:
      dilled, 81
      and sausage biscuits, 80
   flat, Italian, 85
      meat-stuffed, 86
   garlic, 80
   pizza:
      dough, easy, 89
      with topping I, 90
      with topping II, 91
   potato, 84
   stuffing, Italian, 92–93
      with nuts, 93
      with sausage, 92
   vegetable, herbed, 83

Breakfast menus for an Italian
    diet, 301–37 *passim*
Broccoli:
    antipasto mixed fry, 46
    basil-crumbed, 221
    and leeks, 217
    and pine nuts, 218
    salad, 98
        shrimp and potato, 109
    in sherry garlic, 218
Brunch menus and preparation
    tips, 278-82

Cabbage:
    and capers, 219
    coleslaw, Italian, 102–103
    rice, and sweet peppers, 200
    salad, mixed vegetables, 104
Cake:
    fruit-filled log, 265
    lemony coconut, 266
    nut, 267
    spice sponge, 268–69
Calabria, cuisine of, 6–7
Calamari, *see* Squid
Calorie(s):
    content of recipes, 41
    daily intake on Italian diet, 298
    tables of nutritional values,
        339–48
Campania, cuisine of, 8–9
Cantaloupe, pork and, 58
Caper(s), 14
    cabbage and, 219
    carrot soup with, 66
    piquant mayonnaise, 258
    salad, chicken and, 115
    salmon, eggplant, and, 122
    wine-, sauce, 251
    rice in, 201
Carbohydrates:
    complex, 295, 299
    content of recipes, 41
    tables of nutritional values,
        339-48
Carrot(s):
    bread, herbed vegetable, 83

    in cheese sauce, 220
    in orange wine, 220
    pickled vegetables, sweet, 45
    salad:
        coleslaw, Italian, 102–103
        green bean and, 100
        mixed vegetable, 104
    soup with capers, 66
Cauliflower:
    antipasto mixed fry, 46
    basil-crumbed, 221
    in cheese sauce, 220
    and peas, creamed, 222
    pickled vegetables, sweet, 45
    salad, 98
Celery seed, 22–23
Central Italy, cuisine of, 9–11
Champagne chicken with herbs,
    139
Cheddar cheese:
    bread, dilled, 81
    burgers, stuffed, 166
    green beans with mushrooms
        and, buttery, 227
    pizza with topping I, 90
    puffs, fried, 60
    rice with tomatoes and, 204
    salad surprise, mixed, 103
    squash melt, 236
    steak and, 165
Cheese, 14–15
    dip, combination, 59
    low-sodium, 14–15, 22–23
    mushroom-, sauce, 241
        shells with, 191
    puffs, fried, 60
    see also individual types of
        cheese
Chicken, 137-155
    with applesauce, braised, 138
    with artichokes, 140
    champagne, with herbs, 139
    honey-vinegar baked, 150
    lasagna rolls, oyster-and-, 188
    leeks and, in lemon-basil sauce,
        179
    lemon-basil, 150-51
        and leeks, 179

Chicken (*cont.*)
with lemon sauce, 143
liver(s)
rice with, 203
spread, 55
Marsala with peppers and
mushrooms, 178
Milano, 147
and mushrooms, 141
mustard, 151
picante,155
as protein source, 296
in raspberry sauce, 169
rosemary, with green peppercorns, 153
salad:
basil and tarragon, 114
capers and, 115
pasta and, 113
and sausage, 142
simple Italian, 154
spaghetti and, with vegetables,
192
stew Roma, 148
stock, 64
stuffed, Italiano, roast, 152
-stuffed eggplant, 225
stuffed tomatoes, baked, 234
Tetrazzini, 149
tomato salad, stuffed, 106–107
with watercress, braised, 181
in wine, 145
baked wings, 54
parsley, 144
-tomato sauce, 146
wings:
in tomato sauce, broiled, 54
wine-baked, 54
Christmas salad, 99
Cinnamon, 15
biscuits, fruit, 88
Clam sauce:
red, 244
mock, 244
white, 245
mock, 245
Cloves, 15
Cobbler, mixed fruit, 264

Coconut:
apples baked in cranberry-,
sauce, 270–71
cake, lemony, 266
Cod:
baked, Venezia, 118
in herb sauce, parsley, 120
seafood fettuccine, 187
Coleslaw, Italian, 102–103
Cookies:
Easter, 269
pecan, 270
Cornish hens, *see* Hens, Rock
Cornish
Cornmeal for baked polenta with
tomatoes and eggplant,
205
Cottage cheese, 15
combination cheese dip, 59
Cranberry-coconut sauce, apples
baked in, 270–71
Cream:
bananas in strawberry, 271
cauliflower and peas, creamed,
222
fennel in, sauce, 226–27
fettuccine:
in parsley-, sauce, 185
in wine-, sauce 186
meat loaf with, 162
oranges with raspberry, glazed,
272
peach ice, 273
salmon in basil-, sauce, 121
shrimp, zucchini, and peppers
in wine, 136
wine-, sauce, 246–47
Cream cheese for combination
cheese dip, 59
Cucumber:
dressing, 259
asparagus with, 216
hot sauce, 250

Dates:
biscuits, cinnamon fruit, 88
fruit-filled log, 265

Desserts, 261–75
　apples baked in cranberry-
　　coconut sauce, 270–71
　bananas in strawberry cream,
　　271
　cake:
　　fruit-filled log, 265
　　lemony coconut, 266
　　nut, 267
　　spice sponge, 268–69
　cookies:
　　Easter, 269
　　pecan, 270
　fruit:
　　dried, in brandy wine, 275
　　cobbler, mixed, 264
　　creamy rum, 274
　　-filled log, 265
　nut:
　　balls, 268
　　cake, 267
　oranges with raspberry cream,
　　glazed, 272
　peach ice, 273
　pears:
　　brandied, 274
　　in cranberry-coconut sauce,
　　　270–71
　pie, Italian cheese, 263
　pie dough, Italian, 262
Deviled shrimp, 134
Diet, an Italian, 295–338
　daily caloric intake on, 298
　daily tips, 300, 303, 306, 309,
　　312, 315, 317, 319, 322,
　　325, 328, 331, 334, 336
　diabetics on, 299
　duration of, 298
　menus for, 301–38 *passim*
　nutritional basis of, 295–98
　sodium intake on, 298–99
Diet tips, 32–38
Dill(ed), 15
　cheese bread, 81
　sauce, flounder in cheesy, 119
Dough, Italian pie, 262
Dressings, 254–59
　creamy garlic, 256–57

　cucumber, 259
　honey-vinegar, 255
　Italian vinaigrette, 254
　mayonnaise:
　　herbed, 257
　　piquant, 258
　oil and vinegar, 254

Easter cookies, 269
Easter soup, 67
Eggplant:
　chicken stew Roma, 148
　mixed vegetable appetizer, 44
　with mushrooms, 224
　Parmigiana, easy, 223
　pizza with topping II, 91
　polenta with, and tomatoes,
　　baked, 205
　relish, spiced, 61
　salmon:
　　and capers, 122
　　-stuffed, 225
Eggs:
　Genovese, stuffed, 49
　sausage, peppers, and, 175
　spice sponge cake, 268–69
　sweet pepper-stuffed, 50
Emilia-Romagna, cuisine of, 9–
　10
Endive salad, braised, 96, 99
Entertaining, 277–93
　brunch menus and preparation
　　tips, 278–82
　buffet menus and preparation
　　tips, 288–90
　cocktail menus and preparation
　　tips, 291–93
　dinner menus and preparation
　　tips, 285–87
　general tips for, 277–78
　lunch menus and preparation
　　tips, 282–84

Fat(s), 296–97
　content of recipes, 41
　tables of nutritional values,
　　339–48

Fennel, 15–16
  in cream sauce, 226–27
  salad, 100
Fennel seed, *see* Aniseed
Fettuccine, *see* Pasta, fettuccine
Figs:
  biscuits, cinnamon fruit, 88
  fruit-filled log, 265
  fruit in brandy wine, dried,
    275
  shrimp and potato salad with,
    109
Fish, 117–31
  cod:
    baked, Venezia, 118
    in herb sauce, parsley, 120
    seafood fettuccine, 187
  flounder:
    with braised watercress, 181
    in cheesy dill sauce, 119
    in herb sauce, parsley, 120
  haddock, Venezia, baked, 118
  as protein source, 296
  red snapper:
    baked, 123
    deviled, 134
    fish soup, 68
    stuffed with seafood, 124
  salmon:
    in basil-cream sauce, 121
    canned, low-sodium, 24
    eggplant, and capers, 122
    in herb sauce, parsley, 120
    spread, 53
    -stuffed eggplant, 225
  sardines:
    canned, low-sodium, 24
    eggs Genovese, stuffed, 49
    piquant mayonnaise, 258
    salad, zucchini, tomato, and,
      107
    spicy green sauce, 247
    spread, 53
    stuffed artichokes, 215
  soup, 68
  swordfish:
    in basil-cream sauce, 121

    deviled, 134
    fish soup, 68
    in pepper-wine sauce, 127
    rosemary, with green
      peppercorns, 153
    salad, basil and tarragon,
      114
    sautéed in wine, 130
    and sweet peppers, 126
  trout:
    simple broiled, 128
    wine-baked, 129
  tuna:
    baked stuffed mushrooms,
      47
    canned, low-sodium, 26
    cheese, and tomato bake, 131
    salad, 112
    salad, pasta and, 113
    sautéed in wine, 130
    spaghetti in spicy green
      sauce with, 194
    spread, 53
    stuffed artichokes, 215
    stuffed tomatoes, baked, 234
  see also Shellfish
Flounder:
  in cheesy dill sauce, 119
  in herb sauce, parsley, 120
Fritters, potato, 209
Fruit:
  biscuits, cinnamon, 88
  cobbler, mixed, 264
  creamy rum, 274
  dried, in brandy wine, 275
  -filled log, 265
  *see also individual types of
    fruit*

Garlic, 16
  bread, 80
  broccoli in sherry, 218
  dressing, creamy, 256–57
  mustard-, sauce, 256
    meatballs in creamy, 57
  potatoes, creamy, 206

sauce, vermicelli and squid in, 196
shrimp, 52
Gnocchi, 183, 184
    potato, with mustard-tomato sauce, 210
Gouda cheese for carrots in cheese sauce, 220
Grapes for creamy rum fruit, 274
Green bean (s):
    basil-crumbed, 221
    with mushrooms, buttery, 227
    with orange slices, 228
    salad, 98
        carrot and, 100
        potato and, 102
    soup, barley and, 69
Green pepper(s):
    bread, herbed vegetable, 83
    chicken stew Roma, 148
    coleslaw, Italian, 102–103
    meat-stuffed, 230
    pizza with topping I, 90
    rice-stuffed, 231
    salad, roast peppers and beet, 105
    sausage, and eggs, 175
    tomato sauce I, 242
    tomato sauce II, 243
    veal Marsala with, and mushrooms, 178

Haddock Venezia, baked, 118
Hens, Rock Cornish, 156
    and beans, 157
    marinated, 156
Herb(s):
    chicken with, champagne, 139
    flounder in, sauce, parsley, 120
    herbed mayonnaise dressing, 257
        asparagus with, 216
    herbed vegetable bread, 83
    sauce, 249
        asparagus in spicy cheese sauce, 216
    see also individual herbs

Honey-vinegar dressing, 255
    asparagus with, 216
    baked chicken in, 150
Hors d'oeuvres, see Antipasti
Hot sauce, 250
    shells, 191

Ice, peach, 273
Ingredients, 12–26
    an Italian pantry, 12–21
    a low-sodium pantry, 21–26

Ketchup, low-sodium, 23
    hot sauce, 250
    pungent basil sauce, 248

Lamb, 159
    burgers, stuffed, 166
    chops
        in lemon-parsley sauce, broiled, 168
        in raspberry sauce, 169
    Easter soup, 67
    leg of, roast, 170
Lasagna, see Pasta, lasagna
Lazio region, cuisine of the, 11
Leeks, 16
    basil rice and, 198
    broccoli and, 217
    stuffed baked potatoes, 211
Lemon peel powder, 23
Lemon(s):
    -basil chicken, 150–51
    biscuits, cinnamon fruit, 88
    chicken with, sauce, 143
    lemony coconut cake, 266
    -mint artichokes, 214
    -parsley sauce, broiled lamb chops in, 168
    veal scallops and leeks in, -basil sauce, 179
Lettuce, see Salads
Liver, chicken, see Chicken, liver
Lobster:
    in creamy wine sauce, 132

Lobster (*cont.*)
  salad:
    in brandied mayonnaise, 108
    tomato, zucchini, and, 107
  soup, 71
  zucchini, and peppers in wine
    cream, 136
Lombardy, cuisine of, 3
London broil, *see* Beef
Low-sodium adaptations of your
    favorite Italian recipes,
    30–31
Low-sodium ingredients, 21–26,
  33
Lucania, cuisine of, 6–7

Macaroni, *see* Pasta, macaroni
Marches, cuisine of the, 10
Marjoram, 16
Mayonnaise:
  creamy garlic dressing, 256–57
  cucumber dressing, 259
  herbed, dressing, 257
    asparagus with, 216
  lobster salad in brandied, 108
  low-sodium, 23
  piquant, 258
    tuna salad with, 112
Meat, *see* Beef; Lamb; Pork; Veal
Meat stock, 65
Meat-stuffed flat bread, 86
Melon, pork and, 58
Menus:
  for entertaining, *see* Entertain-
    ing
  for an Italian diet, 300–338
    passim
Mint, 17
  artichokes, lemon-, 214
Mock red clam sauce, 244
Mock white clam sauce, 245
Molise, cuisine of, 7
Mozzarella cheese, 14, 15
  eggplant Parmigiana, easy, 223
  pizza with topping II, 91
  salad, tomato and, 106
  tuna, and tomato bake, 131

Mushroom(s):
  baked stuffed, 47
  -cheese sauce, 241
    shells with, 191
  chicken and, 141
  eggplant with, 224
  green beans with, buttery, 227
  in mustard marinade, 48
  soup, rice-, 70
  tomato sauce I, 242
  tomato sauce II, 243
  veal:
    with artichokes and, 180
    Marsala with peppers and,
      178
    stew and, 177
Mustard:
  chicken, 151
  -garlic sauce, 256
    meatballs in creamy, 57
  low-sodium, 23–24
  mushrooms in, marinade, 48
  -tomato sauce, 246
    gnocchi in, 210

Navy beans:
  pork and, 174
  tomatoes and, 212
    Rock Cornish hens and,
      157
Noodles, *see* Pasta, noodles
Northern Italy, cuisine of, 1–5
Nut(s):
  almond(s):
    bread with aniseed, 87
  nut balls, 268
  cake, 267
  cashews for nut balls, 268
  pecan(s):
    cookies, 270
    nut cake, 267
  pine nut(s):
    broccoli and, 218
    nut cake, 267
    squash with orange-, stuffing,
      237

walnut(s):
bread with, Italian flat, 85
nut balls, 268
nut cake, 267
shrimp and potato salad with,
109
stuffing with, Italian, 93
Nutmeg, 17
Nutritional values, tables of,
339–48

Olive oil, 17, 296
Italian vinaigrette, 254
and vinegar dressing, 254
Onion(s):
bread:
herbed vegetable, 83
Italian flat, with, 85
hot sauce, 250
pizza with toppings, 90–91
Orange(s):
acorn squash with, -nut stuffing,
237
biscuits, cinnamon fruit, 88
carrots in, wine, 220
creamy rum fruit, 274
green beans with, slices, 228
with raspberry cream, glazed,
272
salad:
Christmas, 99
fennel, with, 100
mixed, surprise, 103
Orange juice for cucumber
dressing, 259
Orange peel powder, 24
Oregano, 17
Oyster(s):
baked stuffed, 51
broiled, 133
fish soup, 68
lasagna rolls, chicken-and-, 188
mock red clam sauce, 244
mock white clam sauce, 245
snapper stuffed with seafood,
124

soup, 71
tomato salad, stuffed, 106–107
vermicelli and, 195
Paprika, 18
Parsley, 18
beef in brandy, 163
chicken in, wine, 144
fettuccine in, -cream sauce,
185
flounder in herb sauce, 120
lamb chops in lemon-, sauce,
168
spicy green sauce, 247
Pasta, 18, 183, 185–96
fettuccine:
in parsley-cream sauce, 185
seafood, 187
in wine-cream sauce, 186
lasagna rolls, chicken-and-
oyster, 188
macaroni:
bean, pork, and pasta soup,
73
chicken Tetrazzini, 149
Easter soup, 67
and spinach, 189
tuna, cheese, and tomato
bake, 131
noodles, sausage, and
vegetables, baked, 190
nutritional value of, 295
shells:
hot sauce, 191
with mushroom-cheese sauce,
191
spaghetti:
chicken salad and, 113
and pork with vegetables,
192
and shrimp in tomato sauce,
193
in spicy green sauce, 194
tuna salad and, 113
vermicelli:
oysters and, 195
squid and, in garlic sauce,
196

Pastry pie dough, Italian, 262
Peach(es):
  creamy rum fruit, 274
  fruit:
    in brandy wine, dried, 275
    cobbler, mixed, 264
    -filled log, 265
  ice 273
  with strawberry cream, glazed,
    272
Pear(s):
  biscuits, cinnamon fruit, 88
  brandied, 274
  in cranberry-coconut sauce,
    270–71
  fruit cobbler, mixed, 264
  fruit in brandy wine, dried,
    275
  with pork, 228–29
  stuffing with sausage, Italian,
    92
Peas:
  cauliflower and, creamed, 222
  soup with squid, 72
  with sweet peppers, 229
Pecan(s):
  cookies, 270
  nut cake, 267
Pepper(corns):
  green, rosemary chicken with,
    153
  swordfish in, -wine sauce, 127
Pepper(s):
  green, see Green pepper(s)
  red, see Red pepper(s)
  hot cherry, low-sodium, 23
  hot flakes, 16
  sweet, halves, low-sodium, 25
    peas with, 229
    rice, cabbage, and, 200
    stuffed baked potatoes, 211
    -stuffed eggs, 50
    swordfish and, 126
Pickles:
  bread and butter, low-sodium,
    24
  hot sauce, 250

Pie:
  cheese, Italian, 263
  dough, Italian, 262
Piedmont, cuisine of, 2
Pine nuts:
  broccoli and, 218
  nut cake, 267
  squash with orange-, stuffing,
    237
Pinto bean soup:
  pork, pasta, and, 73
  tomato-, 77
Piquant mayonnaise, 258
  tuna salad with, 112
Pizza, 89
  dough, easy, 89
  with topping I, 90
  with topping II, 91
Plum relish, tomato-, 62
Polenta, 183
  with tomatoes and eggplant,
    baked, 205
Pork, 159
  apples and, 58
  and beans, Italian, 174
  braised, 173
  chops:
    in lemon-parsley sauce,
      broiled, 168
    in raspberry sauce, 169
  meatballs, tender, 167
  melon and, 58
  peas with, 228–29
  potatoes with, bits, mashed,
    207
  in raspberry sauce, 169
  salad, basil and tarragon, 114
  sausage:
    biscuits, cheese and, 80
    chicken and, 142
    hot, 171
    noodles, and vegetables,
      baked, 190
    pizza with topping I, 90
    rice and, 198–99
    Sicilian, 172
    soup, 75

soup, bean, pasta, and, 73
stuffing with, Italian, 92
sweet and hot, 173
soup:
bean, and pasta, 73
bean, sausage, and pasta, 73
potato and, 74
spaghetti and, with vegetables,
192
stuffed tomatoes, baked, 234
Potato(es), 183, 184, 206–11
bread, 84
fritters, 209
garlic, creamy, 206
gnocchi with mustard-tomato
sauce, 210
mashed, with pork bits, 207
in pungent basil sauce, baked,
208
salad:
green bean and, 102
Italian, 101
shrimp and, 109
soup:
beef and, 74
pork and, 74
stuffed baked, 211
Pot roast, *see* Beef
Poultry, *see* Chicken; Hens, Rock
Cornish
Preparation methods, 27–29
see also Entertaining
Prosciutto, melon and, 58
Prune stuffing with sausage,
Italian, 92
Puglia, cuisine of, 6–7
Pungent basil sauce, 248
potatoes baked in, 208

Radishes:
antipasto mixed fry, 46
pickled vegetables, sweet, 45
Raisins:
biscuits, cinnamon fruit, 88
fruit:
in brandy wine, dried, 275
-filled log, 265

Raspberry:
cream, glazed oranges in, 272
ice, 273
sauce, 253
lamb chops in, 169
Red clam sauce, 244
mock, 244
Red pepper(s):
salad:
mixed vegetable, 104
roast peppers and beet, 105
shrimp, zucchini, and, in wine
cream, 136
Red snapper:
baked, 123
deviled, 134
fish soup, 68
stuffed with seafood, 124
Regional cuisines, 1–11
Relish:
spiced apple, 61
tomato-plum, 62
Rice, 183, 184
basil, and leeks, 198
cabbage, and sweet peppers,
200
with chicken livers, 203
nutritional value of, 295
primavera, 202
risotto, 184, 197
sausage and, 198–99
soup, mushroom-, 70
in spicy green sauce, 200–201
-stuffed peppers, 231
with tomatoes and cheese,
204
in wine, 199
in wine-caper sauce, 201
Ricotta cheese, 14, 15
combination cheese dip, 59
flounder in cheesy dill sauce,
119
mushroom-, sauce, 241
shells with, 191
pie, Italian, 263
puffs, fried, 60
squash melt, 236

Risotto, 184, 197
Rome, cuisine of, 11
Rosemary, 19
    chicken with green
            peppercorns, 153
    -wine sauce, 252
Rum fruit, creamy, 274

Sage, 19
Salads, 95–115
    arugola:
        braised, 96
        mixed, surprise, 103
    beet, 97
        mixed vegetable, 104
        roast peppers and, 105
    broccoli, 98
        shrimp and potato, 109
    cauliflower, 98
    chicken:
        basil and tarragon, 114
        capers and, 115
        pasta and, 113
    Christmas, 99
    coleslaw, Italian, 102–103
    endive, braised, 96, 99
    fennel, 100
    green beans, 98
        carrot and, 180
        potato and, 102
    lobster:
        in brandied mayonnaise, 108
        tomato, zucchini, and, 107
    mixed surprise, 103
    mixed vegetable, 104
    pasta and tuna, 113
    peppers and beet, roast, 105
    pork, basil, and tarragon, 114
    potato:
        green bean and, 102
        Italian, 101
        shrimp and, 109
    Roma, 104–105
    shrimp:
        potato and, 109
        squid and, 110

    squid:
        shrimp and, 110
        vinaigrette, 111
    swordfish, basil, and tarragon,
            114
    tomato:
        mixed vegetable, 104
        mozzarella and, 106
        stuffed, 106–107
        zucchini, and sardine, 107
    tuna, 112
        pasta and, 113
    watercress:
        braised, 96
        mixed, surprise, 103
    zucchini:
        mixed vegetable, 104
        tomato, and sardine, 107
Salmon:
    in basil-cream sauce, 121
    canned, low-sodium, 24
    eggplant:
        and capers, 122
        -stuffed, 225
    in herb sauce, parsley, 120
    spread, 53
Salt, 32–33, 297
    guidelines for avoiding, 33
    herbs and spices that imitate
            the taste of, 30–31
    labeling of products, 33
    low-sodium ingredients, 21–
            26, 33
    see also Sodium
Salt substitutes, 40
Sardines:
    canned, low-sodium, 24
    eggs Genovese, stuffed, 49
    piquant mayonnaise, 258
    salad, zucchini, tomato, and,
            107
    spicy green sauce, 247
    spread, 53
    stuffed artichokes, 215
Sardinia, cuisine of, 7–8
Sauces, 239–56
    apricot, 253

Bechamel, 240
herb, 249
hot, 250
mock red clam, 244
mock white clam, 245
mushroom-cheese, 241
mustard:
  -garlic, 256
  -tomato, 246
pungent basil, 248
raspberry, 253
red clam, 244
rosemary-wine, 252
spicy green, 247
tomato:
  mustard-, 246
  I, 242
  II, 243
white clam, 245
wine:
  -caper, 251
  -cream, 246–47
  rosemary, 252
Sausage:
  biscuits, cheese and, 80
  chicken and, 142
  hot, 171
  Napoli, 172
  noodles, and vegetables, baked,
    190
  peppers, and eggs, 175
  pizza with topping I, 90
  rice and, 198–99
  Sicilian, 172
  soup, 75
    bean, and pasta, 73
  stuffing with, Italian, 92
  sweet and hot, 173
Scallions for mixed salad surprise,
  103
Shellfish, 117, 132–36
  lobster:
    in creamy wine sauce, 132
    salad in brandied
      mayonnaise, 108
    salad, tomato, zucchini, and,
      107

soup, 71
zucchini, and peppers in wine
  cream, 136
nutritional values of, 296
oysters:
  baked stuffed, 51
  broiled, 133
  fish soup, 68
  lasagna rolls, chicken and,
    188
  mock red clam sauce, 244
  mock white clam sauce, 245
  snapper stuffed with seafood,
    124
  soup, 71
  tomato salad, stuffed, 106–
    107
  vermicelli, and, 195
shrimp:
  antipasto mixed fry, 46
  in creamy wine sauce, 132
  deviled, 134
  fish soup, 68
  garlic, 52
  lasagna rolls, chicken-and-,
    188
  and potato salad, 109
  seafood-fettuccine, 187
  snapper stuffed with sea-
    food, 124
  spaghetti and, in tomato
    sauce, 193
  in spicy tomato sauce, 135
  and squid salad, 110
  -stuffed eggplant, 225
  -stuffed peppers, 232
stuffed tomatoes, baked,
  234
  tomato salad, stuffed, 106–
    107
  zucchini, and peppers in wine
    cream, 136
squid:
  with bread crumb topping,
    125
  pea soup with, 72
  salad, shrimp and, 110

Squid (*cont.*)
    salad vinaigrette, 111
    seafood fettuccine, 187
    vermicelli and, in garlic
      sauce, 196
    see also Fish
Shells, *see* Pasta, shells
Sherry, 20
Shrimp:
    antipasto mixed fry, 46
    in creamy wine sauce, 132
    deviled, 134
    fish soup, 68
    garlic, 52
    lasagna rolls, chicken-and-,
      188
    salad:
      potato and, 109
      squid and, 110
      stuffed tomato, 106–107
    seafood fettuccine, 187
    snapper stuffed with seafood,
      124
    spaghetti and, in tomato sauce,
      193
    in spicy tomato sauce, 135
    -stuffed eggplant, 225
    -stuffed peppers, 232
    stuffed tomatoes, baked, 234
    zucchini, and peppers in wine
      cream, 136
Sicily, cuisine of, 5–6
Sodium, 32–33, 296, 297
    content of recipes, 41
    guidelines for avoiding, 33
    herbs and spices that imitate
      salt's taste, 30–31
    intake on Italian diet, 298–99
    labeling of products, 33
    low-, ingredients, 21–26, 33
    tables of nutritional values,
      339–48
Soup, 63–78
    arugola, 66
    bean:
      pork, and pasta, 73
      sausage, and pasta, 73

      tomato-, 77
    beef:
      potato and, 74
      stock, 65
    carrot, with capers, 66
    chicken stock, 64
    Easter, 67
    fish, 68
    green bean and barley, 69
    lobster, 71
    minestrone, 78
    mushroom-rice, 70
    oyster, 71
    pea, with squid, 72
    pork:
      bean, and pasta, 73
      bean, sausage, and pasta, 73
      potato and, 74
      sausage, 75
    spinach and cheese, 76
    stock:
      chicken, 64
      meat, 65
    zucchini and barley, 69
Sour cream:
    creamy garlic dressing, 256–57
    creamy rum fruit, 274
    herb sauce, 249
Southern Italy, cuisine of, 5–8
Spaghetti, *see* Pasta, spaghetti
Spice(s):
    sponge cake, 268–69
    see also individual spices
Spicy green sauce, 247
    rice in, 200–201
    spaghetti in, 194
Spinach:
    braised, 233
    macaroni and, 189
    soup, cheese and, 76
Sponge cake, spice, 268–69
Spreads, *see* Antipasti
Squash, *see* Acorn squash; Yellow
      squash; Zucchini
Squid:
    with bread crumb topping, 125
    pea soup with, 72

salad:
  shrimp and, 110
  vinaigrette, 111
seafood fettuccine, 187
vermicelli and, in garlic sauce,
  196
Stock, 64–65
  chicken, 64
  meat, 65
Strawberry(ies):
  bananas in, cream, 271
  creamy rum fruit, 274
  fruit-filled log, 265
  peaches with, cream, glazed,
    272
Stuffing, Italian, 92
  with nuts, 93
  for roast stuffed chicken
    Italiano, 152
  with sausage, 92
Swiss cheese:
  asparagus in spicy cheese sauce,
    216
  biscuits, sausage and, 80
  chicken Tetrazzini, 149
  eggplant Parmigiana, easy,
    223
  puffs, fried, 60
  risotto with, 197
  soup, spinach and, 76
Swordfish:
  in basil-cream sauce, 121
  deviled, 134
  fish soup, 68
  in pepper-wine sauce, 127
  rosemary, with green
    peppercorns, 153
  salad, basil and tarragon, 114
  sautéed in wine, 130
  and sweet peppers, 126

Tables of nutritional values, 339–
  48
Tarragon, 20
  chicken salad, basil and, 114
Thyme, 20

Tomato(es), 20
  beans and, 212
  mixed vegetable appetizer, 44
  polenta with eggplant and,
    baked, 205
  relish, plum-, 62
  rice with, and cheese, 204
  salad:
    mixed vegetable, 104
    mozzarella and, 106
    stuffed, 106–107
    zucchini, and sardine, 107
  shrimp, deviled, 134
  soup, bean-, 77
  spice-broiled, 235
  stuffed, baked, 234
  tuna, cheese, and, bake, 131
Tomato paste, low-sodium, 25
Tomato puree:
  hot sauce, 250
  low-sodium, 25
Tomato sauce:
  chicken wings in, broiled, 54
  low-sodium, 25
  mustard-, 246
    potato gnocchi in, 210
  I, 242
  II, 243
  pizza with toppings, 90
  shrimp in spicy, 135
  spaghetti and shrimp in, 193
  wine-, chicken in, 146
Trentino/Alto Adige, cuisine of,
  3–4
Trout:
  simple broiled, 128
  wine-baked, 129
Tuna:
  canned, low-sodium, 26
  cheese, and tomato bake, 131
  mushrooms, baked stuffed,
    47
  salad, 112
    pasta and, 113
  sautéed in wine, 130
  spaghetti in spicy green sauce
    with, 194

Tuna (*cont.*)
  spread, 53
  stuffed artichokes, 215
  stuffed tomatoes, baked, 234
Tuscany, cuisine of, 9

Umbria, cuisine of, 10–11

Veal:
  with artichokes and
      mushrooms, 180
  with braised watercress, 181
  Como, 176
  Marsala with peppers and
      mushrooms, 178
  meatballs, tender, 167
  meat loaf with cream, 162
  sausage Napoli, 172
      peppers, and eggs, 175
  scallops and leeks in lemon-
      basil sauce, 179
  stew, mushroom and, 177
Vegetable(s), 213–38
  antipasto mixed fry, 46
  appetizer, mixed, 44
  bread, herbed, 83
  canned, low-sodium, 21
  frozen, 21
  minestrone, 78
  noodles, sausage, and, baked,
      190
  rice primavera, 202
  salad, mixed, 104
  spaghetti and pork with, 192
  sweet pickled, 45
  see also Salads; *individual*
      vegetables
Venice, cuisine of, 4–5
Vermouth, 20–21
Vinaigrette:
  Italian, dressing, 254
      asparagus with, 216
  London broil, 161
  squid salad, 111
Vinegar, 21
  chicken picante, 155

honey-, dressing, 255
  asparagus with, 216
  baked chicken in, 150
  Italian vinaigrette, 254
  oil and, dressing, 254
  see also Dressings; Vinaigrette

Walnut(s):
  bread with, Italian flat, 85
  nut balls, 268
  nut cake, 267
  shrimp and potato salad with,
      109
  stuffing with, Italian, 93
Watercress:
  salad:
      braised, 96
      mixed, surprise, 103
  veal with braised, 181
White clam sauce, 245
  mock, 245
Wine, 20, 40
  beef stew, Italian, 160
  broccoli in sherry garlic, 218
  -caper sauce, 251
      rice in, 201
  carrots in orange, 220
  chicken in, 145
      parsley, 144
      -tomato sauce, 146
      wings, baked, 54
  -cream sauce, 246–47
  fettuccine in, -cream sauce,
      186
  fruit in brandy, dried, 275
  lobster in creamy, sauce, 132
  rice in, 199
  rosemary-, sauce, 252
  shrimp, zucchini, and peppers
      in, cream, 136
  swordfish in pepper-, sauce, 127
  trout baked in, 129
  tuna sautéed in, 130
  veal Marsala with peppers and
      mushrooms, 178
Worcestershire sauce, low-
      sodium, 26

Yellow squash melt, 236
Yogurt:
    cucumber dressing, 259
    herb sauce, 249

Zucchini:
    appetizer, mixed vegetable, 44
    bread, herbed vegetable, 83

salad:
    mixed vegetable, 104
    tomato, and sardine, 107
shrimp, and peppers in wine
    cream, 136
soup, barley and, 69
squash melt, 236
strips, 48
sweet-and-sour, 238